A PSYCHIC'S HANDBOOK

About the Author

Michelle Welch (Dallas, TX) is the owner and operator of SoulTopia LLC metaphysical store, where she provides intuitive readings and healing sessions in addition to teaching classes on crystals, tarot, energy work, and intuition. She has also presented at Readers Studio, the Northwest Tarot Symposium, and the International New Age Trade Show. Michelle is also an attorney and the host of the *SoulWhat* podcast and the *Michelle SoulTopia* YouTube channel.

To Write to the Author

If you wish to contact the author or would like more information about this book, please write to the author in care of Llewellyn Worldwide Ltd. and we will forward your request. Both the author and publisher appreciate hearing from you and learning of your enjoyment of this book and how it has helped you. Llewellyn Worldwide Ltd. cannot guarantee that every letter written to the author can be answered, but all will be forwarded. Please write to:

Michelle Welch
℅ Llewellyn Worldwide
2143 Wooddale Drive
Woodbury, MN 55125-2989
Please enclose a self-addressed stamped envelope for reply,
or $1.00 to cover costs. If outside the U.S.A., enclose
an international postal reply coupon.

Many of Llewellyn's authors have websites with additional information and resources. For more information, please visit our website at http://www.llewellyn.com.

A PSYCHIC'S HANDBOOK

METHODS AND ADVICE FOR COMMUNICATING WITH SPIRITS

MICHELLE WELCH

LLEWELLYN
WOODBURY, MINNESOTA

First Edition
First Printing, 2025

Book design by Christine Ha
Cover design by Shannon McKuhen
Interior illustrations by the Llewellyn Art Department

Llewellyn Publications is a registered trademark of Llewellyn Worldwide Ltd.

Library of Congress Cataloging-in-Publication Data
Names: Welch, Michelle (Spiritualist), author.
Title: A psychic's handbook : methods and advice for communicating with
  spirits / Michelle Welch.
Description: First edition. | Woodbury, Minnesota : Llewellyn Publications,
  2025. | Includes bibliographical references. | Summary: "Pinpoint your
  psychic strengths, discover a variety of divination methods, and hone
  your spirit communication skills with this guide to creating your unique
  psychic handbook"—Provided by publisher.
Identifiers: LCCN 2024050887 (print) | LCCN 2024050888 (ebook) | ISBN
  9780738771397 (paperback) | ISBN 9780738771564 (ebook)
Subjects: LCSH: Spiritualism—Handbooks, manuals, etc.
Classification: LCC BF1261.2 .W66 2025 (print) | LCC BF1261.2 (ebook) |
  DDC 133.9—dc23/eng/20241121
LC record available at https://lccn.loc.gov/2024050887
LC ebook record available at https://lccn.loc.gov/2024050888

Llewellyn Worldwide Ltd. does not participate in, endorse, or have any authority or responsibility concerning private business transactions between our authors and the public.

All mail addressed to the author is forwarded, but the publisher cannot, unless specifically instructed by the author, give out an address or phone number.

Any internet references contained in this work are current at publication time, but the publisher cannot guarantee that a specific location will continue to be maintained. Please refer to the publisher's website for links to authors' websites and other sources.

Llewellyn Publications
A Division of Llewellyn Worldwide Ltd.
2143 Wooddale Drive
Woodbury, MN 55125-2989
www.llewellyn.com

Printed in the United States of America

Other Books by Michelle Welch

The Magic of Connection
Spirits Unveiled

Disclaimer

Anyone reading this book or listening to it in any form hereby acknowledges and is tacitly assumed to have read this disclaimer. This publication contains the opinions and ideas of the author. The information provided herein cannot be given to any degree of certainty or guarantee, and you should not rely on it to make any decision that would affect your legal, financial, or medical condition. If any condition, inquiry, or situation involves the law, finance, or medicine, then you should seek the advice of a licensed or qualified legal, financial, or medical professional. These methods can only facilitate how you cope spiritually with a given situation.

Furthermore, certain jurisdictions require that those in the field of fortune-telling must state "For entertainment purposes only." To the extent you live in such a jurisdiction, consider yourself on notice thereof. The author and publisher and all their affiliates specifically disclaim all responsibility for any liability, loss, or risk, personal or otherwise, that is incurred therefore, directly, or indirectly, by the use and application of any of the contents of this book.

The author has endeavored to re-create events, locales, and conversations from her memories and conversations with those involved. Therefore, it reflects her present recollections of experiences over time. To maintain anonymity, some names and characteristics have been changed, some events have been compressed, and some dialogue has been re-created.

To all those who walk in between

Acknowledgments

I have so many people to thank for helping write this book and even more who have helped me live it. Due to the overwhelming support I have received, I will limit my acknowledgments to those who specifically helped me on this book.

Thank you to:

Everyone at Llewellyn Worldwide.

Roger Welch for your hard work and support.

Mat Auryn for your encouragement and writing the foreword. You are one of the most gifted yet humble people I know. You, Devin Hunter, Storm Faerywolf, and Chas Bogan truly make the world more magical.

Amy Zerner and Monte Farber for being mentors and friends.

Sally and Andrew Robinson, for endless support and understanding. You are the king and queen of the cons!

Madame Pamita for helping me on my first book proposal. You are always generous with all of your talents. I am forever grateful.

Ethony for always supporting me and making me laugh. You are a lifer.

Lexy Colombe for being my oak tree.

Mary K. Greer for your wisdom and support. The twinkle in your eye always makes me smile.

Charles Harrington and Catiara Marie for being there just when I needed it most.

Premila Patel. You know why.

Neil Marshall for teaching me how to handle walking and operating in between.

Erica Hamilton, Dawn Crosby-Moore, Mary Gates, Nikki Pere, and Leah Curtis for countless edits.

To all of my clients and students. You give me purpose as a psychic.

To those who have stood with me at several crossroads when it was not easy. You know who you are. I am here because of you.

To the spirits that are always with me. You are not paranormal in my life. You are normal.

Most of all, thank you to my higher self for finding a way to make it through the past two years. They were years of severe physical and emotional pain that left me questioning everything. I found out that I should always trust my psychic knowingness regarding situations and people. Never again will I minimize or downplay my psychic knowingness.

CONTENTS

CHECKUPS

TERMINOLOGY

EXERCISES AND
JOURNAL PROMPTS

FOREWORD

I must've been around four or five when I started to think there was more to life than what we see and touch every day. One of my earliest memories was something that, I guess, shook me up pretty good, even as a kid. I remember this one afternoon—I was out in the yard, just doing what kids do, not really thinking about much, when I suddenly felt something. It wasn't anything dramatic or obvious, just a kind of quiet presence that brushed against the edges of my thoughts. But I knew it was there. Funny enough, it didn't scare me. If anything, it felt…I don't know, warm, like the way a hug from someone you love makes you feel safe. I even looked around, expecting to see someone, but there was no one there. The yard was completely empty. Yet that warm feeling didn't go away—it lingered, almost like it was watching over me. Even at that age, I was sure it was my grandmother. She'd passed away not too long before, and somehow, it just made sense to me. I couldn't explain it, not with words, but deep down, I just knew she was there—and that I'd experienced something different, something beyond the everyday.

As the years went by, I started noticing something kind of odd—I'd somehow know things I really shouldn't have, like stuff about the future. I'd say something offhand, not really thinking much about it, and then I'd catch these startled or uneasy looks on my guardians' faces. One moment stands out pretty clearly: I casually mentioned that the neighbor's dog was going to run away soon and come back in three days, and sure enough, a few days later, it did. At first, they just shrugged it off, like it was just me being a kid with a big imagination or something paired with lucky coincidences. But then, when I started getting these predictions right more often, and with this weird accuracy, they began to look more unsettled. Sometimes, they couldn't just ignore what I was saying—those were the times when their reactions got a bit worse. They couldn't really understand what was happening, so they started thinking maybe something nefarious was behind it.

These moments stuck with me, buried somewhere in the back of my mind, until years later when I started looking for answers. The church I grew up in didn't have any explanations for what I had gone through, and everyone around me—my guardians, the community—they just said it was evil, something to be afraid of. But deep down, I knew they were wrong. Their warnings only made me more curious, pushing me to find out the truth, especially after a traumatic experience that really opened up my sensitivity to energy. Shortly after, I read every book I could get my hands on, talked to people who seemed to understand the unseen, and followed every lead that might help me make sense of it all. I knew the things I went through as a small child weren't just something I made up—it was real, and it had a certain power to it. I was finally seeing something that had always been there, just out of sight, even if others couldn't see it.

As I got older, my interest in the unseen just grew stronger. What began as simple childhood curiosity turned into a real drive to understand the hidden parts of reality. As I learned more, I realized these abilities weren't just occasional flashes of something magical—they were real and could be developed into something meaningful. I know in a world where technology and logic seem to rule, focusing on psychic skills might seem a bit unusual or even delusional. But to me, they were really important. They gave me a way to connect with deeper parts of life, to tap into knowledge beyond the usual, and to live with a clearer sense of purpose. Developing psychic skills isn't just about predicting things or reading minds. It's more about tuning in to the little signs around us, listening to that inner feeling, and seeing how everything connects. It's about taking in both the obvious and the hidden parts of life and using them to make things better. I often think having someone like Michelle Welch to help me from the start would've made things a lot easier.

When Michelle Welch first invited me to be on her podcast, *SoulWhat*, I didn't realize how special that moment would become. But from the moment we connected, it felt like meeting a kindred spirit. Michelle doesn't just talk about psychic development and spiritual practices; she lives them with such warmth and authenticity that it feels completely natural. The way she communicates, you can tell she's drawing from a deep well of wisdom. You immediately feel comfortable, as if you're in a place where everyday and special moments come together. Michelle's Texan charm adds to this—her warmth and confidence make you feel at ease, like you're talking with an old friend, even if you've just met her.

What really stood out to me about Michelle was her approach to the psychic world. For her it's not about flashy tricks or big, dramatic displays of ego. Instead, she focuses on the quiet, subtle work that reveals new possibilities to help others. Michelle has a way of helping others shine, never seeking to hog the spotlight herself but supporting those around her. She truly gets what community means—creating connections that empower and support each other.

Michelle is one of the first people I think of when I consider those making a real impact in the spiritual community. My respect for her goes beyond her impressive skills—it's also about her brave choice to leave a successful legal career and fully commit to the spiritual path. Leaving behind the security and prestige of a law career is no small feat, especially for something that might seem unconventional to some. But Michelle knew her calling was much bigger than what her legal career could offer—she was meant to guide others on their spiritual journeys, help them explore the unseen, and create meaningful connections.

Her dedication to this path shines through in everything she does. She runs SoulTopia, a metaphysical shop offering much more than just books, crystals, or tarot cards. These stores have become safe spaces for people on their spiritual paths, growing into lively communities where they can learn, grow, and support each other. The way she's built these spaces shows her commitment to creating a welcoming environment for everyone. She's also behind some major events, like the Northwest Tarot Symposium in Oregon, The International Divination Event in Texas, and the Readers Studio in New York. These events have become key parts of the metaphysical and divination community, drawing in people from all over. They're a chance to learn, connect, and dive deeper into spiritual practices. Through these events, Michelle has really established herself as a true leader. She's focused on lifting others up, giving them space to shine, and building strong, supportive communities. That's what makes her truly stand out. That's the real hallmark of a leader.

As the author of two essential books, she's quickly established herself as a leading voice in psychic development and spiritual growth. When I first read *The Magic of Connection* and *Spirits Unveiled*, even before experiencing her energy in person, I knew immediately that she was the real deal. As a psychic and medium myself, I could sense the authenticity and depth in her words. *The Magic of Connection* explores how energy and intention shape our relationships with others and the universe. *Spirits Unveiled* takes readers further, guiding them through the complexities of working with spirits and unseen forces.

What really stands out to me about this book, *A Psychic's Handbook*, is how it offers more than just advice on psychic development. If I'd had this book earlier, it would've made things clearer and helped me better understand my own psychic nature. This book is meant to grow with you, helping you create something personal. Michelle Welch knows that everyone's psychic journey is different, with its own twists and turns. She honors that uniqueness and offers tools to help you explore your psychic potential in a way that works for you. The book's focus on customization is what makes it special. Michelle encourages you to try different things and see what really fits. It's not just a guide—it's something that evolves with your experiences, questions, doubts, and discoveries.

This book is about empowerment. It's here to help you trust your intuition and explore your psychic abilities with curiosity. Michelle hopes you'll finish the book with a practice to access your psychism in a way that truly feels like your own. *A Psychic's Handbook* is about more than just learning—it's about seeing yourself and your place in the world differently. Michelle dives deep into the psychic world with curiosity and thoroughness. She doesn't just scratch the surface—she explores every detail. Her dedication to research is clear in *A Psychic's Handbook*. She writes like a teacher but with the heart of a mystic, making the book equally approachable and spiritual.

Michelle Welch has done something extraordinary—not just in writing *A Psychic's Handbook*, but in creating a community that radiates warmth and shared purpose. She knows that psychic development thrives in the company of others, where insights are exchanged and every step forward is met with encouragement. Michelle has cultivated this community with grace, creating a space where everyone feels welcome and valued. *A Psychic's Handbook* is undoubtedly another monument in the legacy Michelle is crafting—one that will echo far into the future. She's dedicated to making psychic wisdom a living tradition, accessible to anyone who seeks it. Michelle is a bridge-builder, connecting the wisdom of the past with the possibilities of today. She's setting the foundation for a future where psychic practices are part of our everyday lives, where people won't be questioned or criticized or pressured to be scared of their experiences like people tried to do with me when I was a child. And as Michelle makes clear in the book, you don't even need to feel you were psychic as a child or at any point in your life to begin developing the skills within these pages.

I was already a well-established psychic and author when I met Michelle Welch, but she made a big difference in how I moved forward. From the start, her genuine nature and warmth really struck me. Michelle has this way of being wise and approachable at the same time without ever putting herself above anyone. She meets you where you are, offering guidance that feels both thoughtful and empowering. Michelle Welch has enriched my journey, offering unique perspectives, new layers of understanding, deeper connections, and a shared purpose that has made my journey more meaningful. Most of all, I'm grateful she's in my life and that she is following her True Will of doing the work that she is.

As you begin *A Psychic's Handbook*, keep an open mind. The book isn't about telling you *what* to believe—it's here to help you explore and strengthen your psychic skills based on how you naturally work and perceive energy. With Michelle's guidance, you're in safe hands. Her experience and personal journey are all here to help you get better at your skills, deepen your intuition, and trust yourself.

So take a deep breath and begin. This book meets you wherever you are in your psychic journey, whether you're just starting or wanting to dive deeper.

Mat Auryn
Author of *Psychic Witch* and *The Psychic Art of Tarot*

INTRODUCTION

Many curious about psychic abilities have an intense yearning to dip their toes in psychic waters or dive in and get carried away by psychic tides. Whether you have a curiosity to begin your exploration or a desire to go deeper into your psychic knowingness, it is no mistake that you have picked up this book. With the help of *A Psychic's Handbook*, you will experience guidance on your psychic quest. If you are beginning your psychic journey, it is an ideal time to work through this book because you will chart and steer your experience as a psychic from the beginning. Without proper guidance, some psychics spend much of their lives trying to figure out how to navigate their psychic path. Further, at some point, those already deeply immersed in their psychic knowingness usually have a strong desire to examine how to control their abilities or find a purpose for them. They even try to blend in with the rest of society, but this is often futile for the genuine psychic. For those less-fortunate psychic souls who feel overwhelmed by your psychic senses, do not despair; I walk your path, hear your cries for help, and this book has come into your life when you need it most.

I wrote *A Psychic's Handbook* to help those of you who wish to manage or develop your psychic knowingness and use it positively. A clear manifesto drives me: If you are going to do something, do it with excellence. I am psychic; therefore, I will strive to be the best psychic I can be, and I hope this book will help you do the same. Whether you already feel overwhelmed with your abilities, don't know how to use them, are just beginning to develop them, or have a child exhibiting these characteristics, you are ready to learn your unique psychic style and step into psychic success. Let's get started and figure out our psychic knowingness together.

How Is This Book Different from Other Intuition Books?

This handbook's approach to exercising your intuitive muscles is different from many other approaches you might come across in psychic development resources. You will assemble a method that is the best for you instead of a cookie-cutter book or class that seemingly works for everyone else but not for you. Psychic development is not a one-size-fits-all endeavor. I will share experiences I have seen and encountered through years of teaching thousands of students.

In *A Psychic's Handbook*, you will explore and compare your experiences with what you may have previously learned or read about psychic phenomena. Remember that everything you read or hear is not necessarily the truth. Truth can even change with new paradigms (beliefs). Additionally, the truth may vary between people, cultures, and periods. This book will help you find your truth regarding your psychic journey.

What Is a Psychic Handbook, and Why Will You Benefit from One?

In almost every endeavor, job, school, or training, a handbook provides information to help you succeed. Handbooks are *books on hand*. They are valuable tools that provide facts and information for quick accessibility and use. You can think of a handbook as a cookbook with all the ingredients, recipes, terminology, and explanations to make a wonderful meal. A handbook is a living document that is constantly updated.

To enhance and develop your psychic knowingness, creating your psychic handbook is helpful, allowing you access to general information. Your handbook is a vital resource for your psychic journey. It helps you pinpoint your psychic strengths, ascertain your divination preferences, hone your psychic skills, and track your progress. Unlike standard manuals or books that teach everyone the same methods to increase psychic knowingness, it is necessary to build your handbook yourself to evolve as a psychic. Assembling your psychic handbook includes keeping it updated as your psychic knowingness grows.

What Are the C's, R's, and E's of Psychic Success?

One of the easiest ways to enhance your psychic knowingness, whether you are a novice or professional, is to always remember the Three C's of Psychic Success: clairs (part 1, chapter 6), chakras (part 1, chapter 7), and colors (part 1, chapter 8). You will find the interconnection between the Three C's whether you work with crystals, candles, auras, or other modalities. Once you learn and experience how easily the Three C's tie together, you will be well on your way to understanding how simple it is to make psychic connections.

When using your psychic knowingness, there are four crucial steps that we will refer to as the Four R's of Psychic Success. The Four R's include requesting, receiving, reading, and relaying information or messages. The request is the ask—the answer or information sought. Once you make the request, you receive a message. Next, you read or interpret that message. Finally, you relay the message to the person asking the question and receiving the message (also known as the sitter or querent). Watch for the Four R's throughout this book and when assembling your handbook.

Throughout this book, the Eight E's of Psychic Success will guide you in formulating your style. These E's could be the key to success in many areas of life. The Eight E's of Psychic Success include education, experience, ego, energy, empathy, ethics, entertainment, and excellence. Keep these words in mind while developing your book. The Eight E's will be summarized in part 4 of the book, but feel free to peek at that section anytime.

Who Will Benefit from This Book?

Anyone old enough to read and apply the precepts of *A Psychic's Handbook* will benefit from this book. I wish it had been available when I was a child. It would have helped me learn to navigate psychic waters independently, because I could not access books like this. This book would have helped me write a psychic script to minimize the obstacles and maximize the victories of psychic knowingness.

On the other hand, if you are a professional psychic, please keep reading. This book is also an important resource for you. One of the biggest mistakes professional psychics make is letting their ego run amuck after only a few years of reading. Even if you have known you were psychic for as long as you can remember, you can always learn from others, whether you consider your skill level beginner, advanced, or professional. The best psychics keep expanding their Eight E's, including keeping their egos in check.

It is also important to note that anyone can benefit from this book regardless of profession. I know people from all walks of life who utilize the precepts taught in this book. Everyone uses some level of discernment and intuition every day. It behooves you to mold this handbook into the best format to guide you.

What Is the Format of This Book?

This book contains four parts: Part 1: Assembling Your Psychic Handbook, Part 2: Divination Exercises from the Ancient to the Modern, Part 3: Practice Makes Psychic: Exercises to Sharpen Your Psychic Senses, and Part 4: The Eight E's of Psychic Success. In part 1, twelve chapters equip you with everything you need to begin to step into or advance in your psychic knowingness. Every chapter has the essential components to help you assemble your handbook: checkups, terms, exercises, journal prompts, pitfalls to avoid, and keys to psychic success. The checkups are intentionally at the beginning of each chapter to assess your baseline before you have all the information. Following the checkup is information on the chapter topic and terminology. Next, there are exercises with journal prompts based on those exercises. Each chapter has pitfalls to avoid and a summary paragraph regarding the psychic success you will ultimately achieve. Part 2 covers many ancient divination methods and suggests modern practices you may choose to have as part of your tool kit as you work with different psychic skill sets, styles, or modalities. Divination is the process of getting information through supernatural means. In part 3, you will find numerous exercises I have taught firsthand in my classes. I created many of the exercises. You may also recognize some of the exercises that have been utilized for some time.

How Should You Approach This Book and Assemble Your Handbook?

The beauty of *A Psychic's Handbook* is that you will benefit from reading one section or the whole book. Every aspect of this book has valuable information for you to use in your daily life, whether you are merely curious about psychic matters or are a professional psychic. Suppose you read the book without doing any exercises. In that case, you will benefit from the gems of information dispersed throughout the book. Of course, the deeper you dive into the activities in the book, the more your psychic muscles will grow and expand because practice makes psychic.

This book can be read cover to cover, in parts, or by flipping to a chapter or exercise that catches your eye in the table of contents. In other words, the book is divided into parts and chapters to accommodate each method, and each can stand alone if you prefer reading on one subject. However, the book's overall goal is to help you discover your best personal way of tuning in to your psychic self, style, and knowingness. Everyone is unique in their endeavor. Therefore, consider achieving the goal by assembling your psychic handbook. Please realize that even when constructing such a handbook, everyone may have different ways of approaching the task.

The handbook you assemble will be a sacred text, like a grimoire or book of spells. Each handbook will be unique. Your handbook will be your touchstone, and I will lead you through this journey. If you buy a ready-made journal or spiral notebook, put a label on the front cover and always keep it with your copy of *A Psychic's Handbook*.

You will write a lot in your separate handbook (the one you compile as you read *A Psychic's Handbook*), so it is essential to have something you can always access or at least paper to insert later in your handbook. Perhaps the best option is to buy a 3–5-inch binder with solid rings. I suggest a plastic insert cover on the front for a cover sheet. You can get as creative as possible with dividers and laminated insert sheets. I recommend this because you will always add to your handbook since it is a living document. In this binder, you can put charts, personal readings, notes from classes you attend or teach, and all sorts of things you will learn. Ultimately, it is up to you to assemble your handbook, but the most important thing is that you do what's best for your psychic style.

What Makes Me Qualified to Train You to Assemble Your Psychic Handbook?

I am a natural-born psychic. I didn't strive to become psychic; it is just who I am and always have been. I don't know what it feels like to not be psychic. Early in life, I assumed everyone was just like me until I had the rude awakening that I was significantly different. Although knowing things before they happen can be beneficial, most psychics did not choose this life. Many with extraordinary psychic abilities have struggled or even received a mental illness label at some point in their lives. They often feel different than others and feel like they don't fit in or belong on earth. Natural-born psychics usually have stopped telling people the extent of their psychic abilities because others who want to be psychic think the natural-born psychic is bragging. In contrast, those who are skeptical of psychics believe the psychic is unhinged or a fraud. Some claim that real psychics do not need to tell you they are psychics, and while I agree that over time people rarely, if ever, question my psychic abilities, I have no problem cutting to the chase when time is of the essence. It is who I am, and I hope you learn you can tell others you are psychic.

Having owned metaphysical stores and three divination conventions, I recognize what you want to learn versus someone who sits and writes esoteric theories all day. I am in the trenches with you daily and have helped others walk this path. I hear and see you come to my stores and conferences with a desire to learn. I have also seen the frustration of many of you who take classes and read books only to find that you still need help connecting to your psychic style. This need to determine your psychic style is because everyone learns differently when stretching psychic muscles. Again, there is no one-size-fits-all approach that works for everyone. I have practiced or tried all the methods in this book. I understand everyone learns and practices in various ways, and I provide alternative ways to achieve the same result. Having taught law school, I know that there are many different learning styles. I have worked with many frustrated students when they first came to me for psychic mentoring. They had books or teachers that represented only one way to develop psychic knowingness. Just as there are various learning styles for school, there are different learning styles for psychic development.

Most importantly, I am qualified to help you assemble your psychic handbook because I am passionate about the Eight E's: education, experience, ego, energy, empathy, ethics, entertainment, and excellence. I am a committed ally who will encourage you to use your skills, abilities, and gifts in a dignified and professional manner, which will help you excel.

PART 1
ASSEMBLING YOUR
PSYCHIC HANDBOOK

In part 1 of *A Psychic's Handbook*, you will assemble a handbook unique to your psychic learning style. In doing so, you will examine if or why you want to be psychic and what being psychic means. Additionally, you will explore who you were in previous incarnations and who you are now. This self-awareness will help you understand what kind of psychic knowingness you naturally possess and how to develop it.

Two imperative requirements make a handbook successful: form and function. The structure of handbooks should be such that they allow for ease of use and quick accessibility, which leads to retention. You can choose the form you want for your handbook. The structure could be as simple as a spiral notebook or as elaborate as a binder with tabs, sections, and pockets for inserts. When considering what form to use, remember that you will constantly add to your handbook. The function of handbooks is to improve capabilities and performance, which will ultimately make you a better psychic. When you have a plan, it leaves room for more creativity, which in turn leads to more excellent psychic development. Remember to journal and date all your results, insights, and revelations as you assemble your psychic handbook.

CHAPTER 1

YOUR UNIQUE PSYCHIC KNOWINGNESS

Have you ever noticed that the résumés or biographies of many psychics begin with something along the lines of "I've been this way since I was little"? I am one of those people. I cannot recall a time when I wasn't psychic. Even if the word *psychic* has not resonated with you in the past, a lifelong journey working through your intuition is not a rite of passage. In other words, if you do not remember or believe that you were psychic as a child, it in no way makes you less qualified to be so now. Everyone may be born a psychic, but many have yet to realize, understand, or utilize their abilities. This book will meet you where you are. Whether you remember being psychic or something is just now enticing you to gather information, some part of you wants to explore your psychic knowingness.

Checkup: Psychic Self-Assessment Baseline

This psychic self-assessment checkup determines your baseline for psychic knowingness, which will help you begin assembling your handbook. Let's start with an honest psychic self-assessment. Answer the following questions based on what you are like instead of what you aspire to be. If you answer honestly, you will advance much more quickly because, from the beginning of constructing your handbook, you are releasing the need to be right, or what many call "having an attachment to the outcome." You are acknowledging that you are not omniscient. Write yes next to the statements that apply to you and no next to those that do not.

1. I can tell what others are thinking.
2. I can tell what others are feeling emotionally.
3. I can tell what others are feeling physically.
4. I see or sense spirits that others don't necessarily see.
5. I see or sense auras.
6. I find that electrical equipment malfunctions when I am around.
7. I know something is happening with a friend or family member before they tell me.
8. I can sense illness in others.
9. I am familiar with some of my deceased ancestors even though I have not met them.
10. I have lucid or vivid dreams.
11. I sleepwalked as a child.
12. I had night terrors as a child.
13. I said things when I was young that others thought were inappropriate but were true.
14. I communicate with nature and its beings.
15. I can move objects with my mind, especially when highly emotional.
16. I had an imaginary friend as a child.
17. I was afraid of the dark when I was a child.
18. I know of past lives without a psychic telling me.
19. I experience déjà vu.
20. I can tune out the noises around me.
21. I am often inundated with information that floods my brain.
22. I have premonitions about the future, which are usually correct.

23. I know things and typically have no details or reason to support my knowledge.
24. I have sensed when someone is about to die.
25. I hear my name called when no one is around.
26. I know if someone is watching me.
27. I am in tune with the spirits around me.
28. I win at games of chance more than average.
29. Animals are drawn to me for no apparent reason.
30. I have had out-of-body experiences.

The more yes answers, the more you already utilize your psychic knowledge. The number of yes answers will increase as you develop and practice the skills in your handbook.

What Is Psychic Knowingness?

A huge misconception surrounding psychic work is that you cannot use your imagination, senses, or observation skills. That is silly. Of course you can! These innate abilities help you develop your knowingness. The mind naturally combines imagination, synchronicity, and the collective consciousness (which includes the thoughts of every being in existence) to help humans read situations to survive and thrive. You are not cheating when you use them to read psychic situations, especially initially as you are developing psychically. Trust your senses. They will speak to you and give you clues. Shift your brain. Trust your dreams. Get in tune with nature, and most of all, have fun!

We are born with a gland at our brain's center that is linked to the third eye, the seat of intuition, and shaped like a pinecone. Knowing this shape, the ancient Greeks named it the pineal gland. Children have pliable pineal glands. They also have active imaginations that are initially not questioned. But eventually, conditioning and limiting beliefs often enter the picture. Some may have heard prohibitive phrases, such as "It is just your imagination; stop exaggerating," "It is evil," or "Stop making things up." Over time, you may try to block your psychic senses. Physically, the pineal gland may also start to calcify due to age, toxins, or lack of stimulation. So, while we may all have the ability initially, you can and do lose touch with your psychic abilities without use, much like a foreign language: If you don't use it, you may lose it.

Think of psychic knowingness as a continuum of various terms that describe a range of abilities or skills awaiting development. While everyone may have the inherent ability to sense certain psychic phenomena, only some have honed these skills. Most people can sing. Your voice is an instrument. However, only some have learned to use the instrument properly. For example, only some understand that singing should come from the diaphragm (as should breathing). Only some have trained their ears to sing on key. To some, it comes naturally, and they have perfect or relative pitch, while others work hard to train their ears. The best operatic singers warm their voices up with scales before they sing in full voice. They also know they can lose their voice with overuse or incorrect use. The ear of the listener is also a consideration. The same is true when using your psychic senses.

It is essential to always view your handbook from all angles—not only the way you think is correct. Any good practitioner looks at their handbook from every perspective. Of course, they consider their strengths, but they also identify their weaknesses so they can work on them or protect themselves from damage. Good handbooks also prepare you to examine the ways you interpret something differently from someone else. The point of a psychic handbook is to be ready for any psychic circumstance that comes your way.

Terminology: The Psychic Spectrum

Read through the following terms and take note of similarities and differences between the words used to describe a range of abilities.

Instinct: An inborn and unlearned way of behaving.

Whim: A passing thought or idea that might get dismissed as silly.

Hunch: A feeling something will occur without any evidence to support the feeling.

Gut feeling: A gnawing feeling from the pit of your stomach.

Insight: An intuitive peek or glimpse into a situation.

Intuition: A feeling or perception rather than conscious reasoning.

Faith: A belief despite lack of proof.

Psychic knowingness: A pure awareness based on no outside knowledge or observation.

The psychic spectrum ranges from inborn instinct to psychic knowingness. You may often see the terms above intermingled and interchanged. Still, subtle nuances make all the difference when it comes to psychic abilities.

Exercise: Progression for the Psychic Spectrum (Range of Abilities)

This exercise will help you understand where you think you fall on the psychic spectrum as you begin this book. It will also help you think about how you refer to the psychic knowledge you possess. You are encouraged to revisit this exercise as you work through *A Psychic's Handbook*.

In your handbook, write down your own definitions of the terms *instinct, whim, hunch, gut feeling, insight, intuition, faith,* and *psychic knowingness*. Add other terms if you think of them. Ponder where you fall on the psychic spectrum. Some people will have stronger psychic knowingness than others, but no one will be correct one hundred percent of the time. However, whether it be a strong knowingness or a slight one, at some point you will experience a nagging feeling, a hunch, or a gut instinct. While there is a continuum of knowingness, these are all forms of psychic abilities.

It is important to acknowledge that many people have a negative connotation of the word *psychic*. About ten years ago, I decided to reclaim the word *psychic* and dismiss the negative connotation. But you can call your knowingness whatever you want.

Your feelings about psychic knowingness may vary from moment to moment. One moment they may feel like a gift, and the next they may feel like a curse. For the most part, I find being psychic to be tricky unless I find a purpose for it. I have worked with countless clients who feel the same way. Working through your feelings surrounding relevant terminology may help you feel more positive about your psychic knowingness.

Journal Prompts: Progression for the Psychic Spectrum (Range of Abilities)

1. Which of these words do you feel comfortable using? Why?
2. Do you think everyone is born with some psychic knowingness?
3. Do you think you can develop your psychic knowingness with practice?

Terminology: Psychic Knowingness

Read through the following terms and take note of similarities and differences between the words used to describe psychic knowingness.

Let's examine some terminology used to describe intuitive, sensitive, or psychic abilities. Some are listed here, but be sure to list them in your handbook and provide your definition of these words. Then, determine which words best describe your psychic state.

Fluke: An accidental stroke of good or bad luck.

Skill: An ability that stems from practice, aptitude, knowledge, etc.

Ability: Competence because of training or other qualifications.

Blessing: Implies that someone chose you to have the ability bestowed upon you.

Gift: A unique ability or capacity, natural endowment, or talent bestowed upon you.

Curse: Feeling trapped with your knowingness and no one believing you.

Exercise: Labels for Psychic Knowingness (What You Call It)

The exercise will help you decide what you want to call your psychic knowingness. You are encouraged to revisit this exercise as you work through *A Psychic's Handbook.*

In your handbook, write down your own definitions of the terms *fluke*, *skill*, *ability*, *blessing*, *gift*, and *curse*. Ponder where you fall on the psychic spectrum. Add any other relevant descriptive words that come into your mind.

Recently, a friend corrected me on the use of these words. I told her that I did not care which word described psychic knowingness. The most important thing is if it feels right to the one who exhibits psychism. Knowing the terminology you want to use is essential, instead of arguing about which word is correct. I see groups on social media spend more time arguing over semantics than they do utilizing their gifts, skills, abilities, or whatever they decide to call what they are wasting time arguing about. There are varying degrees of psychic knowingness, and these intuitive muscles must be stretched over time in order to not atrophy with a lack of use. Let's be blunt: most of us cannot become Nostradamus overnight. Further, not every psychic is a Nostradamus psychic. Nostradamus primarily predicted doomsday events in the future; talk about an ability or gift being a curse! Although everyone is perhaps born with some degree of intuition, people are misleading you if they say you can become a professional psychic over a weekend for a certain fee. It is best to be honest and examine why you want to be psychic or are curious.

Whether you believe you read people well, get good gut feelings, have a sixth sense, are intuitive, feel psychic, or think you have a direct channel to the Source (God, the Collective, or a higher power), some part of you has picked up this book because you want to explore or broaden that aspect of your awareness. That curiosity or hunger to learn is where you will best invest your time. So let's get to it.

I will provide exercises and steps to strengthen your psychic muscles. Still, the key is to apply your experiences and experiential filters. It is not an exact science, but the steps, lists, and exercises give you a starting point.

Please do not compare yourself to others, because their handbook is and should be different than yours. It is crucial to build your confidence with a few basic guidelines. This book does not contain all the answers; it ignites the spark that helps light the way to your personalized psychic style.

Journal Prompts: Labels for Psychic Knowingness (What You Call It)

1. Do you believe everyone has psychic knowingness?
2. Do you believe anyone can learn it with practice?
3. Do you believe some people are more psychic than others?

Visualization

One of the quickest ways to begin your exploration is visualization, which is seeing a picture in your mind's eye. This picture may come in the way of a photo, a movie, or even a word or group of words that pop into your head and lead you to envision a message. Some people say they cannot visualize.[1] However, the general problem is usually the connotation they have of the word *visualize*. For example, almost anyone can close their eyes and imagine their car. They can imagine the color of the vehicle. Then, if you ask them to change the car's color to another color in their mind, they can do so. It is simply becoming familiar with the visualization process, and realizing it isn't that mysterious. Remove the word *visualization* if you need to do so. *Visualization* is often misleading because it erroneously implies you must see a photo or movie in your mind. Keep in mind that visualization may come through thoughts, phrases, or words instead of sight.

Exercise: Pinecone Visualization

This exercise aims to help you visualize, hold the visualization, and then change it. Once you have completed the activity, journaling in your handbook will help you bring your visualization from your third eye (I believe it is our first and most potent eye) onto paper.

I have always loved the story of the pineal gland named after the pinecone by the Greeks. I grew up in East Texas, and there are pinecones everywhere. I collect jewelry, photos, paintings, and other pinecones. To me, pinecones

---

1. There is a rare condition known as *aphantasia*. People with aphantasia are unable to form mental images. However, those who experience this can still *visualize* for our purposes because they can form a mental thought of words.

represent our psychic ability. However, as there are different types of pinecones, there are various psychic abilities. Now, let's visualize using a pinecone.

Relax and slow your breathing. Bring one palm to your third eye (the space between your eyebrows). Bring one palm to the back middle of your head. Hold your hands in these positions and begin to envision a brown pinecone. At first, you may see it as a word or thought, but eventually, most will see it as a pinecone. Imagine the shape. If your mind needs to tell you the shape, that is fine. Can you picture the pinecone? What does it look like? If you cannot see the pinecone, it is okay. Stay encouraged. You will eventually see it with practice, or it may come through another sense besides seeing.

If other thoughts or images come into your mind, calmly acknowledge them and return your focus to the pinecone. Now, turn this pinecone red. You might want to sense it feeling hot. When you are ready, turn the pinecone yellow. Now, the pinecone may seem like a bright, sunny day. Go easy on yourself if you cannot automatically visualize the colors. Then, go through the colors green, blue, indigo, and violet. Take a moment and gently spin the pinecone around. See it twirling in your mind's eye. See it shedding anything that is stuck to it. See it begin to sparkle and shine. Make glitter fly off as it turns and spins. Now, slow down the spinning. Slower and slower. Let the pinecone gently drift to the ground at the foot of a majestic pine tree. Calm down your pineal gland. Let the pinecone and pine tree drift away. Remove your hands, shrug your shoulders, and stretch. Now, bring your awareness back into the room.

Journal Prompts: Pinecone Visualization

In your handbook, journal everything you experienced in the exercise. Include those things that came quickly and any area of struggle or frustration. Make sure you always date your notations.

1. Were you able to turn the pinecone into different colors?
2. Did you see a photo or image of the pinecone or experience words or phrases?

3. Did you sense temperature changes with the various colors?
4. Were you able to make the pinecone spin?
5. Did you see the glitter flying off the pinecone?

Avoid These Pitfalls

You can spot someone who has just woken up to their psychic knowingness. They want to give messages to anyone who will listen. They may be in line at the grocery store and see in their mind that the lady in front of them is upset about a breakup. Someone opening to their psychic knowledge often feels they must relay this message to the upset lady. A seasoned psychic will stay silent for several reasons: (1) they get messages all the time and do not want to be talking to strangers constantly, (2) they realize it is unethical to ambush someone at a grocery store with a psychic message, or (3) they know that if the person needs to hear the message, the person will initiate a conversation. Unless someone wants your help, keep your mouth shut. Avoid the pitfall of the overeager newbie psychic.

Psychic Success

I am fortunate to give readings to clients all over the world. I always tell my clients that I am just a psychic. I am not a counselor or life coach; therefore, I do not give advice. I merely relay the message. I also am not a medical doctor. Although I regularly receive these messages, I am often left holding information that I cannot relay. I can smell cancer and have smelled it since I was very young. I saw this as a curse until about ten years ago. A strong man who rode motorcycles for sport came to get a reading from me. There were no visible indicators of any illness in his throat, but I could smell cancer and, with my mind's eye, saw an area of disease in his throat. I carefully asked the man if he had seen his doctor lately. He laughed and explained that he had no use or time for doctors. I encouraged him to get a checkup.

About a year later, I was sitting in my office, and my assistant brought a man to see me. I was busy, but my assistant signaled that I would want to meet with this man. He walked into my office. He was skinny and had an oozing bandage on his throat. He asked if I remembered him, and I sheepishly told him I did not. He proceeded to show me a photograph of him on his motorcycle. He reminded me of my encouragement for him to see a doctor. He went on to explain he had not seen the doctor as I advised and was dying of cancer, and if he had listened to me, they probably would have stopped the cancer. He encouraged me to continue to use my gifts. He explained that I had handled the situation professionally, but he was stubborn.

It is difficult to know when people are terminally ill. Sometimes, I carry a heavy burden. I do not diagnose or play doctor, but I strongly encourage doctor visits. This dear man told me how much I needed to continue using my gifts to help people. He thanked me as he left. I asked why he was thanking me, and he said he appreciated how hard it must have been for me and wanted to assure me that I had done everything possible. He passed away a few months later, but I saw him in spirit. He smiled, and I smiled back.

CHAPTER 2

YOUR PSYCHIC ROOTS

It is time to begin mapping out your handbook. Please know that the root of who you are is the key to embracing your psychic knowingness. Likewise, knowing your psychic self and style is the beginning of assembling your psychic handbook. Right now, let go of all expectations surrounding what it means to be a psychic or what a psychic experience is or is not. Each handbook should always look different. Think of all the judgments we could save if people realized we do not have the same handbook as others in any area of life.

Remember to make this handbook your own. At every opportunity, ask yourself what works for you. It will take practice, but try to never compare yourself to others. Part of psychic development is realizing that while we are all connected, we are also unique in our psychic styles. Only you bring your unique combination of natural gifts and acquired skills to the psychic circle. Many of you may think you lack psychic abilities or become easily frustrated. Using your handbook will cut down on this frustration or do away with the disappointment altogether as you find your unique way of exercising your psychic muscles. You may never realize your full potential if you keep trying to progress like others.

Checkup: What Do I Remember Baseline

This checkup aims to see how far back you remember and what you remember as a young child regarding present, past, parallel, or future lives. Recalling your memories is important because many people begin to identify their psychic experiences once they take the time to allow old memories to surface.

Answer the questions yes or no. Remember, this is a checkup for your benefit. It will only help you to the extent you are candid. If you are honest, you will have a good baseline for knowing what you were like as a child based on your memories.

1. I remember past lives.
2. I recognize future lives.
3. I know I have lived many lives.
4. I believe in reincarnation.
5. I remember much of my childhood, but only after two years of age.
6. I remember things and sometimes feel they are the memories of others.
7. I experience feelings of nostalgia.
8. I do not ever remember feeling young.
9. I do not ever remember feeling old.
10. I feel lost or stuck in life.
11. I believe there is much more than this physical life.
12. I have experienced heartbreak and pain.
13. I follow what society or family expects of me.
14. I dim my light to fit in with others.

The more yes answers, the more you can recall from your memory, not secondary sources. Remember, this checkup is merely a tool to get you to start remembering and thinking about where and when your views originated.

Terminology: Reincarnation

Let's look at a few terms that are important to know in this chapter. The meanings associated with these terms could fill entire books, but we will stick to the essential points.

Blueprint: A life plan mapped out before you incarnated (or were born). It may include karmic contracts that you want to accomplish.

Old soul: A soul that has incarnated to earth many times, probably by choice. Old souls are considered wise because they have empathy, mental understanding, insight, and intuition regarding things on earth.

Reincarnation: Rebirth of the soul in a new body.

Remember to dig deep with every word you read. Take, for instance, the definition of reincarnation as the rebirth of the soul in a new body. Perhaps you should pause and ask if you believe that definition. Break down every part of the definition. For example, do you think that when a soul reincarnates it must be in a new body? Put your definitions and thoughts surrounding the definitions in your handbook.

Exercise: Reincarnation and You

Many psychic development books will refer to the blueprint you created for this lifetime. Someone may have told you, or you sensed, you have lived past lives. Reincarnation is not a New Age idea. Cultures dating back as long as recorded history have believed in reincarnation, or the idea that we repeatedly come back in different forms. This exercise will help you consider what you believe regarding reincarnation and why.

Journal Prompts: Reincarnation and You

1. Do any religions or philosophical organizations that you follow believe in a form of reincarnation?
2. What do they believe?
3. If you believe in reincarnation, write down your thoughts about your beliefs and those who taught you these concepts.
4. If you don't believe in reincarnation, explore your reasons why.

Exercise: Your First Memory

This exercise aims to help you remember what you may have forgotten. Assuming everyone is born psychic, you may have forgotten things about your psychic knowingness because of ridicule, reprimand, repression, or suppression. These memories may be more accessible than you might think.

Your first memory should be direct. In other words, it should not be based on photographs or stories but on your experience. Research suggests that it is impossible to have memory recall before age two.[2] Perhaps those who can remember events before age two are recalling a past life, or they are naturally more psychic.

Close your eyes and slow your breathing. When you are ready, take your energetic self to a safe place you remember from childhood. Be the observer and remember that this is a safe space. Settle in and get comfortable. Start to let little memory clouds float into your space. Take your time. Allow yourself to sense if the memory is from this lifetime.

Assuming you have an early memory, rule out that it is from a suggestion (such as a photograph or story you were told or overheard). Also, consider whether the memory is from a former lifetime (past life) or a parallel life. Think of everything you can recall, including any sensory perceptions. Continue to allow these memory clouds to float into your space until you are ready to return to present reality.

. . . .
2. Shazia Akhtar et al., "Fictional First Memories," *Psychological Science* vol. 29, no. 10 (2018), https://doi.org/10.1177/0956797618778831.

Journal Prompts: Your First Memory

1. What are your thoughts concerning the research asserting you cannot access memories before age two?
2. Why do you think specific memories stand out?
3. Do you think your first memory could have been from a past, parallel, or future life or a false memory? Remember, there are no wrong or right answers.

If you had your psychic knowingness conditioned out of you, journaling about memories will bring intuition to the surface. Remember, you can always revisit these exercises. Do not worry if you don't get anything on the first try.

Do You Have to Be Spiritual to Be Psychic?

At some point, you may have realized or believed that spirituality and religion are different. It is essential to take the next step to explore what you think regarding spirituality. Many New Age, metaphysical, conscious-minded, holistic teachings imply that a psychic must be spiritual. But do they?

It is essential to be clear about what spirituality means to you. You might be surprised that you do not have to be spiritual to be psychic. You do not need a high vibration (often interpreted as higher ascension or enlightenment) to receive messages. It is interesting to see the similarities between the definitions of *psychic* and *faith*. Consider the definition of *psychic*: relating to something outside of natural or scientific knowledge or proof. *Psychic*, as a noun, is someone sensitive to supernatural influences or forces. Now, consider the definition of *faith*: belief and surrender, which are not based on proof. Both definitions are based on a belief or surrender, not based on scientific knowledge or evidence. Remember these definitions the next time you question your psychic knowingness. Neither faith nor psychic hits are based on proof. Consider if you may be searching to fill a void left by leaving or expanding a religion of your youth. Do you want to replace it with yet another creed and dogma?[3]

....

3. "Spirituality Among Americans," Pew Research Center, December 7, 2023, https://www.pewresearch.org/religion/2023/12/07/spirituality-among-americans/.

Exercise: Examining the Role of Spirituality in Your Life

This exercise aims to get in touch with the *why* of your handbook. Why do you want psychic abilities? Are psychic abilities tied to spirituality?

Take a moment to consider what spirituality means to you. Before consulting other sources, write down your thoughts in your handbook. Once you have contemplated and noted your thoughts, consult additional sources.

Spirit and *spirituality* refer to something not physical or tangible. The definitions of *spiritual* and *psychic* also include the mind or intellect. You may feel your religious upbringing makes you hesitant to pursue things of a psychic nature. Perhaps you were told psychic things were evil or, on the other extreme, silly circus cons. It comforts many people to realize that they can integrate psychic pursuits and spirituality, because these are not as mutually exclusive as someone may have led you to believe. Many of my clients, like me, had been led to believe they had to choose between their psychic leanings and their faith. They are relieved and empowered when they realize this is not true. So, while psychic work does not have to be spiritual, it can be integrated into your spiritual beliefs if that is important to you. Remember how important it is to concentrate on your psychic style and not that of others.

Journal Prompts: Examining the Role of Spirituality in Your Life

1. What were you taught about religion or spirituality when young?
2. How have these conditioned beliefs hindered or enhanced your thoughts surrounding psychic matters?

Your Soul's Purpose and Life Purpose

When developing your handbook, knowing your soul's purpose and life purpose is crucial. Those of you who feel you are drowning in your psychic awareness may be desperate to put your psychic knowingness to use. At some point, you have probably been curious about your overriding purpose for all your lifetimes (soul's purpose) and your purpose for this lifetime (life purpose). Do not feel alone if you don't know your soul's purpose or life purpose. Humans have been searching for meaning since the beginning of time. Be careful not to confuse these with an occupation. Your soul's purpose and life purpose may be small, or they may be grand. Still, they have much more to do with the inherent definition of your soul than with the physical or mental aspects of your humanness. In short, you can tell if you align with your soul's purpose and life purpose based on why you do something and how it makes you feel.

Terminology: Your Purpose

Soul's purpose: Your soul's purpose is your overriding purpose for all lifetimes. (A soul's purpose could be joy, for example.)

Life purpose: Your life purpose is your purpose for this lifetime. A lifetime purpose may be to bring joy (soul's purpose) through singing (life purpose).

Mission statement: Your mission statement is what you will do on earth to implement your life purpose. (Someone with a soul's purpose of spreading joy may have a mission statement to smile at someone daily.)

Vision statement: Your vision statement is how you will implement your mission statement. (For example, the mission statement of smiling at someone every day could be fulfilled by a vision statement of making a point to serve others by volunteering or simply making a point to walk by someone and smile at them every day.)

Exercise: Your Purpose

This exercise aims to help you understand your soul's purpose, life purpose, mission statement, and vision statement so that you can make this handbook and your life uniquely yours without comparing yourself to others. Once you understand your purpose and how it does or does not relate to those around you, your outlook on life will improve. This fresh outlook will also free you to exist in your psychic knowingness without caring what others think.

Look at the terms above and then formulate your soul's purpose, life purpose, mission statement, and vision statement.

Journal Prompts: Your Purpose

1. Without looking at other definitions, write down your definitions of *soul's purpose*, *life purpose*, *mission statement*, and *vision statement*.
2. Choose one of the terms. Think through what steps you can take to get closer to your purpose or mission statement.

Avoid These Pitfalls

Mindlessly following what others tell you is one of the biggest mistakes you can make in your psychic development. If you are searching for meaning in your life, decide to own your journey today. Reframe your narrative. Taking charge of your story will help prevent waking up one day only to realize you are still unaware of your beliefs. Although you might not have all the answers, no one does. You can and should spend some time getting to know yourself and what you are comfortable with in your life, where you are okay being stretched, and those areas that are off-limits to you. This handbook allows you to write your manifesto to avoid the pitfall of following someone else's.

Psychic Success

As a lifelong people pleaser, I finally realized I was going along with people to make them like me or to avoid confrontation. I woke up one day and realized that I was still conditioned. I had traded one set of conditioned beliefs for another. To avoid confrontation, I would accept certain beliefs without really knowing what they meant or if I agreed with them. I realized I needed to get to the root of my beliefs. I started by taking a long, hard look at my psychic statements. Now, I question everything I read, hear, or teach. My queries are not contrarian but a search for my soul and authentic being. I arrived at this point because I looked at my beliefs versus those of conditioning.

For a while, I did not want anything closely resembling another box to dictate my life. But I realize now that I don't mind boxes. They serve to bring stability and structure to my life. I now realize success comes from knowing I build the box if I choose to have one.

Further, I can expand or contract the box depending on my reality versus everyone I want to please. Finally, I can get rid of boxes at any time. Once you put what others tell you to your litmus test, you can get to the root of who you are and what you believe. The success comes in knowing that instead of letting others dictate your life, you are creating it yourself.

CHAPTER 3

YOUR PSYCHIC DEFENSE

A Psychic's Handbook does not intend to promote fear, but wisdom and discernment. In other words, you understand that a full spectrum of energy is available to absorb. However, practicing good psychic hygiene is a great habit to cultivate whether you are just waking up your psychic senses or are a professional psychic or energy worker. Many professionals fail to proactively protect their energy field to the point of hurting their health because they inadvertently take on the destructive energy of others.

Checkup: Energetic Body Scan (What Is Mine) Baseline

This checkup aims to assess if you are protecting and managing your energy. Follow this protocol, or something similar, to always be aware of what energy belongs to you and what belongs to someone else.

1. I do an energetic body scan before I go into crowded places. I check my body to see how I feel physically, mentally, emotionally, and spiritually. This scan allows me to ascertain what belongs to me instead of others and better manage my energy.

2. I assess energetic situations and choose a type of defense based on my energy and the other energy. For example, I know I am attending a family holiday dinner that may become heated. In that case, I might put a bubble of light around me like an eggshell.

3. I use protection. Protection might be an energetic shield of armor or a crystal, such as a black tourmaline.

4. I realize that with protection, the energy I send out to others can still surpass any protective barriers. Still, incoming energy is blocked, slowed down, or weakened.

5. I realize that clearing old energy through methods such as a salt bath is critical to protection because knowing the source of unwanted energy is essential. A clean auric field provides a better chance of assessing the energy source.

The more yes answers, the more you are taking responsibility to manage your energy. Remember, this is a checkup for your benefit. It will only help you to the extent you are honest.

Terminology: Psychic Defense

Psychic attack: Mental intrusions from humans or other spirit beings into your energetic self, which may cause physical or mental damage. Some signs of a psychic attack include extreme fatigue, mood swings, fear, anxiety, and self-doubt.

Psychic self-defense: Protecting your energy to ward off undesirable entities or other energy.

Psychic source: The source of a reader or energy worker's information or channel.

Psychic transmuters: Those who can take negative energy thrown at them and change it into energy for good. They do not drain anyone's energy because it was initially directed at (handed over to) them.

Origin of Your Psychic Information

As a psychic, your information, by definition, should come from some source other than your mere opinion. It is crucial at this juncture to begin by asking about the origin of the information you receive. Discovering the origin can be achieved through meditation and interviewing your source of information.

Some people will fall back on the conditioned beliefs of their youth as the source of their information. For example, if you called on saints as a child, you may believe a saint or an angel is providing the information. While this may be the case, you should still exercise due diligence to determine the source of your information. This clarification is significant if, for instance, the saint does not give information in line with the behavior or personality of that saint. For example, suppose you are connecting to a saint who is known to be an animal lover and they are exuding traits contrary to loving animals. In that case, you may question who you are communicating with. If you are not aware of the source of your information, you can also be subject to an unintentional energy attack when you give or receive readings. It is essential to know the source of psychic information, and especially ask when getting readings from others about the source of their information.

Knowing this is important for psychic protection because you need to know if you want to open your energetic field up to the energy (source) of the information. If you cannot pinpoint the source of the information, it is helpful to ascertain how the energy makes you feel. Suppose the energy makes you feel guilty or angry. In that case, you might stop communicating and not open your energetic field to that energy.

Once you know the source of your abilities, it is time to determine if you need to set any energetic or personal boundaries. Boundaries will serve a purpose if you do not know how to transmute the energy into something palatable if something that comes around you or at you is uncomfortable.

Below are various ways to set boundaries. Most are effective for both personal and energetic boundaries. You should set up a personal limitation with a friend who takes advantage of your abilities. For example, an energetic boundary that protects your aura and entire beingness. For our purposes, boundaries fall under a general category known as *protection*.

Exercise: Psychic Source

This exercise aims to help you discover the source of your psychic information. Some psychic source information is crucial for you to protect yourself energetically. You can do all the protection exercises you want. Still, if you are tapping into an energy not in alignment with you, it may not respond to the protection. It is like locking the door to your house and then letting beings in through the window.

Take time to contemplate where you believe your messages originate. We are all portals, and there is no veil. It is a conditioned belief that you do not have direct access to Source. Therefore, everyone has direct access to all information if they learn to tap into the frequency of that information. Practice protecting and minding your energy as you do in every aspect of your life. In other words, you are around portals every second of every day. You are a portal, and so is every form of energy. The protection you need may vary from moment to moment and person to person.

An ideal time to use some form of protection is under anesthesia. You have no control over what enters your auric field during that time. Before going under anesthesia, it is advisable to set protection around you. Also, ask the doctor or nurse to put a black tourmaline or some shungite in the surgery area to transmute any negativity you might not be able to while unconscious.

There are various ways to protect yourself energetically. What is best for you will vary from situation to situation. Once again, nothing is perfect for everyone. We will cover various methods; you can try them to see which works best. The one that will ultimately work the best is the one you will remember to use.

Journal Prompts: Psychic Source

1. Do you know where your messages are coming from or originate? Explain.
2. What are your thoughts regarding portals?
3. Do you see or sense spirits?
4. Do you believe there is a veil?

Exercise: Colors to Surround Yourself with Light

This exercise utilizes colors to help surround your auric field with protective vibrations. Visualize yourself surrounded by color. You can tie the color to the chakra you are protecting. For instance, if you are protecting your words, you would use blue to safeguard your throat chakra and the words that come from your mouth or those you might hear. You could also use crystals or other blue objects. You could even utilize an actual blue light as opposed to visualization. Eventually, try doing this with every color.

Journal Prompts: Colors to Surround Yourself with Light

1. Were you able to visualize one or more colors?
2. Which color was most effortless for you to visualize?
3. We will cover chakras in chapter 7. Once you are familiar with chakras, can you visualize the chakra's color around the area of the chakra? This helps you begin to tie the Three C's—clairs, chakras, and colors—together.

Exercise: Affirmations

The purpose of this exercise is to proclaim statements declaring your protection. A positive, affirming protection statement is a straightforward way to invoke protective measures and stay in a positive vibration. If you were protecting yourself from the hurtful words of another, you could use the affirmation "I am fully protected and surrounded by words of love."

Think of a physical, mental, emotional, or spiritual area where you feel vulnerable to a psychic attack. This vulnerability may stem from a physical illness, cognitive overload, emotional stressors, or spiritual doubts. Start with one area, such as a physical vulnerability. You may go to the dentist and have a cavity filled. You are initially in pain, so therefore vulnerable, and then you may receive a shot or laughing gas. The sedation makes you more susceptible to a sneak attack by insidious energy. Once you realize this (the earlier, the better), you can protect against the attack by stating, "I am safe. I am protected. No negative energy can harm me."

Journal Prompts: Affirmations

1. Is it hard to form a positive statement before you feel it is true?
2. Could you state affirmations for your physical, mental, emotional, and spiritual self?
3. Do you feel affirmations help protect you?

I used to feel like I was lying when I stated positive affirmations. Perhaps I felt on the verge of a migraine, but I knew I should express gratitude to feel better. It was nearly impossible to say a positive affirmation, such as "I am happy and content." I felt utterly inauthentic because the statement was not valid. However, the more I began to understand the power of my words to create my reality, the more I realized I was speaking the affirmation into reality where, in some parallel universe, it already was in existence.

Exercise: Bubble of Protection

This exercise aims to help you visualize yourself in a protective bubble through which your energy can pass. Your energy can go out of the bubble, but any harmful energy cannot pierce the bubble to harm you.

A bubble of protection, or any other shape, allows you total security and comfort. Imagine a bubble surrounding you. The bubble may be egg shaped. In theory, nothing that will harm you can penetrate the bubble of protection. Surround yourself with this bubble of protection for as long as you feel the need. The problem with this type of protection is that while you may feel safe in your bubble, a robust and energetic being can quickly drop-kick your bubble with you in it to the depths of the ocean. In these instances, it might be preferable to call in your big dog, heavy protector guides, such as Archangel

Michael, to stand guard around you. You will learn about these guides in chapter 5. But it doesn't hurt to slap a bubble of protection around yourself first. The same applies to walls or shields of protection.

Journal Prompts: Bubble of Protection

1. Could you visualize a bubble of protection? If so, describe it.
2. Do you believe the bubble of protection will protect you?
3. Are there circumstances when a bubble of protection might not be enough?

The best protection is learning to transmute energy, which is an advanced technique that I teach in my book *The Magic of Connection*. Transmutation takes practice; therefore, at this point, I suggest you meet your guides and get a solid defensive line. Chapter 5 will introduce guides. Transmutation isn't a skill that's covered here; however, the types of protection covered in this book work just fine as you begin exploring your abilities.

Exercise: Design Your Psychic Defense

The purpose of this exercise is to design your ultimate psychic defense. Some spirit beings and energies are best at catching you when you are at your weakest, so the key is to never be caught off guard. This exercise will prepare you while you are strong.

We are all one. If malevolent energy wants access, it will find your weakest link. If the energy can't get to you, it will get to someone or a situation close to you. Design a psychic defense plan in your handbook. You could create strategies such as affirmations, guides, bubbles, energetic shields, crystals, oils, herbs, or other modalities to help protect you. Remember that energy never goes away; it merely changes form.

Journal Prompts: Design Your Psychic Defense

1. Could you think of which means of protection will work best for you at various times?
2. Did you think of vulnerable areas in your life that might need protecting?
3. Were you able to get an excellent psychic defense plan started?

Avoid These Pitfalls

I can tell you without hesitation that where there is light, there is darkness. While this may mean different things to different people, the fact remains that there are some evil energies roaming everywhere you find yourself. They are not just in graveyards or haunted houses. They are all around you, and many prey on those not equipped to deal with them. Take protection seriously. Only get involved with energy beings you understand or are equipped to handle.

The mission of some psychics is to deal with complex frequencies. I am one of those psychics, but it came at a cost when I was not psychically mature enough to do so. Dealing with certain energy beings can be very dangerous and is not a game. Some of these energies come in the form of jealousy and envy. Be very careful of humans who are resentful of you for no reason. Steer clear of that energy and make sure to use protection. Sometimes, the best form of protection is the adage "out of sight, out of mind," because nothing is feeding the energy. Avoid falling into ego and playing above your experience if something or someone feels wrong. Monsters are real, and they do walk among us.

Psychic Success

A lot of information is available about maintaining reasonable boundaries. However, please know that good energetic boundaries only sometimes equal solid protection. The more you find what works to protect you, the more you embrace your psychic knowingness. You will become much more settled in your knowingness when you instantly set up the boundaries and tools that work best for you. Knowing which work best for you will involve trial and error, so get started now!

CHAPTER 4

YOUR OWN WORST ENEMY

The most important thing to advance your psychic skills is to stop being attached to the outcome. In other words, stop caring if you are right. Some claim we forget our abilities as we grow older. While this may be true, another strong possibility is that as we age, we begin to care too much about being right or not making a mistake when using our psychic abilities. Children say whatever comes into their minds. Overcoming your concern about what others think is extremely beneficial when relaying your psychic communications.

Checkup: Are You Your Biggest Roadblock Baseline

This checkup determines how much you are getting in your way regarding your psychic development. Answer the questions yes or no. Remember, this is a checkup for your benefit. It will only help you to the extent you are candid. If you are honest, you have a good baseline for your roadblocks.

1. I operate from logic.
2. I push to get answers when I do readings.
3. I do not trust my intuition.

4. I overanalyze things.
5. I second-guess my messages.
6. I try to tie messages up with a neat bow, meaning speculation enters the message.
7. I am not particularly eager to give a message that doesn't make sense.
8. I filter my messages.
9. I repress particular messages.
10. I am concerned about being wrong.
11. I change messages that sound too out there.
12. I care that I am right, not just for me but the client.
13. I go with statistics and odds in readings.
14. I do not believe in my abilities.
15. I am good at evaluating cues from others.

The more yes answers, the more you hold yourself back in your psychic knowingness. The number of yes answers will decrease as you develop and practice the methods in your handbook.

The Four R's

When using your psychic knowingness, remember the Four R's: request, receive, read, and relay information or messages. The request is the ask—the answer or information sought. Once there is a request, you receive a message. Next, you read or interpret that message. Finally, you relay the message to the person asking the questions and receiving the message (the sitter or querent). The biggest mistakes occur while reading or relaying the message because of overanalyzing or second-guessing. The best thing to do is receive and read the message without filtering it. When you deliver (relay) your interpretation (read) of the message given, always follow the guidelines you impose on yourself. You can relay a message without filtering or adding your own advice while still considering the way in which you deliver it. For example, be honest with the querent and do not add your personal advice or comments. However, also be cognizant of the tone you deem respectful. If you follow your preset rules, it leads to accuracy.

On one occasion, I was reading for a lady. She was highly professional and a bit uptight, so it surprised me that I kept seeing a pink flamingo sitting on her head. Finally, I interrupted her and asked why I kept seeing a flamingo on her head. She laughed and said she was mortified when her friends made her wear a gaudy flamingo hat for her birthday celebration a few weeks before. Even though it made no sense to me, it connected with the querent. It also helped her open her garage door just a little, which is my way of explaining when a querent begins to open up to me.

Terminology: Consciousness

Let's review a few terms that can confuse some people. There is no reason to overthink this. However, you can dive as deep as you want in your handbook. Please return to every section often and update it as you grow.

Conscious mind (ego): Your conscious mind or ego is your thinking, logical, analytical mind. In other words, your ego is your identity and who you think you are. You know your ego has entered a reading when you are reaching for answers or you have received a response to your request, but you begin to scrutinize and reconsider how to relay the message. You do not lose your ego as you become enlightened; however, it stops defining you. Your ego protects you physically and psychologically, but remember, you are not your ego.

Unconscious (subconscious) mind: Your unconscious or subconscious mind holds every memory, belief, feeling, thought, and fear you have learned and observed since you were young. While you aren't aware of the influence the unconscious has on you, it influences nearly every area of your life. You know the unconscious mind is coming into a reading when you suppress, reconfigure, or restrain part of or the entire message you receive.

Superconscious mind (higher self or psychic mind): Your superconscious or higher self enters the picture when things seamlessly float into your mind. You receive information and relay it. You do not filter it— request, receive, read, and relay.

Exercise: Turn Your Back on Them

The purpose of this exercise is to begin to turn off the performance aspect of your psychic knowingness to start to release your attachment to the outcome of being correct.

Go to the front of a room with a few participants. These are people who practice with you, or they are volunteers. When you reach the front of the room, turn your back on the others. Sit or stand, whichever is more comfortable for you, but make sure you are not looking at anyone. The key to this exercise is to request, receive, read, and relay an intuitive message to someone in the room without observing their reaction. Changing or qualifying your message is tempting if you watch someone shaking their head in disagreement or agreement with you. Deliver your message without hesitation—request, receive, read, and relay.

Afterward, you may ask for validation from the person you gave the message to. Validation and honest feedback are great ways to know that you are tapping into your intuition, even though you may feel like you are making something up. It is not your job to judge the message.

As a reader, continually formulate specific requests by drafting brief questions with no wiggle room. Then, tap into your unique psychic knowingness to receive the information. Next, you will read or interpret the data. Then, finally, relay or deliver the message. You must be careful at each step to do your job and not judge it. Request, receive, read, and relay. The querent, or person getting the message, can assemble the puzzle. That is different from your calling as a psychic. Your job is to relay the message you receive. You do not have to figure out how it all fits together. Trying to solve the case or fix an issue is often the sign of someone who may get lucky a time or two but will rarely progress in their psychic knowingness.

Journal Prompts: Turn Your Back on Them

1. Did you feel uncomfortable turning your back to the room, or did it help you not see reactions?
2. Could you limit the relaying of your message to just the information you received?
3. Did you find yourself wanting to fill in the blanks with your speculation to give a complete answer to the subjects?
4. Did this exercise help you overcome some of your fear of being wrong?

Avoid These Pitfalls

One of the biggest pitfalls psychics fall into is wanting to be correct. You may have heard it called *being spot on*. This attachment to the outcome is ego run amuck. Slow your roll and practice the exercises in this book as suggested, especially in relaying messages. Only impart the message. Do not embellish it. It is important to note that most messages come in short spurts, snapshots, and flashes of thought instead of entire paragraphs. Please read the message and relay it without embellishment. If you stick to this, you will never have to second-guess yourself.

Problems arise when you want to be right (either for the accolades or the strong desire to help your client), and the temptation to elaborate on the message rears its ugly head. The desire to be right happens a lot when lawyers cross-examine witnesses. The lawyer may have the witness up against the ropes, but then the lawyer makes the dreaded mistake—they ask one question too many. The witness then has an opportunity to argue their answers, and they come out swinging. One question too many is the equivalent of a psychic relaying a message and trying to put all the information together. Sometimes, the message is not clear. Resist the urge to play God. Just request, receive, read, and relay. The message is not about you being right; it is about relaying the message.

Psychic Success

I teach people to relay messages at least thrice weekly in various classes. I immediately know when someone steps quickly into psychic success versus those who will progress slower. The key is to describe, describe, describe. Those that describe instead of trying to summarize or fill in gaps progress rapidly. They enjoy psychic success at astonishing rates due to realizing they should only relay the information given. They are the psychics who I would want to read for me.

Once you begin experiencing psychic success, please know it can be difficult. Being right can be a significant burden when you don't want to be. It's not fun when you have a difficult message to relay. There are times I say, "I hope I am wrong." You will know you did the right thing if you relay the message lovingly and compassionately. But I will not mislead you; sometimes you may be tempted to avoid a tough message. Sticking with your psychic message and delivering it compassionately will not hurt nearly as much as dismissing it and leading the querent astray.

CHAPTER 5

YOUR SPIRIT GUIDES

The topic of spirit guides is one I always approach with caution. While we can all use helpers in life, I see too much emphasis on spirit guides. The concept is interesting, as we all want to be guided by some unseen force. But sadly, what I observe is overreliance on and obsession with guides, which is directly at odds with their ultimate purpose. A guide directs or points you to your higher self or Source. Instead of being so obsessed with wanting to know who your guides are, it is ultimately more important to know in what way you need guidance. Spirit guides should point you to that part of you that is part of Source—your higher self. Meeting your guides is not the end of the journey; it is scratching the surface. Your guides serve as spiritual bumper pads to help you stay on track to connecting with your higher self and Source.

Spirit guides are energy beings that direct and assist you throughout your life. They ultimately lead you to your higher self so that you can fulfill your soul's purpose, life purpose, mission statement, and vision statement. It is best to cultivate a relationship between you and the guide alone. Therefore, there are better ways to meet your guides than learning who your guide is from a psychic. Try choosing or selecting your guide, perhaps an animal, historical figure (dead or alive), or crystal. You do not have to wait for a guide to come to you or for someone to tell you who your guide is.

It is important to watch for signs and synchronicities. These are some of the best ways to know a guide is with you. Do not dismiss anything as a coincidence. Guides send obvious signs, but you must listen and stop second-guessing. Ultimately, the best measure of whether you want to work with a guide is how they make you feel, and only you can assess that. Always remember that you do not have to see a guide for one to be with you; seeing a guide is less common than sensing a guide.

Many claim that spirit guides must be in spirit or not living. I don't see it this way, so I invite you to consider that we are all spiritual beings and can be spirit guides. Someone living, someone you know who has passed, someone you don't know who is living or has passed, an angel, an animal, or any other kind of being can serve as a spirit guide. There is no reason to put spirit guides in categories. Guides come to you as you need them. Many claim we all have one spirit guide, often called a guardian angel, or even a guide who helped us incarnate; I have found no evidence of this. We may have one or many, but at some point, spirit guides may step away from us to let us mature into reaching our connection to our higher selves and Source. The goal is to utilize the guides when necessary rather than depend solely on them. I cringe whenever I hear people say, "My spirit guide told me to…" or "*They* told me to do such and such." Your spirit guide will rarely, if ever, tell you what to do. If they do, take a long, hard look at whether that guide is guiding you to a connection with your higher self or if the guide wants you to rely on them.

Checkup: Guide Baseline

This checkup aims to get a baseline for your relationship with guides.

1. I know at least one of my spirit guides.
2. I have a relationship with the guide.
3. I discovered my guide without someone else telling me.
4. I am doing things to get to know my guides better.
5. I am helped by my guides.
6. I show gratitude to my guides.
7. I know my level of comfort with psychic matters.
8. I know who and what beings I want to work with.

The more yes answers, the more you already connect with guides. The number of yes answers will increase as you develop and practice the methods in your handbook.

Terminology: Spirit Guides

Duality: The contrast or opposition between two ideas or things. The resistance creates chaos, repulsion or, some might say, positive and negative aspects.

Polarity: The principle that everything has two opposite poles. These opposite poles help us gain understanding in our lives. Without distinction, there is no comparison. Polarity allows the duality aspects to unify or find peace in separateness.

Spirit guide: A being of any type that directs you.

How Do I Get a Guide to Work with Me?

Through the years, I have had many clients come to me and claim they need help getting a guide to work with them. Guides will work with everyone. Remember, this is your handbook, not that of your friend or a guide. It is *yours*! The issue is that you have probably thought your spirit guide had to be a certain way or be up in your face all the time. Guides are often subtle, and you can work with any guide. You can choose your guide, which may be from a culture other than the one you live in during this lifetime. There are some exceptions to this that people love to argue about. Still, my advice is to stop arguing and focus on your handbook instead of trying to manage everyone else's. Deities can also decide if they want to avoid working with someone. Just as you pick friends or employees to fulfill jobs, it helps to know what you are looking for a spirit guide to do in your life. The following are some things to consider regarding the role of a spirit guide in your life.

Be Clear About the Guide's Job Description

Make a list of what you want your relationship with a guide to achieve. Ultimately, your spirit guide should direct you to your higher self, but what else do you want from your guide? Clarifying what you don't want from a guide is equally important. This job description should originate with you, not with what others tell you a spirit guide should do or be in your life.

Set Your Intention—Name It and Claim It

Many advise you to pray when contacting or connecting with your spirit guide. I recommend you set your intention, which is the same as a prayer in many ways. (Hold up before you get upset; I said "in many ways.") Set the intention (make up your mind and claim it) that you will meet a guide. Say it out loud. I often add "For my highest and best good." I add these words because I do not want to set any parameters for anything except my highest and best good. I may even work with a neutral or so-called "low-vibration" guide if that is for my highest good.

Frequency

When you meet spirit guides, you open the door to spirit beings you may not have encountered or do not remember encountering. As I emphasize in my book *Spirits Unveiled*, there are all types, shapes, and varieties of spirit beings. As humans, we have our social mores, ethics, and laws. But the innumerable spirit beings do not necessarily share our views, and who are we to force ours on other beings? Therefore, there will be spirit beings who do not share your sense of morality. They may have your highest and best good in mind when helping you, but you might feel uncomfortable with their methods because your frequencies may need to match. There may also be some who do not have your best interest at heart due to duality and polarity. I am open to every kind of guide because I work in the shadow realms. But many people will tell you to only work with beings of the light. I struggle with this because it implies a vital distinction between light and dark. This distinction is more complex than religions and television shows want us to believe. Like humans, there are many shades of gray with spirit guides.

However, many think that saying the words "I only want to work with beings of the light" will magically involve only what is considered light. I will be blunt: The people who say that probably have yet to work with that many guides, nor do they understand the nature of frequency and energy. Energy has no judgment. We are the ones who assign judgment to energy, and it can become rather comical once you truly meet other beings. Please be aware that the boundaries may not work for specific beings.

Research and Pursue a Guide

Much like friends, the more you think of a guide, the more they will reveal themselves to you. If you show you care and want to get together with a friend, it is more likely that a friendship will form. You can pick your guide. They do not have to choose you. However, if you feel a spirit around you, talk to them like you would when meeting someone for the first time. Wait to sage them. Would you do this to a human you met for coffee? Engage before you sage!

Ask any questions you want, but also ask what they are here to help you with. How are they going to guide you? Make sure to listen to the reply. No, it usually won't be an audible reply, but use your mind's eye to sense and feel the guide. Use your clairs to connect with this being here to help you. Clairs are discussed further in chapter 6. Many will say that you must wait for a guide to choose you. While this might be true with some deities and some practices, countless guides are never written about and do not belong to any group. You can choose these guides. When in doubt, ask. No, not the human trying to control what guides you should work with, but the guide themselves. If you are not supposed to work with a particular deity, they do not need a human to speak for them. They can tell you themselves. Honor them and ask if you have any questions.

Meditate and Journal about It

Journaling and meditation are the two things people seem to resist the most. However, I have learned through the years that they are two of the most important things to do. When you meditate and still your mind, there is a better chance of noticing the energy of a guide around you. Some guides are subtle, while some are bombastic and you can't miss them. Either way, meditation helps you slow down and get into a state to receive information. Once you start receiving information or having thoughts come into your mind, let them flow. You may only get one or two words or pictures in your mind, but write them down. You don't have to write a beautiful essay. Putting your thoughts and revelations to paper will help you remember the details of this guide. It will also help you remember guides from your past when you look at the journal later.

Take That Down a Notch!

Do you know that feeling when you sense someone is with you, but you turn around and see that no one is there? You might feel like that when first becoming aware of your guides. There have always been spirit beings around you, but now you are beginning to connect with them. You might feel a tingling or a subtle shift in the energy. It's as if you know someone or something is with you. Spirit guides are energetic beings just as you are. You just vibrate at different frequencies. If anything feels too intense, tell them to pull their energy back. I have said out loud, "Take that down a notch!"

Make the Relationship a Priority

As with most things in life, consistency and perseverance are critical; the more you work on any relationship, the more you connect with someone. Yes, sometimes the guides will just show up, but cultivating the relationship does help facilitate the process. I find it best to communicate with my guides first thing in the morning. This communication through meditation sets the tone of my day. I am much calmer and more focused when I start my day by quieting my mind and connecting with my guides or higher self. However, this is your handbook. You know your schedule and how you will likely set yourself up for consistency. Once you become consistent, you will also recognize if there is a shift from your typical experience. Any change is something to note and write down in your journal. Your guide will usually match your consistency and show up more quickly.

Chill and They Will Come

It can be frustrating if you feel you are trying to communicate with a guide but have yet to connect. Assuming you are being consistent in your meditation, chill and be patient. Your guide will show up for you. There is a good chance the guide is subtle. Tell the guide to show you a sign. You can even decide on the sign, such as when I see three blue jays at a particular place or time, then that means my guide is communicating. I set that as a sign. Remember that the way someone else connects with a guide does not mean that is how you will. Your psychic knowingness is unique to you. Try not to compare yourself or your experience to others.

Let's Clear Up Some "Mythconceptions"

I have read too many books that echo the same sentiments. The repeated information, in large part, has yet to be my experience. Most of these books are written from a Spiritualist perspective. I am not a Spiritualist, and my experiences sometimes vary from the books written by those who are. Below are some general mythconceptions surrounding spirit guides:

1. *Guides should be worshipped:* Unless it is a guide from a particular practice or religion, spirit guides are here to show us the way. They may desire respect or acknowledgment, but most do not expect worship. They are here to guide you.

2. *Guides have never incarnated:* Guides can be spirits that have never incarnated to earth, incarnated only once, or incarnated thousands of times.

3. *Angels cannot be guides:* Guides can be angels. Remember, guides meet you where you are. They could be angels if you like angels and are comfortable with them.

4. *Ghosts cannot be guides:* Although in theory a ghost could be a guide, I would only recommend this if it was for a short period. If the ghost has something to offer that guides you to your purpose, then the ghost could serve as a guide. The way to tell the difference in all spirit beings is the rate at which they vibrate, which is their frequency. Read my book *Spirits Unveiled* for detailed ways to ascertain and adjust to differences in frequency.

5. *Loved ones cannot be guides:* The guide can be a loved one, a living human being who serves as a spirit guide.

6. *You should know the guide's name before working with them:* Although I used to repeat this because everyone else did, I now realize I was regurgitating something that did not resonate. Knowing or not knowing the name of a guide is less important than how the guide treats you. They may have a name you couldn't pronounce even if they told you. They also may be hesitant to give you their name because you might not work with them if you are afraid of certain types of beings based on the information you have heard or learned in the past. It is best to place the judgment of any being on whether the guide points you to Source, your higher self, or your purpose.

7. *Everyone has a fixed number of guides:* You can, and most likely will, have more than one guide. We tend to be stubborn and often need a team to help us.

8. *Spirit guides and angels do not have free will:* You have free will. You choose whether to follow their guidance. The spirit guide also has free will to not work with you. Angelic guides also have free will, although some erroneously believe they do not.

9. *Spirit guides will be familiar and healthy in appearance:* Spirit guides meet you where you are. You might freak out if a particular type of guide appeared to you. In other words, if you can handle seeing the guide as a gargoyle, then the guide might appear to you as such. Gargoyles are protective and placed on massive cathedrals' tops to ward off evil. Guides often come as human because this might be more acceptable. They may dress in familiar clothing so that you feel more at ease. I have frequently heard it said that guides won't present themselves to you with disabilities. This statement regarding guides is not accurate. Guides come in all shapes and forms because that may be what you need at the time. I suppose the theory is that the guide's disabilities are healed, but this is not how all guides work and is misleading and shortsighted. Many of us have disabilities, and we should not feel ashamed of them. A guide may appear as someone with paraplegia because that may be the guide someone needs. How condescending and arrogant to think otherwise. Guides may appear to us with a disability if they help guide us in some way. Ultimately, everything is energy, so eventually, you may have a guide that appears like a ball of crackling electricity. You may even have a guide that is a group of guides serving as one guide.

10. *Guides must communicate with you in certain ways:* Guides will communicate with you through different means, including, but not limited to, short messages in your mind's eye (yes or no), information downloads, claircognizance (inner knowing), dreams, meditation, clairaudience (inner hearing), outer hearing (audible sound), symbols, signs, songs, conversations, numbers, and books.

11. *Guides must be of the light:* Many people will tell you to only work with guides from the light. I used to set this boundary and intention when calling on guides; however, I now know that beings are not simply of the light or not of the light. All beings have polarity—light and dark, good and bad, salty and sweet. Calling something "of the light" or "not of the light" does not resonate with me. I prefer to set boundaries by saying I welcome guides for my highest and best good. There have been times in my life when a being did not seem of the light, yet they served a purpose that pointed me to Source or my higher self.

Exercise: Meet Your Guide in Five Easy Steps

The purpose of this exercise is to meet a guide. Meeting a guide can be simple. The easier you make it, the more likely you are to meet one. The following exercise is simple and concise. The only tricky part is believing what you experience.

Equipment: Paper and something to write with, and a candle

Instructions:
1. Write down an intention of what you want from a guide. A good start is seeking a guide to show you your purpose and lead you to it. But please use your wording because it will make it specific to you with the vibration of your words.
2. Light a candle and begin to gaze into it. I recommend a tapered candle. Put a fireproof plate or dish under the candle so the wax can drip safely.
3. Ask to meet a guide for your highest and best good (or whatever your intention is).
4. Pay attention to any signs or messages in your third eye. As always, do not dismiss them as your imagination.
5. Ask the guide to reveal information about what they are here to help you with currently.

You can also change this exercise and pick the guide yourself. Decide on a guide you want to work with and call in that guide.

Journal Prompts: Meet Your Guide in Five Easy Steps

1. Could you calm down and be in the moment's stillness?
2. Did a guide reveal themselves to you? Remember, it may be a subtle revelation.
3. What signs were you given?

4. What thoughts regarding a guide came into your mind or senses?

5. Did the guide tell you what they are here to help you with?

6. Did you pick a guide yourself? If so, journal about that.

I have read in book after book that we all have specific guides. While I agree that we can all have guides, I do not agree that there are predetermined kinds that work with us, such as joy, protection, or incarnation guides. They could be of any type, any number, and for anything. We are all different, so the idea that we all have the same category of guides is misleading.

Exercise: Connection to Guides

This exercise aims to help you connect to different types of guides and, eventually, your higher self and Source to receive information. You will also discover your other sources of intuitive information.

Close your eyes and slow your breathing. Feel yourself pull away a little from your body. You are not having an out-of-body experience but are implementing the practice of pulling away from your human form. Now, find yourself at the door to a house. A key appears in your hand, and you know this is a house that you can enter, and you do so. You find yourself in a large entryway with a spiraling staircase. You begin to climb the stairs. Step one, step two, step three, step four, step five, step six, step seven, step eight, step nine, and step ten. You are now at the top of the stairs and see a hallway with a door that you know you are to enter. As you approach the door, you notice another key in your hand. Take a deep breath and insert the key into the door. Before you open the door, take another deep breath, and prepare to meet a guide. Now, open the door. Immediately, you notice all the details in the room. Take in everything you see, hear, taste, smell, and touch. Do not dismiss any detail.

If you see or sense a guide, approach them and ask anything you want in order to get to know them. Spend as much time with your guide as you choose. When you decide to leave, your guide will present you with a wrapped gift. Open the gift and see what is inside. Feel free to ask your guide what the gift is or what it represents.

It is now time to say goodbye to your guide or anyone else in the room you want to bid farewell to. You may choose to invite your guide to leave with you. Gather your gift, leave the room, and lock the door with your key. You can come back to this room at any time. You have the key to the room and the front door.

Descend the stairs. Step ten, step nine, step eight, step seven, step six, step five, step four, step three, step two, step one. Go across the entryway to the front door and exit. Be sure to lock the door behind you. When your feet hit the street, you notice the street is a mixture of stone and grass. You immediately become grounded to earth. You also see the stars and the heavens. You feel your crown chakra connect to a cosmic body. You are now grounded between heaven and earth. When you are ready, open your eyes.

Journal Prompts: Connection to Guides

1. Could you pull away from your body?
2. What did the front door look like?
3. What did the front door key look like?
4. What did the door to the room look like?
5. What did the room key look like?
6. What did you see when you opened the door?
7. Did you meet a guide or guides?
8. Was the guide(s) new or familiar to you?
9. Break down each guide and describe everything you noticed about them.
10. Did you converse with the guide(s)?
11. How was the gift wrapped? What was the gift? What is its purpose?

Avoid These Pitfalls

Refrain from letting anyone tell you who can or cannot be your guide. Such gatekeeping is unnecessary and, frankly, offensive to guides. Guides can let you know if they are off-limits to you. Also, please resist the urge to tell other people what guides they have unless they ask for your psychic message. Be open to allowing yourself breaks from guides so you can operate from your higher self and the Collective. Do not get lost in the spirit guide pursuit when your soul is the best energy guide.

Psychic Success

Being psychic can be very difficult if you do not have guidance. You may have a parent or friend to mentor you; however, you may still want more assistance. Enlisting the help of a spirit guide is a perfect way to help you navigate some of the more challenging aspects of psychic knowingness. However, always remember that you are a powerful force connected to Source or all that is. As you evolve, your higher self will not always need the help of a guide. In fact, you may serve as a guide to others.

CHAPTER 6

YOUR CLAIRS

Through my years of teaching thousands of students, three things that help people advance quickly in developing their psychic knowingness have become apparent to me. The Three C's (the clairs, the chakras, and the colors of auras) are most helpful in quickly getting information that leads to psychic knowingness. The following three chapters will explain the Three C's and introduce checkups and exercises to assist you in formulating your psychic handbook. Because these three chapters are so important, they are robust and lengthy. Keep in mind when working through them that once you have practiced how to use the Three C's in readings, you can deliver strong intuitive messages.

Psychic hits, or moments when a psychic knowingness sweeps over you, are usually fairly clear. Most of us muddy these psychic hits by second-guessing that aha moment. The French word for "clear" is *clair*. The various types of clairs are helpful to ascertain how you receive your information. We will cover eight clairs in this book. As you work through the clairs, you will begin to know how to play to your strengths and bolster the areas where you have weaknesses. You will begin to notice while performing the exercises that the clairs overlap. You will also find you may be more proficient at one or two clairs and must work more on the others to find the clair blend for you. The key to success is to practice consistently. If you take shortcuts in your psychic development, the consequences will become evident when you do not grow or perhaps regress in your skills.

Clairsentience

Clairsentience means "clear feeling." It is acquiring knowledge primarily through empathic feelings and emotions—tuning in to vibrations by feeling what is happening with another person or the surrounding environment. Empathy often mirrors someone else's emotions. Most psychics are clairsentient or empathic; in fact, it is the most common thing I hear someone call themselves when they are beginning to realize they are psychic. Clairsentience is a gut feeling. You may have experienced a time when you heard someone start to tell you about a situation they were in, and suddenly, you felt the emotions of that situation as if they were your own. It is almost as though you soaked them up like a sponge. While it is good to be compassionate, with practice and effort, you will learn to manage your energy and not let it become excessively entangled with the energy of others.

As a responsible and ethical psychic, I encourage you not to blame your issues on your clairsentience but rather begin to use it as a superpower to help yourself and others. Clairsentience is often the beginning of your psychic development. Once you learn to manage your clairsentient energy, you will be much more able to move forward with other clairs. In other words, feeling and empathy are usually signs of beginning psychic exploration.

Checkup: Clairsentience Baseline

This checkup aims to get a starting point for your clairsentience. This makes tracking your future progress much easier because you know your baseline. Answer the following questions honestly with a simple yes or no. Refer to this exercise every time you practice your clairsentience to see if it has changed.

1. I am overwhelmed when I am around lots of people.
2. I experience mood swings around certain people for no apparent reason.
3. I feel someone else's physical, mental, emotional, or spiritual ailments.
4. I know what others need to feel better physically/emotionally.
5. I know when someone is lying.
6. I feel drained after being around people (sick, need a nap).

The more yes answers, the more likely it is you are using your clairsentience. The number of yes answers will increase or adjust as you develop your handbook.

Exercise: Energetic Body Scan (What Is Mine?)

This exercise aims to teach you how to recognize what energy belongs to you and what belongs to others. An energetic body scan is one of the most essential exercises for any psychic work.

Before reading or entering any social setting, scan your energy to see how you feel mentally, physically, emotionally, and spiritually. Record the results of your initial body scan in your handbook. Now, you will know what energy belongs to you and what belongs to someone else. Next, you are ready to enter a crowded or cluttered space. Make a note of where you choose to go and why. The purpose is to see if you can take in some other energy and observe how you react. Once you leave, perform another body scan. As you progress as an empath, you will know what energy is yours. Be sure to record your concluding body scan results in your handbook.

Journal Prompts: Energetic Body Scan (What Is Mine?)

1. What area did you enter for a crowded or cluttered space? Why?
2. Did you do a body scan before entering? What were your findings?
3. Did you take in other energy? How did that feel?
4. Did you do a body scan upon exiting? What were your findings?

Clairvoyance

Clairvoyance means "clear vision." It is gaining past, present, or future information by seeing pictures (objects, actions, or events). There are two types of clairvoyance—outer vision and inner vision. With outer clairvoyance, images may be seen visually (like you see right now). Outer clairvoyance is seeing with your physical eyes. However, people may describe or retell the event differently than others once it goes through their experiential filters. The other kind of clairvoyance is inner clairvoyance, where you see through visions or pictures in what is referred to as the *mind's eye, third eye, brow chakra, inner eye,* or *second sight.* Seeing with the mind's eye is more common than seeing a physical vision or apparition like a ghost. Many people get caught up with wanting to see things, such as an angel, with their bodily eyes, but consider this—seeing with your mind's eye may involve adjusting and trusting how you receive information. One way is not better than the other.

Think back to the pineal gland. It is the seat of the mind's eye, third eye, or inner eye. A clairvoyant has inner vision through the mind's eye. Never discount your imagination. Imagination is a powerful tool shoved away as child's play, but it gives you much information. Therefore, you should never get hung up on questions like "Am I making this up?" or "Is this my imagination?" As stated earlier but is worth repeating, the biggest impediment to your psychic development is the fear of being wrong. Permit yourself to be incorrect. Seeing with your mind's eye may feel like a memory, but you are seeing the past, present, or future. Wanting to be right is where ego enters your mind. Worrying about being right or wrong when practicing hinders your psychic growth. Let that drift away and dare to let the ego be damned. Just spit out whatever comes into your mind—receive, read, and relay. Remember that a group of people who witness the same occurrence or image with their physical or outer eyes will often describe it differently. Witness disparity emphasizes that seeing with your physical eyes is no more reliable than seeing with your mind's eye. Trust what your mind's eye is seeing because no one always sees everything the same. With clairvoyance, you will have a strong feeling and sense of fact. The key is not to question it.

As mentioned earlier, outer clairvoyance is seeing a form with the physical eye. An example is seeing spirit beings such as ghosts, angels, or loved ones in tangible form. If you have this ability, you may already know it. However, it can be developed. Spirit beings understand what you can handle. Some of you might get suffocated by the number of spirits if you realized how many are around you all the time—I have certainly felt crowded by spirits on many occasions. So allow your clairvoyance to develop in the best way for you. Remember that this handbook helps you find the best ways to use your psychic knowledge instead of comparing yourself to others. Further, remember that as you stretch and grow, your ways of receiving and reading information may also change and advance.

Checkup: Clairvoyance Baseline

This checkup aims to establish a baseline for your clairvoyant ability. A baseline makes tracking your future progress much easier. Answer the following questions honestly with a simple yes or no. Refer to this exercise every time you practice your clairs to see if it has changed.

Five Signs of Clairvoyance
1. I see things people do when they are not around me.
2. I see things (such as spirits) other people don't see.
3. I get symbols or images in my head when interacting with others.
4. I've learned to shut my mouth about some things I see.
5. I see things differently than others do.

The more yes answers, the more clairvoyance you are already utilizing. The number of yes answers will increase as you develop and practice the methods in your handbook.

Exercise: Clean Third Eye

This exercise aims to clear your third eye, or mind's eye, of pictures or thoughts that may muddy or distort your message reception. It is imperative to get in the habit of doing this exercise regularly.

Close your eyes and bring attention to your brow chakra (the third or mind's eye). It is located between your eyebrows. Bring a candle into focus. Begin to focus on it. Now, put an umbrella on top of the image of the candle. Next, add a bicycle. Once you have at least three layers of vertically stacked images, ask what message is in those images. The layers of images are indicators of things on your mind or messages trying to get your attention before you clear them away. Once you have considered your messages, visualize a car windshield wiper removing these images from your mind's eye. Make sure it is squeaky clean with no residue left in your mind's eye. Now, state to yourself that your mind's eye is clear. You have a clean third eye. Try incorporating your own images once you have practiced this exercise with the provided images.

Journal Prompts: Clean Third Eye

1. Were you able to visualize a candle? Describe the experience.
2. Could you visualize an umbrella on top of the candle? Describe the experience.
3. Could you visualize a bicycle on the candle and umbrella? Describe the experience.
4. Before wiping or clearing your mind's eye of the images, what messages were there for you?
5. Could you visualize a windshield wiper clearing away the images? Describe the experience.

Exercise: Zener Cards (A)

The purpose of this exercise is to strengthen your psychic skills. You can do this exercise alone or with someone else. Zener cards are a deck of twenty-five cards, each depicting one of five different symbols (circle, cross, square, star, wavy lines). There are five cards of each of the symbols. The cards test extrasensory perception, or psychic knowingness. It is important to remember that this exercise's purpose is not to discover what you did wrong but to make connections in how you perceive and receive information. Refrain from proclaiming you are bad at this exercise. Instead, find what you did right or consistently and look for patterns. Remember, you can practice every exercise in this book on a budget. You can do this exercise using flash cards purchased at a dollar store or made yourself. The cards need to have a variety of geometric shapes.

Equipment: Self-made cards, flashcards, or Zener cards

This exercise takes two people. Pick one person to be the sender and one to be the receiver. Have the sender take the cards and enter a room where the receiver cannot see them. The receiver will need a pen and paper to write down the symbols received. Both the sender and receiver should begin to draw their focus to their third eye. The sender then rings a bell, claps, or makes some noise to indicate they are sending the first symbol. There should be no talking because someone might give clues inadvertently. The receiver should write down the first image that comes into their mind. The bell or other noisemaker then indicates a procession to the next symbol. At the end of twenty-five cards, compare notes.

Journal Prompts: Zener Cards (A)

1. Are you tempted to say something derogatory about your abilities in this exercise?
2. How did you perceive and receive the information?
3. Was there a pattern to your answers? For instance, were you one symbol ahead or one behind? If you were one ahead, you may have been accurately anticipating answers.
4. Did you second-guess your answers?

Exercise: Zener Cards (B)

This exercise may stretch your psychic skills even more than Zener cards (A). It is potentially more advanced than Zener cards (A) because you are alone and unable to pick up on the sender's emotions. However, it may be easier because it takes away a step, which means less room for an incorrect read or interpretation. It is essential to remember that the purpose of this exercise is not to find out what you did wrong but to make connections in how you perceive and receive information. Refrain from proclaiming you are bad at this exercise. Instead, find what you did right and look for patterns.

Equipment: Zener cards (or the cards you made or flashcards)

Lay all the cards face down and see if you can sense which card you are turning over. Try using various clairs to sense the cards. Can you see the card? Does the card evoke an emotion? Note that getting five correct is within the realm of odds.

Journal Prompts: Zener Cards (B)

1. How did you perceive or receive your answers?
2. How did you sense the cards?
3. Did you notice any patterns in your observations?
4. Did you second-guess your answers?

Exercise: Playing Cards (A)

This exercise aims to help you sense the cards by sorting black and red cards into separate piles. However, I feel the heat of the red cards and then intuit what type they are. So I do not use this as much for clairvoyance; instead, I use my clairtangency and clairsentience. Remember, some clairs overlap. My husband uses his clairvoyance as he pictures the card in his third eye.

Equipment: Regular playing cards

Take a deck of regular playing cards and separate the black and red cards into two equal piles. Using as many cards as you choose (it might be best to start with ten of each color), shuffle the cards and then, with your eyes closed, use your clairvoyance to divide the cards into two piles of black and red. As you get better, you can add more cards. You might be tempted to separate the cards into equal piles because you logically know there are similar numbers; however, try to go by what you sense from each card.

Journal Prompts: Playing Cards (A)

1. How did you perceive or receive your answers?
2. How did you sense the cards?
3. Did you notice any patterns in your observations?
4. Did you second-guess your answers?

Exercise: Playing Cards (B)

This exercise will help you sense the cards by sensing the color. This exercise is easy to practice because you only use four cards. As mentioned in the activity above, I feel the heat of the red cards, which narrows it down to a heart or diamond. Then, I discern whether there is emotion or compassion in the card, which narrows it down to a heart. Remember, the clairs can overlap. This exercise is an example of such an overlap. I do not use my clairvoyance. Instead, I use my clairtangency and clairsentience.

Equipment: Regular playing cards

Take out four of a kind, or the same card from each suit. Aces are usually the easiest. Look at each card and get a sense of it. Decide which card is your target card, such as the ace of hearts. Then, shuffle the cards and see if you can turn over your target card.

Journal Prompts: Playing Cards (B)

1. How did you perceive or receive your answers?
2. How did you sense the cards?
3. Did you notice any patterns in your observations?
4. Did you second-guess your answers?

Exercise: Beads

This exercise aims to use your clairvoyance to separate beads by closing your eyes and seeing the colors in your mind's eye. Once again, you may find you mix in other clairs.

Equipment: At least ten beads of two different colors. Howlite beads work great because they are inexpensive and all feel about the same in consistency. Howlite is also absorbent; the beads absorb your energy, and you can connect well. Fun fact: They are so porous that they used to be dyed in blue toilet bowl cleaner to imitate turquoise.

Look at the beads and get a sense of them. Visualize the colors using your clairvoyance. Place the beads on a towel to keep them from rolling away. With your eyes closed, divide the beads into two piles of colors.

Journal Prompts: Beads

1. How did you perceive or receive your answers?
2. How did you sense the beads?
3. Did you notice any patterns in your observations?
4. Did you second-guess your answers?

Exercise: Inverted Cup Game

This exercise is for practicing your clairvoyance. Use your third eye to see what or where an item is under the inverted cup.

Equipment: Three identical cups, permanent markers, paper, pens, and (a) one item that is the same but in different colors or (b) three different items. You can find these items at your house or purchase them at a dollar store.

1. Have a moderator place three inverted cups on a table or the floor. It helps to number 1, 2, or 3 on the bottom of each cup.
2. Then, the moderator will place either (a) one item, such as a little toy car, under one of the cups while the participants are not looking, (b) three toy cars of varying shapes or colors under each of the cups, or (c) three different items, such as a toy car, hand sanitizer, and a dollar bill, under each of the three cups.
3. Now, the participants will use their clairvoyance to see (a) which cup the item is under, (b) which of the three similar but different-shaped or different-colored items is under which cup, or (c) which

of the three different items is under the three different cups. Using descriptive words instead of defining the item is the best way to work toward accuracy.

4. *Alternative exercise:* Before showing the items, have the participants write down what they see under the cups.

Journal Prompts: Inverted Cup Game

1. How did you perceive or receive your answers?
2. How did you sense the item(s)?
3. Did you notice any patterns in your observations?
4. Did you describe the item(s), or did you immediately guess? Remember, the key to progressing is using descriptive language instead of immediately guessing.
5. Did you second-guess your answers?

Exercise: Remote Viewing

This exercise aims to teach you to be okay with partial information, ambiguity, and unanswered questions when using your psychic knowingness.

Equipment: Previously unseen photos (called *targets*) of people, places, or things

Remote viewing is gathering information about a distant place, thing, person, or situation without using your physical senses. Although it is not pertinent to your handbook, it is interesting that government programs have utilized remote viewing.

Many make remote viewing much more difficult than it is. There is really only one thing to remember if you want to excel at remote viewing: the most important thing is to describe the minor nuances instead of jumping to conclusions and identifying the bigger picture or what it means. Using descriptions is why remote viewing principles are the best way to develop psychic knowledge. It removes your need to combine all the pieces and reach a conclusion. It helps you be okay with partial and obscure information that may never form an entire story. If someone always claims to be spot on, eventually people might choose to doubt such claims. Being comfortable with ambiguity is paramount.

If you will approach all readings using descriptive words, you will advance more quickly and improve your accuracy. Always refrain from the temptation to complete missing details with conjecture.

Start with a photo you have not seen. Someone can help you by placing a photo in an envelope or finding a photo on the internet. Keep your mind still and draw or write down descriptive words that come to you. Can you resist the urge to guess what it is? Instead, describe it! When describing what you see in this type of exercise, it is tempting to predict the item. That is not the purpose of the training. The purpose of the exercise is to describe what you see instead of saying what it is. Describing instead of guessing is essential to advancing as a clairvoyant in psychic development. We often only get one small part of the big picture. Describe, describe, describe!

Your accuracy will skyrocket in all areas if you understand the irony that being spot-on is not the goal.

Journal Prompts: Remote Viewing

1. Were you able to write descriptive words?
2. Were you able to draw shapes that came into your mind?
3. Could you resist the urge to guess the entire item but describe even the smallest detail?

Clairaudience

Clairaudience means "clear hearing" and the ability to perceive sounds, words, or extrasensory noise from sources as if they were broadcasting to you. The tones are often beyond rational human experience, space, and time limitations. Please note that you do not need silence to receive clairaudient messages. Many times, the messages will come amid a noisy crowd, which sometimes makes it even easier to realize you are receiving a message.

Clairaudience doesn't always refer to an outward sound but may be heard in the inner mental ear, much like how people think words without auditory impressions. You can be clairaudient in two primary ways: audibly (outer ear) or with your inner ear.

A sound from your inner ear feels like it is coming from your inner being. It comes to you as thoughts that are sometimes hard to distinguish from your own. With practice, you can tell the difference. It is not information you are reaching for or trying to remember. It is the information you receive. It feels like hearing a song you know in your inner ear or a conversation from the past.

Hearing spirit audibly is hearing clairaudiently with your outer ears. Outer hearing can sometimes be quite startling. You will know a difference in the voice. You may look around and realize no one else heard the voice, yet it was said out loud. Spirit uses this only in times of urgency, such as hearing a voice yell "Get out!" before a fire breaks out or "Swerve right!" seconds before a semitruck almost runs your car off the road.

Checkup: Clairaudience Baseline

This checkup establishes a baseline for your clairaudience. This baseline makes tracking your future progress much easier because you know your starting point. Answer the following questions honestly with a simple yes or no. Refer to this exercise every time you practice your clairaudience to see if it has changed.

1. I hear things that others do not hear.
2. I either hear an audible sound or a sound whispered in my inner ear.
3. I may hear a voice or sound when it is deafening around me.
4. I may hear a voice or sound when it is quiet around me.
5. I may hear sounds when I do not want to listen to them.
6. I am attuned to sounds around me.

The more yes answers, the more you are already utilizing clairaudience. The number of yes answers will increase as you develop and practice the methods in your handbook.

Exercise: Happy Song

This exercise uses an upbeat or happy song to tap into your clairaudience.

Listen to your favorite upbeat or happy song. The song can be any genre. No music has a higher vibration than other music—that is a construct of humans who place a value judgment on frequencies. Remember, energy does not judge; we do. Set your intention that you will receive a message from the music.

Journal Prompts: Happy Song

1. Was it challenging to pick a song?
2. What song did you play?
3. Did the song make you feel happy?
4. Why do you think the song did or did not make you happy?
5. Could you stay in the present, or did the song pull you back to memories associated with it?
6. What message did you receive from the song?

Exercise: Ballad

This exercise aims to develop your clairaudience using a ballad or sad song.

Listen to your favorite ballad in a quiet meditation space. This song can be any genre of music. No music has a higher vibration than other music—that is a construct of humans who place a value judgment on frequencies. So give yourself permission to listen to any type of music you like.

Journal Prompts: Ballad

1. What song did you listen to?
2. Could you stay in a meditative space, or did it pull you back to memories associated with the song?

3. How did this song make you feel?
4. What message did you receive from the song?

There is no specific way this song should make you feel. A common mistake many beginner readers make is assuming that a slower, seemingly depressing, or heavy metal song is a lower vibration. Everyone has different emotions attached to music. Do not make assumptions based on your experience or play the odds by going with what is logically or typically the answer. Read separately each time for every type of message; in other words, do not make any assumptions based on likelihood or other readings. Be sure to avoid going with what you assume. Instead, go with what you receive as your message.

Claircognizance

Claircognizance means "clear knowing" and is a form of psychic knowingness in which knowledge is acquired without being able to explain how one knows the information. It is the ability to understand things without pictures or hearing and with few, if any, details as to why. It includes precognition (knowledge of the future) and retrocognition or postcognition (knowledge of the past). There are no restrictions as to what may be known with claircognizance.

One of the most significant indicators of claircognizance is that it often comes out of left field. Claircognizance usually turns you into a human lie detector of sorts. You don't know how someone is lying, but you know they are. Many readers make the mistake of believing the person they are reading for is always telling the truth. Most clients will only tell you partial truths, so resist the temptation to jump to their side. Your claircognizance will help you discern the truth and relay the message.

Claircognizance will also help you solve problems without knowing how you arrived at the answer. Using claircognizance as a psychic is quite beneficial.

Checkup: Claircognizance Baseline

This checkup aims to establish a baseline for your claircognizance. Knowing your baseline makes tracking your future progress much more accessible. Answer the following questions honestly with a simple yes or no. Refer to this exercise every time you practice your claircognizance to see if it has changed.

1. I have always just known things—even as a child.
2. I have always known if things are good or bad ideas but can't explain why.
3. I know if I should do things or not but can't explain why.
4. I experience a strong knowingness, but the details as to why, how, when, etc. are vague.
5. I don't have a lot of tolerance for questions, since I somehow just know the answers.

The more yes answers, the more you are already utilizing your clair-cognizance. The number of yes answers will increase as you develop and practice the methods in your handbook.

Exercise: Claircognizance

This exercise aims to enhance your claircognizance. Once again, you may find you mix in other clairs.

Equipment: None needed

Randomly pick a subject you don't know anything about, or have someone else pick one from the internet. Close your eyes and slowly count from ten to one while slowing your breathing. Write down what comes to your mind without reading anything on the subject. Break down what comes into your mind into separate statements. Again, resist the compulsion to read what is written on the subject. Practice this as often as possible. This exercise may also give birth to inventions and new ideas. Here is a subject to get you started: Write down everything you can about fractals in one minute.

Journal Prompts: Claircognizance

1. Were you able to pick a subject you know nothing about?
2. Did you resist the urge to look it up?

3. Did you have any previous familiarity with the subject?
4. Were you able to make a list without second-guessing yourself? What was the list?
5. How do you feel you did? Based on your journaling, can you distinguish some consistencies, patterns, or tells?

Clairtangency

Clairtangency means "evident touch." It is the ability to handle an object or touch an area and perceive psychic knowledge about the article, the owner, or the history surrounding it. Clairtangency can also apply to handling anything from small or large objects to a living being to the wall of a building. Clairtangency is much more common than people realize, and it is easy and fun to practice. Psychometry is a form of clairtangency. In psychometry, you hold an item and receive intuitive impressions from the object.

Even though I did not ask for an object to hold to relay messages, a client once brought me a straw hat. I immediately asked if she knew where her uncle was in Mexico. The hat quickly connected me to her uncle, who was kidnapped in Mexico. I did not know the country's geography, but I could point out on an online map where she and her family would find their uncle. I told them he was alive but needed his medicine. He was indeed found alive and needed his insulin. The straw hat was helpful when time was of the essence.

Checkup: Clairtangency Baseline

The purpose of this checkup is to let you know you are not alone. You will meet many people with these same characteristics. Another goal of this checkup is to get a starting point for your clairtangency. This baseline makes tracking your future progress much easier because you know your starting point. Answer the following questions honestly with a simple yes or no. Refer to this baseline every time you specifically practice your clairtangency to see if it has changed.

1. I do not like wearing used clothing and jewelry (clothes have energy transfer).
2. I don't know why used furniture or antiques feel strange.

3. I am bothered by pawnshops (desperate energy).
4. I am uncomfortable in cluttered spaces. It sometimes affects my mood (scattered energy).
5. I am bothered by a messy house or workplace (scattered energy).

The more yes answers, the more you are already utilizing your clairtangency. The number of yes answers will increase as you develop and practice the methods in your handbook.

Exercise: Psychometry (Clairtangency)

This exercise aims to help you learn to sense energy from tangible objects.

Equipment: An object with known history but unknown to the reader

Although psychometry and clairtangency are not necessarily exactly the same thing, psychometry exercises are beneficial for increasing your clairtangency. This exercise can be done by yourself or with a group, but you will need at least one item and someone to provide the history behind the item. Make sure to have a sheet of paper to write down the information you receive. This exercise can also involve a large object, such as walls in a building. The idea behind psychometry is that the touching of the object triggers the message. Many people think holding an object to feel its energy is just used for mediumship. While clairtangency may be utilized for mediumship, it is not limited to such a reading. It can help solve crimes, find missing people, or connect with the querent's energy.

Have someone pick out an item they know the history of—the more history they know about the item, the better. Take the item and hold it or touch it.

You may choose to look at the item or not. If you look at the item, you might think that will make it easier to write things about it; however, sometimes it inhibits you because you might think what you write down is too apparent. Set that inhibition aside and write down the obvious things, such as "It is a watch." Then, begin to go deeper. Do not hold back. Write down every thought, color, feeling, or picture that comes into your mind. Remember not to second-guess it. Give yourself 2–3 minutes with the item to write down the things that first come into your head.

If you choose not to look at the item, note whether it is wrapped in something to disguise it from you. Consider that you may pick up on the energy from the packaging.

Once you have noted your impressions, ask for the meaning associated with the item. These impressions can involve many different aspects, including who owned it, where it is from, all the people it has passed through, who manufactured it, and all the energies surrounding any aspect of the object.

Although I stated earlier that you need to be okay with being wrong, this is where things get a little tricky. While you should resist becoming attached to outcomes, you also should resist the tendency to consider anything you wrote as wrong. Many people may think this is contriving a correct answer and is a scam. On the contrary, when you are learning, you must be open to making what seem like mistakes, and then you may see how those perceived mistakes are accurate. You will learn to spot how information comes to you. Sometimes, it will seem wrong, but recognizing your patterns and tendencies will make you a better psychic. Go easy on yourself!

Journal Prompts: Psychometry (Clairtangency)

1. Did you choose to look at the item? Did this make it harder or easier? Why or why not?
2. What clairs did you use to sense the item?
3. Write down every sensation that came to you, whether you feel it was essential or not.
4. Begin to write quickly or have someone else write for you. Filter nothing.
5. If the item was wrapped in something, did you feel you picked up on the energy of the wrapping?
6. Make connections with everything you wrote down. If the owner cannot validate what you wrote, do not dismiss it, because perhaps someone else will later.

Clairgustance

Clairgustance means "clear taste," allowing you to taste a substance without putting it in your mouth (obtaining psychic knowledge through taste). Another aspect of clairgustance is gaining information from physically tasting substances. It is connected to your sense of smell and is a common way to receive messages. Clairgustance includes wet or dry mouth, food cravings, belching, hiccups, or vomiting. An example of clairgustance is having the taste of strawberry in your mouth and then having someone ask you whether they should have a chocolate or strawberry wedding cake.

Checkup: Clairgustance Baseline

This checkup aims to establish a baseline for your clairgustancy. Knowing this baseline makes tracking your future progress much easier. Answer the following questions honestly with a simple yes or no. Refer to this exercise every time you practice your clairgustancy to see if it has changed.

1. I can taste something when nothing is in my mouth.
2. I am not limited to food in the things I taste that are not in my mouth.
3. I may taste things that are pleasant or unpleasant.
4. I realize my sense of smell is often connected to the taste.
5. I broaden my ability by broadening my palette.

The more yes answers, the more you are already utilizing your clairgustance. The number of yes answers will increase as you develop and practice the methods in your handbook.

Exercise: Clairgustance

This exercise aims to help you begin to taste things you cannot associate with a direct source.

Imagine something sweet, such as your favorite chocolate. Think about the taste. Try and taste the sweet food in your mouth. Who or what do you think of when you think of this taste? Does it recall a particular memory? Now, imagine something salty, such as a type of nut. Think about the taste. Try and taste the salty food in your mouth. Who or what do you think of when you think of this taste? Does it recall a particular memory? Repeat the exercise with something spicy and something bland. Hold something in your hand to advance in this exercise and focus on the taste that comes to your mouth.

Journal Prompts: Clairgustance

1. Could you visualize a sweet, salty, spicy, and bland taste in your mouth?
2. Could you taste the sweet, salty, spicy, and bland flavor?
3. What came to mind with the sweet taste?
4. What came to mind with the salty taste?
5. What came to mind with the spicy taste?
6. What came to mind with the bland taste?
7. Did intuitive impressions come to you?
8. What object did you hold in your hand? Did you see it, or did someone randomly give it to you? What did you taste?

Clairolfactory (Clairalience)

Clairolfactory means "clear smelling" and is where a person acquires psychic knowledge primarily by smell. It usually involves smelling a fragrance, person, place, or animal that is not physically present. The physical nose is not necessarily used. Just as olfactory nerves are some of the strongest to trigger memory, so are psychic smells. You can sense danger using clairolfactory. I realized early in life that I could smell a specific odor that I later learned was cancer. The smell hits me hard and fast. It is difficult because I am not a doctor, but when I smell the odor of cancer, I most certainly will implore someone to see a doctor. I never scare the client, but I emphasize the need for them to visit the doctor of their choice. I have had many clients thank me for sending them to their doctor. I also had a few who came to see me before they passed and encouraged me to keep using this gift and said they wished they had listened.

If clairolfactory sense doesn't come naturally, it is important to practice. We can intuit many things with this ability alone.

Checkup: Clairolfactory Baseline

This checkup aims to establish a baseline for your clairolfactory. Knowing your baseline makes tracking your future progress much easier. Answer the following questions honestly with a simple yes or no. Refer to this exercise every time you practice your clairolfactory to see if it has changed.

1. I am not using my nose to smell but have a psychic sense of smell.
2. I smell things when they are not there.
3. I smell things that are pleasant and unpleasant.
4. I realize that clairolfactory is strongly connected to clairgustance.
5. I often receive a message with my ability to psychically smell.

The more yes answers, the more you are already utilizing your clairolfactory. The number of yes answers will increase as you develop and practice the methods in your handbook.

Exercise: Clairolfactory

This exercise aims to help you begin to smell things you cannot associate with a direct source.

Imagine something sweet, such as your favorite chocolate. Think about the smell. Try and smell the sweet food. Who or what do you think of when you think of this smell? Does it recall a particular memory? Now, imagine something salty, such as a type of nut. Think about the smell. Try and taste the salty food in your mouth. Who or what do you think of when you think of this smell? Does it recall a particular memory? Repeat the exercise with something spicy and something bland. Hold something in your hand to advance in this exercise and focus on the smell that comes to you.

1. Could you sense a sweet, salty, spicy, and bland smell?
2. Could you smell the sweet, salty, spicy, and bland scent?
3. What came to mind with the sweet smell?
4. What came to mind with the salty smell?
5. What came to mind with the spicy smell?
6. What came to mind with the bland smell?
7. Did intuitive impressions come to you?
8. What object did you hold in your hand? Did you see it, or did someone randomly give it to you? What did you smell?

Claireloquence

Claireloquence means "clear speaking" and is using the right words to communicate. It also may be the sound, cadence, tone, or word grouping that achieves the desired result. Claireloquence is not necessarily eloquent speaking as the name implies. You may have heard it called the *gift of gab, channeling, automatic speaking,* or *guided speaking.* Typically, these are words you rarely use but mean something unique to the querent. They confirm your message because they are a particular word, words, or phrase to the querent. Still, they are words the reader would only use sometimes. I rarely use the word *courtship* for dating, but I was reading for a sweet older lady once, and old-fashioned words such as courtship began flowing out of my mouth. The lovely lady shed a few tears and spoke of her long-since departed husband. The words were not words I would typically use, but they were the words she needed to hear. Another example is saying a phrase such as "Winner, winner chicken dinner" that the reader never uses but the querent has recently or does frequently. Finally, words may be spoken in a different language or dialect.

Checkup: Claireloquence Baseline

This checkup aims to establish a baseline for your claireloquence. Knowing your baseline makes tracking your future progress much easier. Answer the following questions honestly with a simple yes or no.

1. I find that words easily flow when I receive messages.
2. I receive messages in complete thoughts instead of one to two words.
3. I am guided by the words when I deliver a message.
4. I realize that people listen when I speak.
5. I often feel detached from the words I am saying.
6. I find the words mean something unique to the person to whom I am giving a message.

The more yes answers, the more you are already utilizing your claireloquence. The number of yes answers will increase as you develop and practice the methods in your handbook.

Exercise: Claireloquence

This exercise's purpose is to help you begin to state things that you cannot associate with a direct source.

Get yourself in a setting where you can speak with people who use different word choices or vernaculars. They may be from a different part of the world or country. Perhaps they are from a different era than you. In other words, they use phrases different from what you would use. Let thoughts flow into your third eye, and do not question them. Repeat or write down the phrases to the querent. Repeat this as much as possible.

Journal Prompts: Claireloquence

1. What phrases came into your mind?
2. Where was the querent from, and is this a phrase used in that area?
3. Did the words mean anything to your querent or someone they knew?

Exercise: Activate Your Clairs with Symbols

This exercise aims to help you start using your clairs more quickly and efficiently. Go to your handbook and journal to strengthen your clairs as you go.

Go to your sacred or safe space. This may be a physically real space or a place in your mind's eye. Wherever it is, find a place of comfort and begin to relax. As you sit in your safe space, ask your higher self to provide symbols for your clairs. Draw your attention to your breath as you fall into meditation. Remember to receive instead of reaching for answers. What is the first image or thought that comes to you? Take one question at a time and, while staying quiet and calm, write down the symbol that will trigger your memory when you journal in more detail. Define your symbols and write down a symbol for each in your handbook.

As you sit in your sacred space, ask your higher self:

1. If my clear feeling had a symbol, what would it be?
2. If my clear seeing had a symbol, what would it be?
3. If my clear hearing had a symbol, what would it be?
4. If my clear knowing had a symbol, what would it be?
5. If my clear touching had a symbol, what would it be?
6. If my clear tasting had a symbol, what would it be?
7. If my clear smelling had a symbol, what would it be?
8. If my clear communication had a symbol, what would it be?

Journal Prompts: Activate Your Clairs with Symbols

1. What is your clear-feeling symbol?
2. What is your clear-seeing symbol?
3. What is your clear-hearing symbol?
4. What is your clear-knowing symbol?
5. What is your clear-touching symbol?

6. What is your clear-tasting symbol?
7. What is your clear-smelling symbol?
8. What is your clear-communication symbol?

Avoid These Pitfalls

While it is easy to use only one clair, try to stretch your psychic muscles so that you can grow. On the other hand, it is okay to refine your strengths. Balance is vital to any psychic work. Resist the urge to compare clairs. No clair is better than the others. They are all useful for different purposes. Do not feel you must be proficient in every clair. Over time, you may use different clairs at different times, creating your own clair blend.

When doing the exercises, the biggest mistake you can make is to guess the item. While you may call it correctly now and then, you will grow your psychic abilities less than when describing. Describing instead of guessing is one of the most significant suggestions I see go unheeded by beginners.

Psychic Success

The last thing many of us want is more information flooding our senses. We are already tired of years of information that many of us never asked to receive. However, if we control how we receive that information, we will feel much more balanced overall. For instance, if we receive information primarily through clairvoyance, we may be exhausted from constantly receiving messages in image form. If we let our other clairs step up, it will help us feel more balanced overall. I call this a *clair blend*. Clair blending works. I know from years of experience. Try it, and you will experience it too.

CHAPTER 7

YOUR CHAKRAS

The second of the Three C's is chakras. Your body has primary chakras (energy centers within your body) and transpersonal chakras (energy centers outside of your body). Although you cannot see chakras physically, these energy centers are instrumental in working with your intuition and psychic knowingness; therefore, it is essential to have a familiarity with them. Many psychics can sense these energy centers, and with practice, most can at least get intuitive information. Chakras relate to almost everything in our lives, including, but not limited to, colors, emotions, organs, musical notes, musical instruments, power animals, mantras, crystals, herbs, and essential oils. Knowing which chakras are at work in any given situation is extremely helpful in psychic discernment.

Chakra comes from Sanskrit (ancient India's sacred language) and means "wheel" or "turning." Chakras are centers of awareness in the human body and are means by which various energy fields exchange power. The chakras have been described in a variety of ways, including funnel-shaped cones, suns, spirals, horns of plenty, or gears. They go from the front to the back of the body, and when in balance, they should be spinning smoothly and evenly. The chakras have individual functions, but recognizing that they all work together is important.

Cleared chakras are free of unwanted energy. *Aligned* or *balanced* chakras mean that the chakras are all spinning gently and evenly at about the same rate. The idea is for the energy to flow evenly between all the chakras. I steer clear of the word *blocked*. You will hear many people use this term, but there is a reason I have chosen not to use the phrase *blocked chakra*. It is simple: I do not see the chakras as blocked. Yes, they may have ground to a stop and are not moving. Could energy be stagnant or clogging up the chakra? The issue is that it is underactive or overactive. An underactive chakra is sluggish, while an overactive chakra is working overtime. These descriptions are much more helpful than describing them as blocked. There are exercises such as yoga, pendulums, and visualizations to get them back in balance. Another reason I do not use the term *blocked* is because it immediately causes my clients to become concerned when there is no reason for such alarm.

I cannot emphasize enough the usefulness of chakras in your psychic handbook. They can help you with every psychic endeavor primarily because they are the connection or link between our physical bodies and the universal collective body. If you can learn to read the chakras, I give you my word that you can learn to increase your psychic knowingness. The problem is that many people know, teach, or write about the chakras but fail to realize how much psychic information you can gather from them. Chakra exercises are some of the most essential things in your handbook to utilize for yourself and others.

Checkup: Chakra Baseline

This checkup aims to see which chakras are functioning smoothly and spinning correctly. It will also help you pinpoint any that are overactive or underactive. This chakra checkup is helpful for anyone at any time. The answers will vary from day to day. It is best to answer the questions honestly so that you know your chakra situation or that of a potential client.

Root Chakra

Sit quietly and get in tune with your body before answering these questions.

Scale: 1 = Never, 2 = Rarely, 3 = Sometimes, 4 = Often, 5 = Always

I have lost the ability to trust.

I do not feel at home in my own body.

I worry about the future, particularly regarding obligations.

I feel emotionally ungrounded.

I feel chronically tired and lack energy.

I do not get enough exercise.

I have cold extremities.

I have problems with my colon or bowels.

I have back pain (lower).

I have sciatica and leg or knee pain.

Total Root Chakra Score:

Tally the score at the end of each chakra. If the score is 10 to 23, the chakra is overactive. If the score is 24 to 38, that chakra is balanced. If the score is 39 to 50, the chakra is underactive.

This information is helpful for a variety of reasons, including psychic knowingness. Determining if a chakra is balanced, overactive, or underactive leads to psychic information.

Examples of psychic messages based on findings of a balanced, overactive, or underactive root chakra:

Balanced root chakra: You feel secure and stable at this time.

Overactive root chakra: You spend too much money due to a false sense of security. This overactive root chakra is taking a toll on your body in your lower back.

Underactive root chakra: You are constantly worrying about money. This worrying has led to chronic stomach and bowel issues.

Sacral Chakra

Sit quietly and get in tune with your body before answering these questions.

Scale: 1 = Never, 2 = Rarely, 3 = Sometimes, 4 = Often, 5 = Always

I feel unenthused with life.

I feel unfulfilled sexually.

I lack appreciation for life.

I put too much importance on self-discipline and self-control.

I am hard on myself.

I feel blocked creatively.

I have feelings of jealousy.

I have feelings of guilt.

I have back pain.

I have bladder or kidney problems.

Total Sacral Chakra Score:

Examples of psychic messages based on findings of a balanced, overactive, or underactive sacral chakra:

Balanced sacral chakra: You feel vital, creative, motivated, and joyful. You focus on things that bring you joy instead of those that drag you down, which creates more joy and vitality.

Overactive sacral chakra: You are going overboard, engaging your passions, and confusing passion with lust. Your lust is turning into an addiction.

Underactive sacral chakra: Find one thing each day that brings you joy. Often, this is an act of service to someone else. Get outside yourself, help someone else, and your joy will return.

Solar Plexus Chakra

Sit quietly and get in tune with your body before answering these questions.

Scale: 1 = Never, 2 = Rarely, 3 = Sometimes, 4 = Often, 5 = Always

I have a hard time setting and reaching goals.

I give in to others easily.

I have a hard time accepting criticism.

I notice that my emotions get the best of me, and I do or say things I regret.

I suffer from nightmares or insomnia.

I suffer from anxiety.

I have stomach or intestinal issues.

I have a complicated relationship with food.

I have jealous or aggressive tendencies.

I turn my anger inward.

Total Solar Plexus Score:

Examples of psychic messages based on findings of a balanced, overactive, or underactive solar plexus chakra:

Balanced solar plexus chakra: You feel worthy of every good thing in life.

Overactive solar plexus chakra: You not only feel worthy, but you also feel better than everyone else and do not consider the feelings of others. You are angry, but you mostly take it out on yourself.

Underactive solar plexus chakra: You feel anxiety and will do almost anything to avoid a confrontation. You do not stand up for yourself.

Heart Chakra

Sit quietly and get in tune with your body before answering these questions.

Scale: 1 = Never, 2 = Rarely, 3 = Sometimes, 4 = Often, 5 = Always

I find it difficult to let other people into my life.

I feel lonely or isolated.

I have relationship problems.

I have problems sustaining friendships.

I am overly compassionate toward others.

Social situations leave me tired and worn out.

I have a hard time genuinely accepting myself.

I have or have had coronary or circulatory problems.

I suffer from respiratory or asthma problems and colds.

I have skin problems.

Total Heart Chakra Score:

Examples of psychic messages based on findings of a balanced, overactive, or underactive heart chakra:

Balanced heart chakra: You love and feel loved.

Overactive heart chakra: You do too much for those who do not care about you. You try to please people to try and win affection. You end up hating yourself for this cycle.

Underactive heart chakra: You do not open up to or trust anyone. You are isolated and closed off, and you continue to harden your heart more and more.

Throat Chakra

Sit quietly and get in tune with your body before answering these questions.

Scale: 1 = Never, 2 = Rarely, 3 = Sometimes, 4 = Often, 5 = Always

I have a hard time expressing myself.

I feel I am not heard.

I find myself being shy or uncomfortable around others.

I say things I later regret.

I suffer (or suffered) from a speech defect.

I feel uninspired by my work.

I tend to be manipulative.

I talk about others behind their backs.

I have thyroid issues.

I suffer from frequent sore throat, ear, neck, or shoulder pain.

Total Throat Chakra Score:

Examples of psychic messages based on findings of a balanced, overactive, or underactive throat chakra:

Balanced throat chakra: You speak your truth, feel heard, and listen.

Overactive throat chakra: You interrupt others and rarely listen.

Underactive throat chakra: You are afraid to speak up, and when you do, no one seems to listen or care what you say.

Brow (Third Eye) Chakra

Sit quietly and get in tune with your body before answering these questions.

Scale: 1 = Never, 2 = Rarely, 3 = Sometimes, 4 = Often, 5 = Always

I often have the feeling that life is meaningless.

I suffer from anxiety or depression.

I have difficulty using my imagination.

I have trouble hearing my inner voice.

I have trouble knowing my path in life.

I have frequent headaches or sinus issues.

I have eye or vision issues.

I want to bring more light and joy into my life.

I strive for a higher realization but can't seem to reach it.

I have little psychic ability.

Total Brow (Third Eye) Chakra Score:

Examples of psychic messages based on findings of a balanced, overactive, or underactive brow chakra:

Balanced brow chakra: You discern and see the truth with ease.

Overactive brow chakra: You pick up on almost every emotion and thought of those around you, which causes you angst and gives you migraine headaches.

Underactive brow chakra: You are clueless to the subtle messages that are the truth of who people are. You miss out on clues because you choose to remain oblivious.

Crown Chakra

Sit quietly and get in tune with your body before answering these questions.

Scale: 1 = Never, 2 = Rarely, 3 = Sometimes, 4 = Often, 5 = Always

I often feel depressed and have a lack of joy in life.

I feel worn out even if I sleep deeply.

I suffer from chronic illness.

I suffer from a weakened immune system.

I find it difficult to connect to higher levels of being.

I believe there is nothing after this life.

I have migraines.

I want to escape this world.

I do not connect with people on earth.

I know there is more to life than this.

Total Crown Chakra Score:

Examples of psychic messages based on findings of a balanced, overactive, or underactive crown chakra:

Balanced crown chakra: You feel connected to everything and everyone in life.

Overactive crown chakra: You not only feel connected, but you think you know it all.

Underactive crown chakra: You don't feel connected to anything more significant than yourself and feel you do not deserve connection.

In conclusion, a close and candid evaluation of the state of the chakras at any given time provides valuable psychic information.

Terminology: The Chakras

Chakra: As stated earlier, *chakra* comes from Sanskrit (ancient India's sacred language) and means "wheel" or "turning." Chakras are centers of awareness in the human body and are means by which various energy fields exchange power. Many psychics can feel or sense the chakras.

Nadi: This word comes from Sanskrit and means "flow," "tube," or "channel." Many nadis flow through our bodies, giving us life force. In this book, we will focus on the hand nadis, which connect to the heart chakra, and the feet nadis, which connect to the root chakra.

Light column: The flow of energy running up and down in a loop in the human body.

Exploring the Chakras

The purpose of the following exercises is to help you begin to associate chakras with almost anything you think you might receive a message about. It will also help you realize how chakras can serve as tools to receive that message. There is a brief introduction to each chakra followed by an exercise to get you thinking about that chakra. In short, these exercises will help stretch your ability to connect to your psychic knowingness. Here, we will use animals, places, songs, and people, but you can do this same exercise in your handbook with any category that interests you, such as crystals, trees, instruments, books, movies, etc. Be sure to put your dated notes and results in your handbook.

Seventh Chakra (Crown)—
Violet

Sixth Chakra (Brow)—
Deep Indigo Blue

Fifth Chakra (Throat)—
Sky Blue

Fourth Chakra (Heart)—
Green

Third Chakra (Solar Plexus)—
Yellow

Second Chakra (Sacral)—
Orange

First Chakra (Root)—
Red

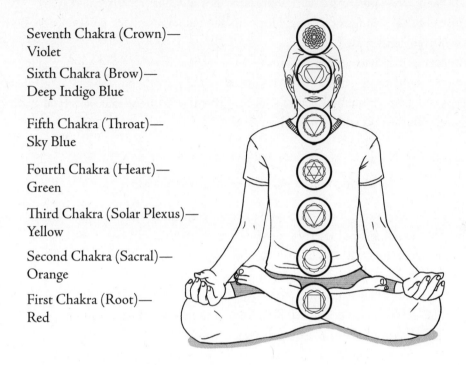

The Root Chakra (First Chakra)

The root chakra is also known as the base chakra. It is the first chakra at the base of the spine (where you sit down). It is associated with red and the element earth. The root chakra is about stability, self-preservation, security, and survival. It is also tied to the sense of smell. When thinking of the root chakra, think of anything that connects you to earth. The mantra or intonation for the root chakra is *Lam* (pronounced like Tom, not ham). Your bones, kidneys, spinal column, colon, and adrenal glands are connected to your root chakra.

When your root chakra is balanced, you feel steady, safe, secure, self-assured, and grounded. When your root chakra is underactive, you might feel unsteady, unsafe, insecure, spacey, unfocused, flighty, untrusting, fearful, out of touch, and ungrounded. You may lack self-assurance. You might have a fight-or-flight response. An underactive root chakra might also cause physical feelings of dizziness, restlessness, and perhaps even diarrhea. When your root chakra is overactive, you might feel stuck, heavy, lazy, greedy, angry, paranoid, nervous, aggressive, oppressive, or materialistic. When overactive, it can also cause physical feelings of lethargy, leg pain, hip pain, lower back pain, tension, body aches, and even constipation.

Crystals can help balance the chakras. Some excellent crystals for the root chakra are black onyx, bloodstone, garnet, hematite, lodolite, red jasper, ruby, smoky quartz, and red tiger's eye. You can hold the crystals, sit near them, wear them, make a crystal grid, or tape them to the chakra with soft medical tape.

Exercise: Exploring the Root Chakra

The following exercises explore associations with the various chakras. Most books, including my first two, provide you with lists of people, places, or things associated with each chakra. However, this is your handbook. This exercise encourages you to begin thinking of how intuitive messages might come to you when evaluating chakras. In order to facilitate such integration of chakras into messages, it will help for you to think of the correspondences instead of having them spoon-fed to you.

To help associate the root chakra with messages, use the keywords *earth*, *grounded*, *secure*, and *stability* for animal, place, song, and person, respectively. If some don't come to mind, use anything you connect with and feel will help you with that chakra.

1. When I think of the earth, I think of [insert an animal here].
2. When I am grounded, it reminds me of [insert a place here].
3. When I feel secure, I think of [insert a song here].
4. When I think of stability, it reminds me of [insert a person you know or don't know here].

Now, you can visualize working with different scenarios when gathering information or reading the root chakra, such as instruments, archetypes, herbs, or anything else that is affiliated with the root chakra.

The Sacral Chakra (Second Chakra)

The sacral chakra is the second chakra, located two finger widths below the navel. It is associated with orange. The sacral chakra is associated with vitality, passion, creativity, sensuality, sexuality, and fertility. While the root chakra is related to the earth element, the sacral chakra is associated with water. When thinking of the sacral chakra, think of anything that connects you to water. The mantra or intonation for the sacral chakra is *Vam* (pronounced like Tom, not like ham). Your sex organs, bladder, circulatory system, prostate, womb, glandular ovaries, and testes are connected to your sacral chakra.

When your sacral chakra is balanced, you might feel vital, energetic, sexy, sensual, or creative. When your sacral chakra is underactive, you might feel isolated, have a low sex drive, have low sexual confidence, be fearful of intimacy, sluggish, stuck, or even depressed. You might not feel vital. An underactive sacral chakra might also cause physical feelings such as impotence, kidney pain, bladder or prostate pain, or lower back pain. When overactive, you might feel hypersexual, have the urge to overeat, feel manic to create, hyperfocused yet not focused, jealous, possessive, or be prone to addiction to things such as porn. An overactive sacral chakra might also cause physical feelings of restlessness, uterine or bladder infections, or kidney stones.

Crystals can help balance the chakras. Some excellent crystals for the sacral chakra are amber, carnelian, citrine, fire opal, moonstone, orange calcite, and orange aventurine. You can hold the crystals, sit near them, and make a crystal grid. Wear them or tape them to the chakra with soft medical tape.

Exercise: Exploring the Sacral Chakra

To help associate the sacral chakra with messages, use the keywords *water*, *passionate*, *creative*, and *vitality* for animal, place, song, and person, respectively. If some don't come to mind, use anything you connect with and feel will help you with that chakra.

1. When I think of water, I think of [insert an animal here].
2. When I am passionate about something, it reminds me of [insert a place here].

3. When I feel creative, I think of [insert a song here].
4. When I think of vitality, it reminds me of [insert a person you know or don't know here].

Now, you can visualize working with different scenarios when gathering information or reading the sacral chakra, such as instruments, archetypes, herbs, or anything else that is affiliated with the sacral chakra.

The Solar Plexus Chakra (Third Chakra)

The solar plexus is the third chakra below your ribs. It is associated with yellow. The solar plexus chakra is associated with worth, confidence, willfulness, personal power, and joy. The solar plexus chakra is related to the fire element and the sense of sight. When thinking of the solar plexus, visualize burning flames like a fire in your belly. The mantra or intonation for the solar plexus chakra is *Ram* (pronounced like Tom, not like ham). Your pancreas, adrenals, kidneys, stomach, liver, gallbladder, metabolism, digestion, sympathetic nervous system, and core muscles are all connected to your solar plexus chakra.

When your solar plexus chakra is balanced, you might feel self-confident, worthy, energetic, upbeat, optimistic, and joyful. When your solar plexus chakra is underactive, you might feel insecure, unworthy, underconfident, overly emotional, fearful of expressing your opinion, worried about what others think of you, or sorry for yourself. You might feel that no one gives you recognition or attention. An underactive solar plexus chakra might cause physical feelings like stomach or digestive issues. An underactive solar plexus might also cause sleep disorders, weight around the midsection, allergies, diabetes, loss of muscle mass, and stomach ulcers. When overactive, you might feel overly powerful, possessive, and overbearing and strongly need accolades and recognition. When overactive, you may think others are not respecting you, which causes anger and perhaps volatility. An overactive solar plexus chakra might also cause physical digestive problems. Some excellent crystals for the sacral chakra are amber, citrine, golden tiger's eye, sunstone, yellow apatite, yellow aventurine, yellow calcite, and yellow jasper. You can hold the crystals, sit near them, or make a crystal grid. You can also wear them or tape them to the chakra with soft medical tape.

Exercise: Exploring the Solar Plexus Chakra

To help associate the solar plexus chakra with messages, use *fire, warmth, worth,* and *confidence* for animal, place, song, and person, respectively. If some don't come to mind, use anything you connect with and feel will help you with that chakra.

1. When I think of a fire, I think of [insert an animal here].
2. When I think of warmth, it reminds me of [insert a place here].
3. When I feel my worth, I think of [insert a song here].
4. When I feel confident, it reminds me of [insert a person you know or don't know here].

Now, you can visualize working with different scenarios when gathering information or reading the solar plexus chakra, such as instruments, archetypes, herbs, or anything else that is affiliated with the solar plexus chakra.

The Heart Chakra (Fourth Chakra)

The heart chakra is the fourth chakra. It is located near your actual heart, but in the middle of your chest. It is traditionally associated with green, but we have also come to associate it with pink in modern times. The pink higher heart chakra (thymus) represents the soul's purpose and universal love. The heart chakra is associated with self-love, love for others, compassion, empathy, tolerance, forgiveness, and openness. The heart chakra is related to the air element and the sense of touch. The mantra or intonation for the heart chakra is *Yam* (pronounced like Tom, not like ham). Your heart, chest, lungs, arms, hands, thymus, and circulatory system are all connected to your heart chakra.

When your heart chakra is balanced, you might feel calm, trusting, fearless, peaceful, generous, grateful, connected, committed, empathic, and tolerant. When your heart chakra is underactive, you might feel melancholy, fearful of loneliness, and codependent. You might also have poor boundaries and relationship problems (specifically, you give too much). You may have a deep-seated fear of getting hurt. An underactive heart chakra might also cause physical feelings such as low blood pressure, heart issues, and shallow breathing. When your heart chakra is overactive, you might feel overly giving, possessive, overbearing, and emotional. When the heart chakra is overactive, you may give too much of yourself and eventually resent it because it often involves a lack of boundaries. An overactive heart chakra might cause physical problems such as high blood pressure and insomnia.

Some ideal crystals for the heart chakra are azurite, chrysoprase, emerald, green aventurine, green calcite, jade, malachite, rhodonite, rhodochrosite, rose quartz, ruby fuchsite, ruby zoisite, and watermelon tourmaline. You can hold the crystals, sit near them, and make a crystal grid. You can also wear them or tape them to the chakra with soft medical tape.

Exercise: Exploring the Heart Chakra

To help associate the heart chakra with messages, use the keywords *green*, *pink*, *love*, and *compassion* for animal, place, song, and person, respectively. If some don't come to mind, use anything you connect with and feel will help you with that chakra.

1. When I think of green, I think of [insert an animal here].
2. When I think of pink, it reminds me of [insert a place here].
3. When I feel love, I think of [insert a song here].
4. When I feel compassion, it reminds me of [insert a person you know or don't know here].

Now, you can visualize working with different scenarios when gathering information or reading the heart chakra, such as instruments, archetypes, herbs, or anything else that is affiliated with the heart chakra.

The Throat Chakra (Fifth Chakra)

The throat chakra is the fifth chakra and is located at the throat or base of the neck. It is associated with the color sky blue. The throat chakra is associated with communication, written and verbal expression, music, writing, speaking the truth, discernment, and listening. The throat chakra is associated with Akasha or ether (spirit). When thinking of the throat chakra, think of anything that connects you to the unseen or heavenly realms.

It is also connected to the sense of hearing. This connection to hearing is interesting because we often think of the throat chakra as being about talking, but it is as much, if not more, about listening. The mantra or intonation for the throat chakra is *Ham* (pronounced like Tom, not like ham). Your throat, ears, nose, teeth, mouth, and neck are connected to your throat chakra.

When your throat chakra is balanced, you might feel peaceful, wise, kind, knowledgeable, and able to express yourself confidently. When your heart chakra is underactive, you might feel unheard, shy, shut down, or out of touch. You might not feel you can speak your truth. You might resent others who seem to express themselves easily. An underactive throat chakra might also cause physical feelings such as thyroid ailments, neck pain, speech defects, sore throat, teeth grinding, hearing or ear issues, tinnitus, and asthma. When overactive, you might feel like you have all the answers and don't need to listen to others. You may begin interrupting or be opinionated, gossipy, bombastic in speech, and overbearing. An overactive throat chakra might also cause physical feelings such as throat pain, mouth ulcers, dental problems, thyroid issues, neck pain, speech defects, sore throat, hearing or ear issues, tinnitus, and asthma. These physical ailments would likely be a sore throat from talking too much and stopped-up ears, representing an unwillingness to listen.

Some excellent crystals for the throat chakra are aquamarine, blue lace agate, blue topaz, celestite, lapis lazuli, sodalite, and turquoise. You can hold the crystals, sit near them, and make a crystal grid. You can also wear them or tape them to the chakra with soft medical tape.

Exercise: Exploring the Throat Chakra

To help associate the throat chakra with messages, use the keywords *blue*, *communication*, *speaking the truth*, and *listening* for animal, place, song, and person, respectively. If some don't come to mind, use anything you connect with and feel will help you with that chakra.

1. When I think of blue, I think of [insert an animal here].
2. When I think of communication, it reminds me of [insert a place here].

3. When I speak the truth, I think of [insert a song here].
4. When I think of listening, it reminds me of [insert a person you know or don't know here].

Now, you can visualize working with different scenarios when gathering information or reading the throat chakra, such as instruments, archetypes, herbs, or anything else that is affiliated with the throat chakra.

The Brow or Third-Eye Chakra (Sixth Chakra)

The brow chakra is the sixth chakra and is located at the center of the forehead between the eyebrows. It is associated with the color indigo (dark bluish-purple). It is associated with intuition, wisdom, realization, insight, awareness, imagination, discernment, and clairvoyance. The brow chakra is associated with light. When thinking of the brow chakra, think of anything that connects you to your higher self. It is connected to what many call the sixth sense or telepathic energy. The mantra or intonation for the brow chakra is *Om* (pronounced Ohm). Your pituitary gland, pineal gland, eyes, and skull base are connected to your brow chakra.

When your brow chakra is balanced, you might feel connected to your psychic knowingness. When your brow chakra is underactive, you might feel disconnected from your higher self and keen intuition. You may feel like you cannot discern the truth, making you less assertive and more indecisive, especially regarding your psychic powers. An underactive brow chakra might also cause physical feelings such as a heaviness in your nose, eyes, or ears. When overactive, you might experience nightmares, learning difficulties, hallucinations, anxiety, and poor concentration. You might also experience physical problems such as sharp ice-pick headaches, poor vision, neurological disturbances, and dizziness. You would need a good chakra alignment and a ground between heaven and earth.

Some excellent crystals for the brow chakra are amethyst, apophyllite, azurite, charoite, iolite, lapis lazuli, lepidolite, moldavite, and phenacite. You can hold the crystals, sit near them, and make a crystal grid. You can also wear them or tape them to the chakra with soft medical tape.

Exercise: Exploring the Brow (Third Eye) Chakra

To help associate the brow chakra with messages, use the keywords *intuition*, *wisdom*, *insight*, and *awareness* for animal, place, song, and person, respectively. If some don't come to mind, use anything you connect with and feel will help you with that chakra.

1. When I think of intuition, I think of [insert an animal here].
2. When I think of wisdom, it reminds me of [insert a place here].
3. When I think of insight, I think of [insert a song here].
4. When I think of awareness, it reminds me of [insert a person you know or don't know here].

Now, you can visualize working with different scenarios when gathering information or reading the brow chakra, such as instruments, archetypes, herbs, or anything else that is affiliated with the brow chakra.

The Crown Chakra (Seventh Chakra)

The crown chakra is the seventh chakra located at the top of the head. It is associated with violet (and sometimes white light). It is associated with spirituality, the experience of higher planes, enlightenment, self-realization, and cosmic consciousness. The crown chakra is associated with thought and will. When thinking of the crown chakra, think of anything that connects you to your higher self. The mantra or intonation for the crown chakra is silence or *Om* (pronounced Ohm). Your pituitary gland, pineal gland, upper skull, cerebral cortex, and skin are all connected to your crown chakra.

When your crown chakra is balanced, you might feel connected to a higher power and all that is. When your crown chakra is underactive, you might feel disconnected from a higher power or beings besides those evident on earth. An underactive crown chakra might also cause feelings such as lethargy, frustration, lack of joy, and a lack of purpose, which can lead to all kinds of physical ailments, including chronic illness. When overactive, you might experience depression, obsessive thinking, confusion, dizziness, hallucinations, and escapism. You might also experience physical problems such as sharp ice-pick headaches, poor vision, neurological disturbances, and dizziness. You would need a good chakra alignment and a ground between heaven and earth.

Some excellent crystals for the crown chakra are amethyst, apophyllite, clear quartz, Herkimer diamond, lepidolite, moldavite, phenacite, and selenite. You can hold the crystals, sit near them, and make a crystal grid. You can also wear them or tape them to the chakra with soft medical tape.

Exercise: Exploring the Crown Chakra

To help associate the crown chakra with messages, use the keywords *spirituality*, *higher self*, *enlightenment*, and *self-realization* for animal, place, song, and person, respectively. If some don't come to mind, use anything you connect with and feel will help you with that chakra.

1. When I think of spirituality, I think of [insert an animal here].
2. When I think of the higher self, it reminds me of [insert a place here].
3. When I think of enlightenment, I think of [insert a song here].
4. When I think of self-realization, I think of [insert a person you know or don't know here].

The more you associate chakras with every aspect of being, the more they will enter your readings, giving you clear and almost-immediate insight into any situation. Then, when you combine them with the clairs and colors (auras), you will find few situations that will psychically stump you.

Exercise: Pendulum Chakra Test

The purpose of this exercise is to test the energy flow of the chakras using a pendulum. If the chakra needs correction, use the pendulum to help balance it. This assessment of the state of the chakras at any given time provides valuable psychic information. See part 2 of this book, where pendulums are discussed, if you need more information on how to work with them.

Equipment: Pendulum, chair or massage table

You can use this to test chakras by holding a pendulum over the chakra. The chakra is balanced if the pendulum moves evenly and smoothly. The chakra is underactive if the pendulum won't move or barely moves. If the pendulum spins fast or acts erratically, the chakra is overactive. You can also ask yes-or-no questions about the chakras; for example, Is the root chakra balanced? If the pendulum indicates no, you would ask if it is underactive. If the pendulum does not indicate that it is underactive, then ask if it is overactive.

One of my favorite ways to use a pendulum is to balance the chakras. I have the pendulum spin clockwise if it needs more activation. If it requires less activation, I spin the pendulum counterclockwise. You can also use pendulums to clear away something, such as a headache. You are simply imagining the headache leaving as you spin the pendulum counterclockwise. Then, replace the headache energy with healing energy by spinning the pendulum clockwise.

Journal Prompts: Pendulum Chakra Test

1. Could you ascertain information about different chakras from your pendulum?
2. Were you able to use this information not only to balance the chakras but also to provide insight into psychic information?

Exercise: Your Chakra Path

The purpose of this exercise is to meaningfully connect with each of your chakras. The more you connect with chakras, the easier intuitive information will flow. Slow your breathing and calm your mind.

You find yourself on a path that is a deep red in color. You may feel great warmth as you walk on this red path. It is not uncomfortable, yet you know it could be if you heat it up. You begin traveling down this path. As you continue down the way, you come upon a tree blocking your path. Take note of the tree. What does it look like? Look at the roots, trunk, branches, leaves, and flowers or fruit. Please take note of how it is blocking your way. Now, find a way to get around the tree and continue your chakra journey.

Your path turns vibrant orange in color. As you travel this warm orange path, you allow a person or memory that ignited your passion or creativity to float gently into your mind. You feel safe and protected as the observer. Observe the person or memory that ignited your feelings of love and creativity.

You now find that your path is turning to a vibrant, warm yellow. As you travel down your yellow path, you come upon a small, contained fire on the trail. You feel drawn to sit down by the fire. Sitting down, you see a pen and paper upon a stone beside you. You pick it up and write down the name of someone who took your power or whom you allowed to take away your power. Now, you accept the paper, place it in the fire, and watch it burn. You get up to continue your journey.

Your path turns to a lush green. You see a pink building and enter one large room. Things are cooler now. The temperature is perfect for you. In the middle of the room, you see an image of your heart on a crystal pedestal. Take note of your heart. What does it look like? Look around the room. You see all sorts of tools you could use to help you heal your heart. Grab whatever tools you feel are necessary to mend and send healing to your heart.

Now, you leave your pink structure and head back on your path, which is sky blue. You may begin to get even cooler. While you are on your path, state something that you want. Be clear in your mind that this is something you desire. It might be something you also need, but allow yourself to know it is all right if you want it instead of needing it. State it again as if you already own or have what you want.

Your path turns to a deep bluish-purple (indigo), and you may feel much cooler. Look in your mind's eye (your third eye) on this path and see the first thing or thought that comes into your mind. This thought or image should appear quickly—try not to second-guess or change your mind. Do not question it.

Now, your path turns violet, or you see white light. Travel this road and check in with your feelings. Note your physical, mental, emotional, and spiritual senses. This awareness is much like the body scan you perform daily to mind your energy (see chapter 6). As you continue to travel, you notice the path turns to a path of every color imaginable and unimaginable. It is full of beautiful crystals. Reach down and pick one up. Keep it in your heart as a gift.

You have reached the end of this chakra journey. Bring your awareness back to the here and now. When you are ready, open your eyes.

Journal Prompts: Your Chakra Path

1. What type of tree was on your red path? Did you have trouble moving around it when it was time to continue down the path?

2. What person or memory ignited your passion or creativity on your orange path? Was this a positive or negative experience?

3. Was the pen, paper, and fire exercise on the yellow path challenging for you? Did it bother you to burn the name?

4. What did your pink building on your green path look like?

5. Describe your heart. Were you able to send your heart healing if necessary?

6. Did you use tools to heal your heart?

7. On your blue path, were you able to state something you need or want that you haven't been able to communicate before? Did it make you uncomfortable to ask for a "want"?

8. On your indigo path, could you visualize your third eye or mind's eye? Did you get a thought? Did you question it? What was the first thought that came to your mind? Do you know the message? If not, ask when you meditate.

9. How did you feel when you reached your violet path? Describe.

10. What color was your crystal? Shape? Do you know which crystal it was?

11. What chakra, if any, did the meditation draw your attention to most? Does this chakra need work?

Exercise: Grounding with Chakras

This exercise aims to help you ground between heaven and earth using visualization with the chakras.

Get comfortable and begin to focus on your breathing. Pay attention to your breath—your life force. You might want to visualize sitting with your back to a tree or standing with your arms around the tree. Become aware of your feet. Begin feeling energetic roots extending from your feet, going deep into the core of Mother Earth. Out of gratitude to her, send some loving energy out through those roots. Now, bring some of Mother Earth's energy up through your feet. Give it a little tug in your mind to make sure the energetic roots have wrapped around Mother Earth's core. Send the energy up your legs to your root chakra. Your root chakra is warm, and you may feel great warmth. Quietly say or think, "I am safe and secure." Picture a nurturing red jasper connected to your base.

Next, draw your energy into your sacral chakra, about two finger widths below your navel. The energy is still warm, like a bright orange sun in your sacral chakra. Say with your inner ear, "I am vital." Picture a lovely orange carnelian connected to your sacral chakra.

Send your energy up into your solar plexus chakra below your rib cage. It is still warm, like a yellow sun at your solar plexus chakra. Say with your inner ear, "I am worthy." Think of yellow jasper, citrine, or aventurine connected to your solar plexus.

Next, begin to explore the heavens or cosmos. You may stay in earth's atmosphere or choose to travel even farther. Go where you feel it might be your original home. Pick a planet or star and send a beautiful silver cord to wrap around the star. Give it a little tug to make sure it is connected.

Now, go to the top of your head—your crown chakra. Feel beautiful light like diamonds pouring into your crown. Then, begin to feel a violet amethyst connected to your crown chakra. It may feel cold at the crown but is still comfortable. Say quietly or to yourself, "I Am One with All."

Begin to draw your energy down into your third eye or brow chakra. Allow yourself to feel the cool energy. Imagine a bluish-purple crystal like an iolite connected to your third eye. Say quietly or to yourself, "I am seeing and discerning truth."

Now, send energy through your light column. Your light column runs the length of your body and seems like a ball of energy on your spinal column and beyond the top of your head. Let it run up and down your entire body a few times.

Draw the energy down into your throat chakra, where you have an indentation between the collarbones. Feel the cool, crisp energy. You may even feel a tickle in your throat. Imagine a blue lace agate connected to your throat chakra. Say quietly or to yourself, "I listen, speak the truth, and am heard."

If you desire, bring your hands to the middle of your chest to your heart chakra in a prayerlike position. Think of a green aventurine. Bring your attention to something you are grateful for today. Remember to acknowledge your gratitude before you sleep tonight and your feet hit the floor the following day. Let all the energies mingle at your heart chakra. Say quietly or to yourself, "I am loved."

You are now equally grounded between heaven and earth. Slowly and gently open your eyes.

Journal Prompts: Grounding with Chakras

1. How did the energy feel at your root chakra?
2. Could you feel the heat?
3. How did you feel when you stated the affirmation regarding safety and security?
4. Were you able to visualize a red jasper?
5. How did the energy feel in your sacral chakra?
6. Could you feel a warm energy?
7. How did you feel when you stated the affirmation regarding vitality?
8. Were you able to visualize a carnelian?
9. How did the energy feel at your solar plexus chakra?

10. Could you feel the warmth?

11. How did you feel when you affirmed your worth?

12. Were you able to visualize a yellow jasper, citrine, or aventurine?

13. Were you able to go out into the heavens and beyond?

14. Did you sense a place that felt like it was home?

15. How did the energy feel at your crown chakra?

16. Were you able to visualize a beautiful violet amethyst?

17. Could you feel the energy turn cold?

18. How did you feel regarding the affirmation I Am One with All?

19. How did the energy feel at your third eye or brow chakra?

20. Could you feel cool energy?

21. Were you able to visualize an iolite?

22. How did you feel about affirming that you are a discerner of truth?

23. How did the energy feel at your throat chakra?

24. Could you feel cool energy?

25. Could you visualize a blue lace agate?

26. How did you feel about affirming that you listen, speak the truth, and are heard?

27. When the energy all mingled at your heart chakra, how did it feel?

28. Could you visualize a green aventurine?

29. Were you able to give gratitude for something specific?

Exercise: Slowing Down Your Chakras

This exercise aims to slow down your chakras' movement at the end of a psychic session. It can be done in pairs of two or solo. If you do this exercise in pairs, face one another and place your hand in the other person's energy field without touching them.

Equipment: None needed

While standing, get comfortable and begin to focus on your breathing. Pay attention to your breath—your life force. Bring your attention to your root chakra and crown chakra. Place one hand about four inches away from the area of your root chakra. Place the other hand about four inches above your head. While doing so, imagine the wheels of the chakras slowing down to a calm rhythm. Allow yourself to feel the root chakra's warm red and the crown chakra's cool violet. Note how these two chakras come into accord as you say, "I am secure and one with All."

Next, move the root chakra hand up to your sacral chakra about two finger widths below your navel, and move the crown chakra hand down to your third eye or brow chakra. While doing so, imagine the wheel of the chakras slowing down to a calm rhythm. Allow yourself to feel the warmth of the orange sacral chakra and the coolness of the indigo third eye. Take note of how these two chakras come into accord as you say, "I am vital, and I am discerning."

Bring the sacral chakra hand up to the yellow solar plexus chakra below your ribcage and the brow chakra hand down to the blue throat chakra. While doing so, imagine the wheel of the chakras slowing down to a calm rhythm. Allow yourself to feel the sunny warmth of the yellow solar plexus and the coolness of the blue throat chakra. Take note of how these chakras come into accord as you say, "I am worthy, and I am heard."

Finally, bring your hands together in a prayerlike position in the middle of your chest at your heart chakra. Feel the mixing and mingling of the pink and green energy. Slow the turning of the wheel of the chakra to a calm rhythm. Take note of how you feel as you say, "I am loved." Give gratitude for one specific moment. When you go to bed tonight, give gratitude once again, and then give the same gratitude before your feet hit the floor to begin your following day.

Journal Prompts: Slowing Down Your Chakras

1. Were you able to slow down your root and crown chakras?
2. Could you feel the root and chakra energies intermingle?
3. How did the colors red and violet come into your meditation?
4. How did you feel about stating your chakra affirmation of "I am secure and one with All"?

5. Were you able to slow down your sacral and brow chakras?

6. Could you feel the sacral and brow energies intermingle?

7. How did the colors orange and indigo come into your meditation?

8. How did you feel stating your chakra affirmation of "I am vital and discerning"?

9. Could you slow down your solar plexus and throat chakras?

10. Could you feel the solar plexus and throat energies intermingle?

11. How did the colors yellow and blue come into your meditation?

12. How did you feel stating your chakra affirmation of "I am worthy, and I am heard"?

13. Were you able to slow down your heart chakra?

14. Could you feel the heart energy intermingle?

15. How did the colors green and pink come into your meditation?

16. How did you feel stating your chakra affirmation of "I am loved"?

17. Could you think of a specific statement of gratitude?

18. Did you say it before you went to sleep?

19. Did you say it before you left your bed the following day?

Chakra Summary

Chakras are part of the Three C's (clairs, chakras, and colors [auras]). Once you learn how to sense if they are balanced, overactive, or underactive, you will have undeniable and quickly apparent intuitive information.

Avoid These Pitfalls

Do not fall for the often-stated principle that if a chakra is blocked, energy cannot flow into the other chakras. Energy can still flow, but it may be impeded and will not flow as fluidly. Don't concentrate on one chakra so much that you neglect others. While one chakra may need special attention, remember to ultimately activate all the chakras at once. Then, they can work together simultaneously, flowing as one activated and balanced unit with a wealth of intuitive information about the physical, mental, emotional, and spiritual bodies.

Psychic Success

Learning to work with the chakras significantly contributes to expanding your psychic knowingness. Many times, your psychic hits will only give you part of the picture. You are left guessing to fill in the blanks, which leads to inaccuracy and frustration. However, when you layer your psychic hits with all the knowledge that comes with the chakras, many questions will naturally be answered, and the disappointment from information gaps will dissipate. Remember to pay attention to the value of the Three C's, including chakras.

CHAPTER 8

YOUR AURA COLOR

Remember I told you that you could cull down your handbook to the Three C's: clairs, chakras, and colors? Learning to use your psychism is related to colors but also involves clairs and chakras. When you combine the Three C's, you will find everything begins to connect and realize how easy it is to read and relay messages.

Checkup: Seeing Auras Baseline

This checkup aims to establish a baseline for seeing auras. Knowing your baseline makes tracking your future progress much easier. Answer the following questions honestly with a simple yes or no. Refer to this exercise every time you practice seeing auras to see if it has changed.

1. I have seen the aura around someone.
2. I have sensed the aura around someone.
3. I can soften my gaze and look past a physical body to see the aura.
4. I can see or sense different auric fields, shapes, and colors.
5. I have a favorite color and my aura color typically matches my aura.

The more yes answers, the more success you have seeing auras. The number of yes answers will increase as you develop and practice the methods in your handbook.

Auras (The Energetic Colors of Living Things)

Everything has its aura or electromagnetic energy surrounding it. *Aura* comes from the Greek word meaning "breeze" or "air." The aura around living things (the auric field) usually has seven layers connected to the seven primary chakras. These layers sync up with your chakras, connecting to your inner body. The aura also connects you to the outer world or universal energy. Like the chakras, the auric field is composed of varying colors.

Many people think auras are hard to see, but everyone can learn to detect them. However, they are most easily seen around humans, plants and flowers, crystals, or animals. Understanding these auric fields is essential so that you can learn to sense where energy is held. You can learn to see the color of these auras and even the shape of the auric field. Your subtle body (the unseen layers of the auric field surrounding your body) is not your physical body. However, a genuine part of you stays with you even when you leave your body.

Picking up information in an auric subtle body by utilizing the clairs, realizing how it corresponds to the chakras, and then looking at the meaning of the energetic color gives you almost all the information you need to read any energy. The Three C's, at the least, give you a baseline or starting point for your reading.

The aura surrounding a healthy human body is typically an oval-shaped field. This egg shape extends from the body. However, it often expands farther at the head and heart. It also rises above the head and descends below the feet into the ground. You have probably seen photographs or renderings of religious figures with a halo above their heads. That halo represents what we now know to be the aura.

An unhealthy human body might not have the perfect egg shape that surrounds the body. When someone is unwell physically, mentally, emotionally, or spiritually, the egg may have indentations, curves, waves, and even other colors that seem to be attached.

The aura consists of seven layers (subtle bodies). Each of these subtle bodies has its unique frequency; however, even though they each have their frequency, they are also interrelated and affect one another. They can change color and consistency due to a person's feelings, emotions, thoughts, behavior, and health. Living beings are holistic. If one layer is out of whack, that may lead to an imbalance in the others. Odd-numbered layers are more structured and hold a proactive energy. Even-numbered layers are more fluid and have a reactive energy. It is essential to become familiar with the different layers because they, along with chakras, are helpful to psychics. Everything about you is stored in your aura—all past, present, and future information is stored in the auric layers. Memories are also held in the layers. In some ways, your aura is your Akashic Record.

Auras are vital for you to understand when creating your handbook because if you can learn to read your aura and that of others, you will know everything about them. The aura serves as a failproof polygraph or lie detector because you cannot trick your aura into presenting a lie. If you learn to see auras, and everyone can do so with practice, then the only mistake you can make is incorrectly reading or interpreting what you see. So, as with everything in your handbook, it is crucial to practice reading or interpreting auras as much as you practice seeing or sensing them.

One common analogy is that the layers of the aura are like an onion and that when you peel one away, you'll reach the next. Although this may be true, the layers are not entirely separate; they vary in vibration while holding the same space, working together, and building on one another. Think of nesting, or cupping, Russian matryoshka dolls.[4] As you go inward, the aura layer before is also present within the next aura layer. For example, the outer body is the causal (or ketheric) body. The next layer is the celestial body, which contains itself and the causal body. As you go inward toward the first layer (the etheric), each layer will become denser because each holds all subtle bodies before it.

Each aura level has the seven bodily chakras nested within it. As each layer extends outward, the chakras vibrate at higher rates. So the seven chakras within the etheric body (the layer closest to the physical body) will vibrate at a much lower frequency than those within the causal body (the layer farthest away from the physical body). Remember, it is helpful for psychic development to know that energy flows between all bodies and is connected to all seven chakras in the body.

. . . .

4. Laura Styler, *The Little Book of Aura Healing: Simple Practices for Cleansing and Reading the Colors of the Aura* (Rockridge Press, 2020), 12.

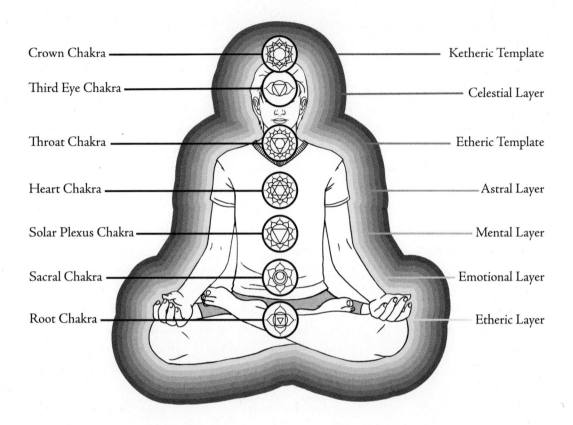

Crown Chakra — Ketheric Template

Third Eye Chakra — Celestial Layer

Throat Chakra — Etheric Template

Heart Chakra — Astral Layer

Solar Plexus Chakra — Mental Layer

Sacral Chakra — Emotional Layer

Root Chakra — Etheric Layer

First Layer (The Etheric Body)

This etheric layer is the closest energy body to the physical body. Kirlian photography, named after Semyon Kirlian, shows this layer and the electricity around living things when a photograph is taken. The etheric layer is right next to the physical body. It is a duplicate (or blueprint) of the physical body. You can sometimes detect physical illness by looking at the etheric layer. This layer is connected to the root or base chakra. It has the slowest vibration (or rate of vibration: *frequency*). When you first begin to see auras, you will see the etheric layer because it is the easiest to see. It is often seen as white, off white, or bluish gray.

Second Layer (The Emotional Body)

Since the second layer is the emotional body, it is associated with feelings. It is more fluid and does not duplicate the physical body. The color of this aura changes depending on what kind of emotions you are experiencing. As we discuss aura colors later in this chapter, you will find that, typically, clear colors are more of what we consider positive emotions, such as love, joy, and excitement. If the colors are muddy, the sentiment is perhaps what we would consider a complex or negative emotion. The emotional body contains all the colors in the rainbow. However, it is associated with the sacral chakra, which is orange and connected to the element of water. You can probably see and make connections between the auric layers and the chakras at this stage. The emotional body contains information about the etheric and emotional bodies.

Third Layer (The Mental Body)

The mental body or mental layer holds our thoughts and cognitive processes. It is related to the solar plexus, so it is generally yellow. The yellow will become brighter if a person is deep in thought or concentrating on mental activities. Although the color associated with this body is yellow, other colors are evident if there is an emotion associated with the thought. Remember that each layer takes on the energy of the layer before it. Therefore, the mental layer contains the information from the etheric and emotional layers.

Fourth Layer (The Astral Body)

If you want to take your psychic training seriously, the astral body is a great place to start. It bridges the three physical bodies with the three spiritual bodies. When you begin to work with this level and above, your abilities will leap from the physical to the more subtle. The state of the chakras can be analyzed from this layer. The astral body is composed of clouds of pink, plus potentially a rainbow of colors. It has the same colors as the rainbow, like the emotional body. Still, pink is often present, especially if the person is loving. The astral, also called the emotional plane, ties it firmly to the heart chakra and the second subtle body (the emotional body). It is closely tied to emotions. When people fall in love, pink comes from their heart chakra. The astral layer is where you connect with spirit guides and ascended masters.

Fifth Layer (The Etheric Template)

The title of this layer may seem confusing at first, but not if you break down the words. It is a template for the etheric or first layer. This template exists before the physical body is formed. This layer is not easy to see unless you practice, but remember, practice makes psychic. In this case, it is beneficial if you can see it. This layer is dark cobalt blue. It represents self-expression or personal truth. It is connected to the throat chakra and is a place of non-judgment and pure potential.

Sixth Layer (The Celestial Body)

The sixth layer, or the celestial emotional body of the spiritual plane, is where you will feel bliss and spiritual ecstasy. This layer is your connection to the source of divine love and is thought to contain a blueprint or life plan. It is related to the brow chakra, so you will also sense and know the truth. Discernment is heightened when you are operating at this layer. The colors of this body are shimmering pastel. However, this layer can sometimes be bluish-purple (indigo), like the brow chakra, since that is the chakra to which it is connected. Remember that this layer contains all the previous layers within it.

The Seventh Layer (The Ketheric Template or Causal Body)

This layer is the mental level of the spiritual plane. If this is confusing, recall that the previous layer, the celestial body, is the emotional level of the body. The Ketheric template contains all the other bodies within it. It typically consists of gold, silvery-gold, or violet. It oscillates or vibrates at a high speed, and, in the crown chakra, we begin to *know* we are one with God, Source, or all that is.

Exercise: Eye Training for Aura Readings

This exercise aims to train your eyes to see lingering colors known as after-images. Although afterimages are not auras, training your eyes to see them helps you eventually see auras.

Equipment: Different-colored construction paper or felt cut into 4 × 4-inch squares, blank white typing paper, scissors

Get colored construction paper or felt pieces that have been cut into 4 × 4-inch squares. Place one on a blank white sheet of typing paper turned to landscape. Stare at the color with a soft gaze. Then, move the color away and see if you can see the color on your white sheet of typing paper. Don't overthink it. Be patient and remember that practice makes you psychic.

Journal Prompts: Eye Training for Aura Readings

1. Were you able to see the color when you moved it away and looked at the white paper?
2. What colors, if any, gave you trouble?

Exercise: Magic Eye Images

The purpose of this exercise is to train your eyes to see auras.

Equipment: Magic Eye images (pictures that have a hidden 3D image)

Go online and find some Magic Eye images. Stare at the picture with it about twelve inches from your eyes. The trick is to look through the apparent photo to find the underlying one. Seeing auras will come naturally to some of you, while others may require more patience and practice. Those who see the underlying image more quickly are more naturally advanced in this area, but remember, everyone can learn.

Journal Prompts: Magic Eye Images

1. Were you able to look through the photo?
2. Were you able to see the underlying image?
3. How quickly did the image appear to you?

Exercise: Sensing, Seeing, and Reading Auras

This exercise aims to help you practice reading the auras of others with your outer or physical eyes. Everyone can physically do this with enough practice. Remember that auras can change due to moods, habits, health, and other factors.

Equipment: Blank wall, white clothing for subject, subject

Get your subject to stand with their back about one or two feet away from a blank wall. Ideally, the wall or backdrop should be white or off-white, with natural or soft lighting (however, some find it easier to see the aura on a black background). The subject will ideally wear white or wrap themselves in a white sheet, something like toga style. You can then stand about six to twelve feet away as the room allows. Get comfortable and quiet.

Pick your focal point, such as the nose tip or third eye. The trick is to gaze through your subject with peripheral vision. If you blink, don't worry; start again. Remember to gaze through or past the subject. Think of the Magic Eye images and how to look beyond the subject. Another way to create a focal point is to use a shiny object that you can see from six to twelve feet. Pin or tape a metal thumbtack or star to the wall a couple of inches to the left or right of the subject's head. If you begin to see colors, great. If not, keep practicing.

Be conscious of afterimages. Staring at the same spot will produce afterimages that are the direct inverse of what you are gazing at. Afterimages are not auras. You'll know the difference because the afterimage will appear briefly before your eyes, no matter where you look. Afterimages are typically color-paired: black and white, red and turquoise, orange and blue, yellow and violet, and green and pink.

Journal Prompts: Sensing, Seeing, and Reading Auras

1. What kind of background did you use?
2. Were you able to see color around the subject's head? If so, what color? Were there any spikes or bubbles in the texture?

3. Were you able to see color around the subject's heart? If so, what color? Were there any spikes or bubbles in the texture?

4. Based on what you saw, were you able to draw any conclusions about the aura? If so, describe your conclusions.

Benefits of Seeing or Sensing Auras

It is helpful to learn how most colors are sensed but not pigeonhole yourself into those typical definitions. They are an excellent place to start while adding knowledge of the meanings of chakra colors. However, over time, you may realize that your sense of red, for example, may mean something different than how others perceive red.

It is also essential to take note of the shape, clarity, texture, and even smell of the aura. The point is to integrate the clairs as needed. Then, you look at your subject and say the first color that comes into your mind's eye. Don't allow the color of clothes they wear or any other material-world assessment to jade your reading as you advance. However, an important point to remember is that the color we wear does affect our aura. So when you grow even more, you can add that to your feedback. For example, if someone wants to feel more stable and secure, it will help them to wear red. As they wear red, they will begin to gain some stability and security. You might let them know that immersing in a certain color through clothing, food, and lights, for example, will help the associated chakra and ultimately aid in changing the aura.

Aura Color Meanings for Aura Interpretation

The meanings of aura colors may vary depending on your approach, but here are some general guidelines. Remember, these are close to colors in chakras. Once you learn the chakra colors and what they represent, you will find it easier to ascertain what each color represents in other situations. However, resisting the urge to oversimplify the meanings of colors in the auric field is vital. Think about picking out white as a paint color for your walls. At first, you may think that you want the color white. It's easy. But then, when you see all the hues, tones, and shades of white, you realize that the color white is not so simple.

Typically, if an aura color is crisp and clear, then the aura is healthy. But with any troubles, the color may become dull and muddy. An aura color can be affected by the environment around it and can change from moment to moment. I use an aura and chakra computer program to help me show my clients. While the aura may not change drastically from one moment to the next, if I do energy work between aura photos or interject a surprise event, the aura color may change quite quickly. As with any divination, there may be differences in the interpretation and message delivery depending on the person reading and relaying the message. This does not mean the interpretations are incorrect, but that they represent different messages the recipient may need to hear. As you go through the various colors, remember that you will also need to consider the clarity or muddiness of the color. Clear red, for example, might represent passion, while a muddy red might indicate jealous passion or perhaps heartache. Once you see or sense a color, think of all the sayings or phrases that come to mind that are affiliated with that color, such as "I feel blue," "I am green with envy," "My world went black," or "I am pure as the white snow." Do the phrases apply to what you are seeing or sensing?

Knowing how your querent feels about a color is essential as a psychic. Perhaps the querent is drawn to green, which shows up in their aura. This might mean they are comfortable with healing and heart issues. However, you may realize the client needs more grounding; therefore, red must be introduced into the client's life. If the client detests red, it may mean they resist working on their safety and security (root chakra). Therefore, the querent may need to wear red. If the querent dislikes purple, then it might be a sign they need to work on connecting to all that is. They may need to immerse themselves in purple. As a psychic, you can get all sorts of intuitive information from these simple scenarios when working with a psychic situation.

> *Clear red (root chakra):* Red is the densest color (slowest vibration); it creates the most friction. Friction can attract or repel; a vibrant red indicates powerful passion, enthusiasm for love and life, consistent drive, and a healthy, strong ego, all at a demanding pace. Because it is the color assigned to the root chakra, it may indicate security, survival, stability, physicality, or lack thereof. Red is the color associated with blood, so a red aura may mean life force, blood circulation, or a feeling of insecurity, anxiousness, or anger. Some people mistakenly think a red aura always indicates anger and aggression. While this may be the case, red will usually have a cloudy or muddy appearance (like brick red) when someone is angry or aggressive.

> *Dark red (root chakra):* Dark red is associated with the root chakra. It may indicate someone who is overly grounded. If this red comes in flashes, it could

mean passion. If it sticks around, it will eventually indicate exhaustion from needing to hold your ground. A person with a consistently dark red aura may become physically worn out over time.

Muddy red (root chakra): Muddy red indicates intense, repelling anger, trauma, frustration, and aggression. Someone with this aura may become impulsive and take their offense out on others, like a bully would transfer their rage.

Light pink (heart chakra): One of the rarest aura colors, pale pink indicates someone loving, tender, empathic, sensitive, sensual, artistic, affectionate, pure, compassionate, philanthropic, and loyal. A light pink aura may show the beginnings of a relationship that seems more platonic than romantic. It may also indicate love for a friend or a child. Those with light pink auras tend to be kind and gentle to all creatures.

Fuchsia pink (heart chakra): People with fuchsia-pink auras are energetic and excited. They are usually happy and fun to be around. They know how to make everything seem beautiful.

Muddy pink (heart chakra): Someone with this aura struggles to love themselves, much less anyone else. They lack compassion or empathy, and this lack of empathy is primarily for themselves.

Orange (sacral chakra): Orange relates to reproductive organs, sexuality, passion, vitality, courage, creativity, and motivation. Someone with an orange aura is likely in good health and excited about living. They probably have lots of energy and stamina, which helps them enjoy adventures. They are courageous and outgoing and make friends easily with the help of their social nature, happy demeanor, independence, and healthy self-confidence. However, they need to be careful because they rarely do things halfway. They go all in, and this can lead to addictive behaviors.

Dark orange (root and sacral chakra): Dark orange is an indicator of someone optimistic and hungry for challenge and adventure. They probably have a very persuasive personality.

Orange red (sacral chakra): Orange is connected to the sacral chakra and red to the root chakra. Someone with this aura feels confident, courageous, and brave. They usually have a healthy ego.

Orange yellow (solar plexus): Someone with an orange-yellow aura is self-confident. They feel at home in their skin and enjoy life. They are also intelligent and creative, which helps them combine their left and right brain.

Muddy orange (sacral chakra): A cloudy-orange aura indicates someone who lacks confidence in their abilities. They second-guess themselves and their leaders all the time. Those with a muddy-orange aura usually do not enjoy life because they question everything instead of being in the moment.

Yellow (solar plexus): Someone with a yellow aura is intelligent, analytical, self-assured, optimistic, and confident about life. They don't worry a lot because they are hopeful things will always work out for the best. People with yellow auras are usually happy and optimistic. The brighter the yellow, the more intelligent, while the broader the aura, the more friendly.

Pale yellow (solar plexus): Those with a light, pale aura are easygoing and optimistic. They tend to be calm and rarely anxious. They are a laid-back version of yellow.

Neon, bright, lemon yellow (solar plexus): While a bright, lemon yellow might seem happy, it indicates someone struggling to maintain power and control in a personal or business relationship. This color of aura usually means fear of losing control, prestige, respect, or power. This is the desperate (trying too hard) version of yellow. Think of the busy neon doing anything to get attention.

Metallic, shiny, bright gold (crown chakra): Metallic gold indicates awakened spiritual energy. A person with this aura is typically inspired.

Muddy, dark, brownish yellow (solar plexus): Someone with this aura color might be a student or worker pushing hard in their studies. They are overly analytical to the extent of feeling fatigued or stressed. They have possibly fallen behind due to procrastination and are trying to make up for lost time by cramming everything simultaneously. The result is that they do not feel confident.

Green (heart chakra): Green is the aura color of self-love. It is also a comfortable and healthy color of nature. It relates to the heart and lungs. When green is seen in the aura, this usually represents growth and balance, and most of all, something that leads to change. A transparent green aura may indicate a love of people, animals, and nature.

Bright emerald green (heart chakra): Bright emerald green is the aura of a healer. The healer is typically empathic and a love-centered person.

Yellow green (solar plexus and heart): Someone with a yellow-green aura is intelligent and clearheaded. They love to help others, are good listeners, and may open up to strangers.

Muddy forest green (also dull gray green) (heart chakra): Dark or dirty forest green indicates jealousy, resentment, or feeling like a victim. People with this aura typically blame themselves or others for everything instead of trying to fix the situation. They are insecure and have low self-esteem. They are sensitive to perceived criticism.

Turquoise (throat or brow chakra): A turquoise aura relates to the immune system. This aura represents someone who is sensitive, compassionate, a healer, or even a therapist. Those with turquoise auras are adventurous and enjoy travel. They bring happiness to others.

Blue (throat chakra): Blue relates to the throat chakra and thyroid. It usually indicates someone cool, calm, collected, caring, loving to others, sensitive, and intuitive.

Soft blue (throat chakra): A soft blue aura indicates peacefulness, clarity, communication, truthfulness, empathy, and intuition.

Bright royal blue (throat chakra): A bright royal-blue aura almost always indicates someone who is clairvoyant, spiritual, generous, and on the right path. This color is associated with mental alertness and emotional control. It may mean new opportunities are coming.

Muddy blue (throat chakra): Muddy blue indicates fear of the future, fear of self-expression, fear of facing or speaking the truth, and one who does not listen. Dark, dingy blue is often seen in those with depression. Think of the saying "I feel blue."

Indigo (brow chakra): Indigo relates to the third eye, vision, and pituitary gland. These auras have sensitive, deep feelings. Someone with an indigo aura searches for truth and can sniff out deception in others. An indigo aura is an excellent sign that the person is tuning in to their higher self, developing their psychic muscles, and understanding their purpose. Many with indigo auras are on a spiritual path.

Muddy indigo (brow chakra): A muddy indigo aura indicates someone who may be delusional or mentally ill. This aura may also indicate a God complex.

Violet (crown chakra): A violet aura relates to the crown chakra and nervous system. Violet is the most sensitive and wisest of colors. This is the intuitive color in the aura and reveals the psychic power of attunement with the self and all that is. It is visionary, futuristic, romantic, artistic, and magical.

Lavender (crown chakra): Someone with a lavender aura has imagination and vision. They are daydreamers.

Muddy violet (crown chakra): A muddy-violet aura may indicate someone who needs clarification with all the messages and information they receive. They may have frequent migraines, hallucinations, and nightmares. This is equivalent to an overactive crown chakra.

Silver (crown chakra): Silver is the color of abundance, both spiritual and physical. Lots of bright silver in an aura indicates plenty of money and an awakening of the cosmic mind. Those few that have silver auras are the dreamers, not necessarily the doers.

Bright, metallic silver (crown chakra): This aura indicates someone receptive to new ideas.

Dark and muddy gray (various chakras): Dark or cloudy gray indicates fear accumulating in the body. This creates health problems, especially if gray clusters are seen in specific body areas. The area that is gray may indicate an area or source of disease.

Gold (crown chakra): Gold is the color of enlightenment and divine protection. When seen within the aura, it indicates the person is governed by their highest good and divine guidance. It signifies protection, wisdom, inner knowledge, a spiritual mind, and intuitive thinking. People with gold auras are charismatic, which can also indicate a prosperous mentality.

Muddy gold (crown chakra): Muddy gold indicates confusion or fear regarding divine guidance. The person may be confused or questioning their connection with Source.

Black (various chakras): Black draws or pulls energy to it and, in so doing, transmutes it. It captures light and consumes it. Black usually indicates long-term unforgiveness (toward self or another) collected in a specific body area, leading to health problems; entities within a person's aura, chakras, or body; past-life hurts; and unreleased grief. Many people claim that areas of white or black may be seen in an aura but are never the total color of the aura; I have found this to be untrue. Although it is rare, I have seen a pure black aura. This aura was that of a sociopathic criminal legal client who had committed murder. I have also seen a black aura photo taken of a woman with a strong entity attachment. After a free energy healing, the aura photo changed to a pale yellow.

White (crown chakra): White reflects other energy. It is a pure state of light and often represents a new, not-yet-designated energy in the aura. A white aura indicates a spiritual, etheric, nonphysical quality. The person with this aura is part of higher dimensions, is pure, values truth and has angelic qualities. Angels or other spirit guides may be nearby if there are white sparkles or flashes of white light.

Earthy (root chakra): An earth-tone aura represents soil, wood, minerals, or plants. These colors display a love of Mother Earth and someone who is grounded. It is often seen in those who live and work outdoors.

Rainbow (various chakras): Rainbow auras indicate many positive traits—intelligence, philanthropy, intuition, generosity, and optimism. Rainbow-colored stripes, sticking out like sunbeams from the hand, head, or body, indicate an energy worker. While those with rainbow auras tend to be leaders and successful, they are also highly susceptible to aura interference that throws them into a tailspin.

Pastels (various chakras): A blend of light and color, pastels show sensitivity, empathy, and a need for serenity.

Dirty brown: Dirty brown usually indicates someone is holding on to harmful energies, usually due to insecurity about moving forward.

Dirty gray (various chakras): Dirty gray indicates someone with messy energy, usually due to codependency with these energies that the person is afraid to release.

Aura Shape and Texture Meanings for Aura Interpretation

When analyzing auras, it is important to remember to look at the shape and texture as well as the color. Any anomalies in the typical oval aura that surrounds the subject should be taken into consideration. The more auras you analyze, the better you will become at interpreting them. A few common ones to look for are listed below, but you will add to this list as you begin to read auras on a regular basis.

Spikes into aura: When points stick into any area of the aura, this is intrusive into the auric field. Often, this is the energy of another person or a spirit trying to harm the subject. It is essential to examine the color and region of origin. Energy healing is indicated. Then, recheck the aura to see if the spikes are gone.

Spikes away from aura: When spikes point away from any area of the aura, the subject is often trying to either get rid of some energy that does not feel good or send harmful energy to someone or something else. It is important to examine the color and region of origin.

Blobs connected to aura: Something bulging out from the aura that is not the aura itself but is attached to the aura is usually not good for the subject. There is a good chance this energy is a hitchhiker (entity) draining the subject's energy. The most insidious ones are usually muddy or black. In this case, an energy healing session would be helpful, followed by a reassessment.

Blobs detached from aura: If a blob is floating around in the auric field but doesn't seem to be attached, it may be a guide or a loved one. However, if it is muddy or black in color, it may be more ominous. Clear the blob, if necessary, then retest the auric field.

Orbs around aura: Orbs are usually round, disklike, or oval. Depending on where and what color they are, you can ascertain more about why they are there. They are often spirit beings that may be malevolent or benevolent.

Exercise: Hypothetical Aura Readings

The best way to learn to interpret aura colors is to practice. As always, get your journal ready for this exercise. Feel free to look at how I have described certain aura colors. You will get more and more comfortable as you practice. Eventually, you will add in your own interpretations of aura colors.

1. Scenario one: A querent's aura is dark red. Part of the aura is muddy red. Close to the area that is muddy, the oval shape around the querent has what looks like needles piercing into the aura. How do you interpret the dark red? How do you interpret the muddy red? How do you interpret the spikes going into the aura? What is your message regarding this aura?

2. Scenario two: A querent's aura is primarily white. There are some vertical lines extending from the aura. How do you interpret the white? How do you interpret the vertical lines extending from the aura? What is your message regarding this aura?

3. Scenario three: A querent's aura is muddy green. There are even darker green blobs of energy attached to the oval shape. How do you interpret the muddy green? How do you interpret the darker green blobs attached to the aura? What is your message regarding this aura?

4. Scenario four: A querent's aura is muddy gray and almost black. There are orbs floating near the oval shape, but they are not attached. How do you interpret the muddy gray and almost black aura? How do you interpret the orbs floating near, but not attached to, the oval shape? What is your message regarding this aura?

Journal Prompts: Hypothetical Aura Readings

1. Do you have experience with reading auras already?
2. How did this exercise feel?
3. Were you confident in your assessments?

4. Where do you think you could improve?
5. Did you agree with the colors as described? Do you want to add to them?

Avoid These Pitfalls

Although most people can learn to see auras with practice, most mistakes are made during the reading or interpretation phase. Color meanings can vary from culture to culture, and errors can be made when relaying the message to the querent.

Psychic Success

One of the most beautiful things to witness is someone with a lovely aura. It is like a fail-proof polygraph test. Being psychic becomes an incredible gift when you can focus on the beauty of spiritual beings at their finest moments. But here's the rub: The aura can change at any time. People will always let us down if we put them on pedestals. It helps to acknowledge our humanness and be determined to celebrate success with others instead of focusing on their shortcomings. Doing so will teach us to bask in our moments of glory instead of beating ourselves up when we fall short. With our intention set to celebrate small victories, we can find much more happiness in our psychic knowingness.

CHAPTER 9
YOUR FOUR R's

The word *divination* comes from the word *divine*, which implies that you are tapping into the sacred. Since you are part of one collective body connected to everything and everyone, you are part of the Divine, or at least have direct access to divine information. You can be a direct messenger or conduit of information. When you realize your interconnectedness, knowing that you have access to past, present, future, parallel dimensions, and multidimensional information should not surprise you.

We have already touched on the Four R's throughout this book, but let's go into a little more detail. The Four R's include requesting, receiving, reading, and relaying information. The request is the ask—the answer or information sought. Once you make the request, you receive a message. Next, you read or interpret that message. Finally, you relay the message to the person asking the questions and receiving the message (the sitter or querent). The biggest mistakes occur while reading or relaying the message because of overanalyzing or second-guessing.

The best thing to do is receive and read the message without filtering the essence of the message. This is tricky and why lots of mistakes are made at this juncture. You do not want to take away from or embellish a message; however, you may need to think about the tone and delivery of the way you relay the information. You do not want to fall into the trap of contriving a message or giving personal advice, but you do need to consider the way in which the particular querent can receive the information. There is a fine line between delivering an honest message in the right tone for someone and changing the message just to appease them.

Checkup: The Four R's Baseline

This checkup aims to establish a baseline for your ability to use the Four R's. Knowing your baseline makes tracking your future progress much easier. Answer the following questions honestly with a simple yes or no. Refer to this exercise every time you practice utilizing the Four R's to see if it has changed.

1. I am succinct in my intention when requesting (the ask) information.
2. I realize the form of the question is essential when requesting information.
3. I am connected to all information from all space and time, yet I might not always get the answer to my request.
4. I prepare myself to receive information, and I might have a routine or ritual that helps me receive (the imparting of the information to the reader) the message.
5. I know that when receiving information it may come through divination tools, signs, or guides or straight from my higher self.
6. I pay attention to all my clairs and do not embellish or filter the data when I receive messages. I simply receive the information.
7. I do not interject bias or advice when reading (the interpretation) the information.
8. I combine receiving information with my skills surrounding the use of certain modalities and with my intuition (the Eight E's) at the reading stage.
9. I think of myself as the researcher putting all the information received together and then using spirit allies, if needed, to glean the message when I read the information.

10. I do not give my opinion or advice when relaying (imparting or delivering) the message to the sitter or querent. I am merely the messenger or conduit of the information.

11. I do not filter or embellish the message; however, I do use discernment regarding the way in which a querent will best hear the message, which I realize comes with experience (the Eight E's).

12. I realize it is not about me when relaying the message. The entire process involves helping the sitter or querent look at a situation and then course correct if there is a need to pivot.

The more yes answers, the more you are already utilizing the Four R's. Remember, this is a checkup for your benefit. It will only help you to the extent you are honest.

Terminology: The Akashic Records

Akasha: *Akasha* is Sanskrit for "sky," "space," and "ether."

Akashic Records: The Akashic Records represent recorded past, present, future, parallel dimensions, and multidimensional history for everything and everyone in all space and time.

Request: Asking a question. The request could also be called a *petition.*

Receive: The step when the reader receives information based on the tools and modality used. Think of this information as just the facts.

Read: Compiling the received information with the reader's abilities, skills, and knowledge. This step is putting it all together before imparting the message to the querent. It is crucial not to let bias or judgment influence the message at this time. In order to remain unbiased, it is helpful to always ask yourself if you are allowing your experiential filters to influence the reader.

Relay: The delivery of the information to the querent. Relaying the message is a time for honesty but with a compassionate tone.

Akashic Records

One school of thought is that the cosmic information of everything is called the *akasha* and stored in the Akashic Records. As explained above, *Akasha* is Sanskrit for "sky," "space," and "ether." The Akashic Records represent recorded past, present, future, parallel, and multidimensional history for everyone and all space and time. There are many philosophies regarding opening the Akashic Records. Consequently, some people make a lot of money teaching you how to open the records. You do not need a complicated method or expensive certificate to open the Akashic Records. They are part of all you are and all that is. There is a record for everything and everyone for all time in all space. When you use your psychic connection, you are opening the Akashic Records.

Exercise: Giving a Divination Message That Automatically Opens the Akashic Records

The purpose of this exercise is to let you know that everyone opens the Akashic Records. You do not need to know legal names, spellings, or dates. You do not need a class to teach you how to open the records. You do not need to spend money to become certified to read the Akashic Records. You only need to request information with clear intentions. Receive the information by applying all of your clairs. Read the info by processing what you intuit and ask any further questions. Take it all in and then spit it all out without filtering. This relay of information should be done compassionately.

1. Relax and breathe in through your nose to the count of four while expanding your belly. Then, exhale deeply with an open mouth while pulling your belly in tightly. Continue this breathing three to five times.
2. Let yourself relax and go deeper and deeper into a space between. A space between is where you are conscious but feel very relaxed.
3. Approach the Akashic Records, where all records are stored. The Akashic Records building may look different every time you approach it, or it may look the same. Close your eyes and let an

image of the Akashic Records float into your mind. You do not need to worry if you are getting it right. You are part of all that is; therefore, you helped create the records.

4. Two large bouncers often greet me at the door to the Akashic Records. These bouncers ensure no one with ill intent is allowed into the records. Ask them to allow you to enter. It is not up to us to know why someone might not gain entrance. We are not meant to understand all mysteries. This answers the question posed in many psychic or intuitive books: Is everyone psychic? Everyone is psychic to the extent they receive information from the hive mind, the Collective, or all that is. The fact that we are not meant to know all mysteries is also why we receive some answers and not others.

5. Upon entering, glance around. The record building may look like anything from a dusty library filled with books to a laboratory in outer space filled with test tubes. Feel free to explore.

6. You can request that the keeper of the records provide you access to the records of the person, place, event, or issue for which you seek information. When looking into the records, some allege you must use a legal last name and a birthday. This is not necessarily true. You might not know the name of a tree from a thousand years ago, but that may be the record you seek. The key is to be clear about what you want to know.

7. Take a good look at the record you have sought. Receive all of the information. Take note of everything about it using all your senses. What does the record look like? Is it heavy? How does it make you feel? This is how you read the information.

8. Now, it is time to relay the information or message. Open your mouth and describe what you have interpreted or received. The correct information will come; therefore, speak it forth with confidence. Be clear in your mind about what information you seek.

9. When you finish the records, put them back or have the keeper of the records help you. Tell the Keeper goodbye until next time.

10. Exit the building or structure and see the bouncers nod knowingly at you. Nod back at them or even tell them thank you. Sometimes, they will speak, but sometimes they are too serious.

11. Feel your consciousness coming back into the earthly room. You have visited the Akashic Records. You do not need to feel any responsibility to close the records. That job is not left to you. Your only job is to relay the information accurately.

Everyone enters the collective records every time they receive information. They may not realize that all information comes from the collective resource known by some as the Akashic Records. When we ask if everyone is psychic, look no further than the Akashic Records to provide the answer to one of the mysteries of the universe.

Journal Prompts: Giving a Divination Message That Automatically Opens the Akashic Records

1. Could you relax by focusing on your breathing? What else, if anything, helped you get into a place where you could let yourself go?

2. What did the structure that housed the Akashic Records look like?

3. Were you greeted by bouncers at the door?

4. Once you entered, describe, describe, describe.

5. Did you need help from the keeper of the records when you requested the information sought?

6. How did you receive the information? How did you read the information?

7. Did you relay the information while in the records building or once you were present back in your meditation space? You can do so in either place.

8. If you remember returning the records, what was your experience?

9. If you remember exiting the building or structure, what was your experience?

10. Did you feel present in your body when you relayed the message, or did you feel like you were in a trance?
11. Is this an aha moment for you? Do you understand that opening the records is often overcomplicated by those who teach it?

Do not doubt yourself. You have opened the Akashic Records and do it more than you probably ever realized.

Requesting Information

The primary purpose of divination is to get information. This information will vary from reading to reading, but at the heart of the matter, the querent wants insight, clarification, or guidance in some area of their life. There is a legal principle that applies perfectly in psychic readings. It is known as the *eggshell skull* or the *thin skull doctrine*. It means that the defendant takes the plaintiffs as they find them. In other words, the defendant is liable for the plaintiff's unforeseeable and uncommon reactions (preexisting vulnerabilities) to the defendant's negligence or intentional acts. For example, suppose the defendant slaps a plaintiff and causes a seizure due to a preexisting brain tumor. In that case, the defendant is liable for the slap and anything preexisting. There is also an *eggshell psyche doctrine*. The defendant may be liable when the plaintiff has an abnormally low threshold for emotional distress.

These doctrines are very helpful when reading for querents. As a reader, you must know that everyone seeking a reading differs. Each comes with their preexisting expectations and ways of reacting to what they are told. It is imperative that the reader clearly explain what the reading encompasses and what it does not. There should always be a meeting of the minds regarding expectations between the reader and the querent. Part 4, the Eight E's of Psychic Success, discusses this in more detail.

Once the administrative portion of the meeting is handled (I suggest a pre-appointment), you may have your process or ritual before you begin. This may also change with various clients. I never start with a prayer, as many suggest. I would only do this aloud in front of the querent if I knew they wanted such a preamble to their reading.

How do you get to the first step, which is request? Many clients do not come with questions and want a general reading. I encourage questions, but I prefer that the questions do not suggest an answer. If they have a question related to a job, I will get a general read on that energy first, and then we can break it down further. I do not want to know if they want the job or which job they want. I like a clean reading (as little information as possible that suggests an answer). This is discussed in detail in part 3 of this book.

Another thing that many people do is correct the querent's question. In other words, the querent may ask if and when they will get a job. Some readers are quick to try and teach the querent how to rephrase the question. This is condescending. If you must reframe a question, reframe the request in your intention setting. There is no need to school the client. The client is seeking an answer to the request. The only time it might be appropriate to correct the form of the question is if it steps into unethical waters.

Receiving Information

Once you have formulated your request, you should receive an answer. The answer may come in various ways, such as through a divination technique discussed in this book, signs, a spirit guide, or directly from your higher self, which is connected to all that is.

When you receive information, act as the researcher. At this point, you are merely gathering all the information and evidence. Allow it to flow to you without immediately trying to figure out what it means. Some of it may never make any sense to you, and that is okay.

Reading Information

Once you have received information, it is time to read (interpret) the message. This process is usually done silently and not stated to the querent. This is where many mistakes are made due to bias or judgment entering the reading. Take the information you have received and decide what it means. You must set your intentions. If you have been clear in what you are asking and how you will receive the information, the reading should be the easiest thing to do. However, it is mucked up on many occasions because the reader is not educated in the modality they use, they are not experienced in reading, they let their ego get in the way, they are too worried about entertaining the client, or they do not control their energy. The Eight E's are pivotal in checking yourself in every type of reading. If you are following the Eight E's, you should never second-guess your reading.

Relaying Information

When you relay the information, you deliver the message to the querent. At this point, you only need to focus on your delivery. Be aware of the way this querent likes to receive messages. Knowing their zodiac sign, life numbers, or tarot birth cards is great for knowing the best delivery style for the client.[5] Just as you are different in your psychic style than others, querents also differ in how they can hear or grasp the message. Many querents will tell you they want straight-shooting readings only to tune you out if you don't adapt to the way they will listen. For instance, a Cancer may want things worded in a more sympathetic way. You do not change the message; you merely assess the best delivery form. You will be honest in your delivery, but you will also be effective because you deliver the message to the querent in the style they can best comprehend. This is the way to get a slam dunk, spot-on reading because you realize the delivery and tone are just as important as the words you are saying.

Avoid These Pitfalls

We have touched on some mistakes that can be made when utilizing the Four R's, but here are eleven to watch out for when acting as a psychic messenger.

1. *Do Not Correct the Querent's Request (or Their Question):* While the form of a question may be important in a reading, the intention that is set when working with the Four R's is much more important. When you make a request, you can tweak the form of the question, but there is no need to school a querent on the proper format. It is not the querent's job to know all the ins and outs of a reading. They have come to you for a message, not a sermon.

2. *Don't Forget to Set Your Intention:* Many mistakes are made in the reading (interpreting) of information because the reader failed to set an intention for what the modality would represent. An example of this is using fabric to do a reading. Suppose the querent wants to know if they should move to another house. If the reader immediately asks the querent to draw three pieces of fabric, then the reader may have trouble interpreting the information they receive. Instead, the reader could say either out loud or in their mind, "Fabric one will represent what it will look like if the querent moves, fabric two will represent what it will look like if the querent doesn't move, and fabric

....
5. Life numbers are covered in part 2 of this book. See Mary K. Greer's book *Archetypal Tarot: What Your Birth Card Reveals About Your Personality, Path, and Potential* in the additional resources at the back of this book to learn more about how to calculate and understand someone's tarot birth cards.

three will tell us the information we did not think to request." If fabric one (move) is a shiny orange, the read might be that a move will bring renewal and vitality. If fabric two (not moving) has a rough texture and a brown color, the read might be that while brown can represent stability, the rough texture does not feel like a smooth path. The querent may be roughing it for a while. If fabric three (more info) is baby blue and looks delicate, this may indicate a child is on the way, which would need to be considered. These are hypothetical, and the reading could go other ways, but the point is that setting clear intentions of what each fabric would represent makes the read and relay much easier.

3. *Do Not Prejudge a Querent:* Make sure to clear your third eye as taught in part 1 of this book. Approach each session with a fresh outlook and clean slate. Some will teach to watch the client before they make it to your office. I totally disagree. Do not size up a querent. Just do your job—request, receive, read, and relay.

4. *Be Sure to Modality Match:* When picking which modality to use for the reading, make sure your modalities match. In other words, has the querent expressed a desire for a specific type of reading, and will the chosen modality lend itself to the questions the querent wants answered?

5. *Receive the Information Instead of Creating Your Own Story or Opinion:* Pull yourself and your stories out of the reading. When you receive the information, get the facts. Do not interject odds, statistics, or your opinion. The querent has hired you as a psychic, not a counselor.

6. *Put All the Received Information Together:* When you receive the information, resist the urge to throw out or ignore something that does not make sense. That piece often ends up being the most critical piece of information. You do not have to understand it.

7. *Read and Relay the Information Given Without Speculation:* Do not fill in the blanks with speculation when reading (interpreting) and relaying (delivering) the message. It is very tempting to do so. If you begin to say things such as "maybe," "I think," or "perhaps," these are indicators that you may be stepping beyond the message you have been given and are speculating. Only read and relay what is given to you as part of the psychic message.

8. *Don't Make It About You:* Always remember that the reading is not about you unless you are reading for yourself. If you feel an anecdotal story may help the querent, then try it, but most clients do not want to pay to hear about the reader's issues.

9. *Don't Represent Yourself as Something You Are Not:* Be very honest with querents regarding your modality skill sets. Refer a client out if they want a type of reading that you are not qualified to give.

10. *Don't Forget to Honor the Reading the Querent Requested:* Many clients will request a specific modality. Do not try to push another modality on them. I do not do many rune readings. If a client wants that, then I will refer them to someone else.

11. *Don't Elevate Yourself to Fixer (You Are the Messenger):* Remember your place. You are not the fixer for the querent's issues. Your job is to deliver the message in a way that empowers the client to course correct. They are the hero of their story, not you.

Psychic Success

The ultimate psychic success is for you to request, receive, read, and relay a message without becoming attached to the outcome. Do your job. Yes, you can care. However, it is not your job to course correct for the querent. Deliver the message. Do not speculate. Do not try to crack the case. Simply request, receive, read, and relay.

Many readers will say their job is to empower clients. I am hopeful that my message does so; however, I do not believe that is my job as a psychic. My job is to deliver only the message I channel. If I embellish it in any way to help empower the client, I believe this is interfering. So I do pause when readers say they love to read or give psychic messages to empower their clients. Again, that is not necessarily my job as a reader.

CHAPTER 10

YOUR MEDITATION PRACTICE

You are mapping out what works best for you in your psychic handbook. There is no need to waste time debating whether something is or is not a specific type of meditation. However, it will help if you determine what is best suited for your needs at any given time and place. You may try guided meditations, visualization, mantras, music, silence, and active meditations. Ultimately, the only thing that matters in the context of your handbook is what works for you to enhance your psychic knowingness healthily. Meditation improves your psychic knowing because the more you sit and listen, the more you will grow in sensing the subtle clues and signs trying to get your attention.

Checkup: Meditation Baseline

This checkup aims to establish a baseline for your meditation practice. Knowing your baseline makes tracking your future progress much easier. Answer the following questions honestly with a simple yes or no.

1. I meditate at least once a day.
2. I look forward to my meditation time.

3. I benefit from meditations.
4. I connect and channel easier when I meditate.

The more yes answers, the more you are utilizing meditation. Remember, this is a checkup for your benefit. It will only help you to the extent you are honest.

Exercise: Simple Breath Awareness Meditation

This meditation exercise prepares you for longer meditations. It is a great way to calm down and start so you don't quit meditating because you jumped into the deep end too soon.

Sit still for one minute first thing in the morning, right when you leave the bed. Make sure you are sitting up comfortably with your legs crossed if you are on the floor. Let your hands rest on your knees. Spend this one minute in total silence, focusing only on the natural in and out of your breathing. After a week of doing this consistently in the morning and at night, increase this to three minutes, then to five. Be aware of your breath—that which gives you life.

Journal Prompts: Simple Breath Awareness Meditation

1. Were you able to sit for one minute?
2. Were you able to get into a consistent routine?
3. How did this exercise help you with your ability to become one with your breathing?

Exercise: Inhale and Exhale Meditation

This meditation aims to get you in the habit of audibly exhaling. Then, you can add inhaling anything positive you want in your life, and audibly exhale the opposite of that emotion or feeling.

Sit with your legs crossed or sit in a chair with your legs uncrossed and your feet on the floor. Take a breath through your nose to the count of three while raising your shoulders to your ears. Then, forcefully and audibly exhale as you lower your shoulders. Make sure to exhale audibly. It is interesting how many people resist letting their breath out forcefully.

Inhale peace. Exhale war.

Inhale joy. Exhale sadness.

Inhale health. Exhale disease.

Inhale acceptance. Exhale rejection.

Inhale worthiness. Exhale unworthiness.

Inhale gratitude. Exhale ungratefulness.

Journal Prompts: Inhale and Exhale Meditation

1. Why do you think it is difficult for some people to exhale their breath forcefully and, perhaps, loudly?
2. What about you?
3. Did you feel a release when you exhaled forcefully?
4. Could you come up with some of your own words representing things you want to inhale and exhale?

Exercise: Switching Up Third Eye Images

This meditation exercise aims to help you learn to see things in your mind's eye. It is okay if you are unable to actually see an image. Thoughts are often strong impressions in your mind's eye. Start with something you know and try to see it differently by interjecting yourself into the imagery.

Take a deep breath and focus on your third eye. Once you are ready, think of a pleasant memory. Begin to see pictures of this event in your mind. Allow the images to float into your mind's eye in color or black and white. It may seem like a movie or a still photograph. Now, change the image. See yourself in the image or detached from it. Try to shake things up and view it from different angles and perspectives.

Journal Prompts: Switching Up Third Eye Images

1. Could you think of a pleasant memory?
2. Describe how you pictured the memory in your mind's eye.
3. Could you change the image or see yourself in the image?
4. Could you detach from the image?

Exercise: Five Senses Guided Visualization

This meditation exercise aims to get you more in touch with your clairs.

Get into a comfortable position and a sacred or safe space for guided visualization meditation. Close your eyes. You find yourself on a path. You look down to see what your path looks like. Up ahead on the path, you see a bench in a garden. You follow the path to the bench and sit down. Take a moment to glance down and notice how you look sitting on the bench. You begin to look around the garden. Note what you see. Something that has a beautiful aroma attracts your attention. What is it that smells so good? You decide to taste something in the garden. You find yourself at that item in an instant. You feel safe and comfortable as you take a bite of that which drew you to it. Now, you hear something in the garden. Knowing you are safe, you look around to see what is making noise. You also take note of all the things you touch in the garden. You can wander around the garden a little longer. Before leaving, you notice a wrapped gift sitting on your bench. Notice the packaging and then open the gift. This gift is from your guides to help you develop your clairs. When you are ready, stroll back down the path. Then, slowly and gently open your eyes.

Journal Prompts: Five Senses Guided Visualization

1. What did your path look like?
2. What did you see?
3. Describe your bench or seat.

4. Describe how you looked in the garden.
5. What did you see and smell in the garden?
6. What did you see, smell, and taste?
7. What did the items you saw, smelled, and tasted look like?
8. What animals or birds came into the garden making the noises you heard?
9. What did you see, smell, taste, and hear?
10. What did you see, smell, taste, hear, and touch in the garden?
11. What gift was left on your bench?
12. How did the gift make you feel?
13. What other senses did you use with your gift on the bench?
14. Describe the packaging of the gift.
15. How will the gift help you with your clairs?

Avoid These Pitfalls

Perhaps the biggest pitfall to meditation is the pressure to do it right. Let yourself off the hook and just try to start with short periods. It is better to be consistent than to try to meditate too long and then quit. Stay calm if your mind wanders. The diversion may lead you to unexpected answers. The goal of meditation is to relax and release the need for perfection. If you are hard on yourself, you defeat the purpose. Stop worrying about how others meditate or if you are doing it right. The term *right* implies there is a correct way for everyone. This thinking is contrary to developing your handbook.

Psychic Success

Psychic success comes with meditation over time. If you are consistent and meditate even five minutes a day, you will see a pattern evolve where you yearn for that solitude and moment of respite. Over time, you will realize you are calmer and receive information with more clarity.

CHAPTER 11

YOUR SIGNS, SYMBOLS, AND SYNCHRONICITIES

In poker, there are certain tells. These signs or changes in behavior reveal a player's inner state, letting you know when the player has a particular hand. Knowing the players helps you see if they are bluffing. The same is true in learning how you receive psychic information. For example, you may get an image of or feel a neck ache. At first, you may interpret this to mean the querent has a neck ache. However, as you keep track of your tells in your handbook, you may realize that when you get an image of or feel a neck ache while reading, it means the person you are reading is stubborn. Some people will have different tells for neck ache. To interpret a message correctly, you must get to know your individual tells and not be led by those of others or what a book or teacher tells you. However, you can set a meaning to certain tells, and if you choose for it to be the ordinary or common meaning, that is fine. The key is to learn your tells and to keep track of them.

Many of you may let your old nemesis, doubt, creep in and wonder if something is a coincidence or a synchronicity, symbol, or sign. Let's spend a few minutes getting these terms straight in your handbook. Carl Jung coined the term *synchronicity* for "meaningful coincidences."[6] Although you cannot always explain them, synchronicities bring together things or events that are not linked by logic or cause but seem uniquely connected to you. They relate to one another symbolically. The more you understand the universe's interconnectedness, the more you can connect an unconscious event or symbolic representation coinciding with another event. Often, this will occur because combining your inner world with an outer symbol provides a shortcut to your psychic knowingness. While Jung believed synchronicity was rare, internationally known astrologer Ray Grasse suggests a symbolist view.[7] This view acknowledges the interconnectedness of everything and, therefore, the interwoven correspondences of all things. The interconnectedness of all things means that synchronicity is always happening and is not a rare occurrence. Unfortunately, we don't take the time to notice it.

A *symbol* is something to represent something else. Careful interpretation of the symbolism is one of the most important things to do when reading your intuitive messages. It is also imperative not to impose your culture or beliefs on someone else. The best way to explain this is by a few examples. I have seen a lot of mistakes made with this first example: dogs. Most readers will see an image of a dog and automatically jump to the conclusion of a beloved family pet. However, they miss the mark if someone is afraid of dogs or has been attacked by a dog. Jumping to conclusions because you, as the reader, feel a certain way or most people think a certain way is the mark of an inexperienced reader. Another more obvious example is with police officers. Some may view them as protectors, and others view them as bullies or worse. When using your psychic knowingness, you must set aside your experiences, biases, and odds. I have seen far too many readers falter in their interpretation using logic or odds rather than pure intuition.

It is also important to note that there will be times when what you believe to be a tell is not a tell, but rather a clear representation of the word or thought you picked up on intuitively. For instance, a rocking chair may be your tell for someone needing to soothe themselves or be comforted. However, you may have a situation where you see a rocking chair and begin to think it is your tell for calmness only to realize that the message is actually that the querent bought a new rocking chair. I once had a student who would always get pain in her elbow when reading for mothers of toddlers. She would ask

. . . .

6. Carl Jung, *The Structure and Dynamics of the Psyche*, 2nd ed., vol. 8. *The Collected Works of C. G. Jung*, Bollingen Series 10, eds., Herbert Read, Michael Fordham, Gerhard Adler, and William McGuire, trans. R. F. C. Hull (Princeton University Press, 1972), 427.
7. Ray Grasse, "Synchronicity and the Mind of God," *Quest* 94, no. 3 (2006): 91–94, https://www .theosophical.org/publications/quest-magazine/synchronicity-and-the-mind-of-god.

the mothers weekly if their elbows were sore, only to be told no. Finally, she took my suggestion and asked one of the mothers if she was tired of cleaning up dishes and toys. The mother replied yes. Then, another mother later confirmed the same feeling. You see, my student's tell for too much work with no assistance was a sore elbow. She had discovered her first tell.

Checkup: Your Tell Baseline

This checkup aims to establish a baseline for awareness of your tells. Knowing your baseline makes tracking your future progress much easier. Answer the following questions honestly with a simple yes or no. Refer to this exercise every time you work on your tells to see if anything has changed.

1. I notice signs and know they have an intuitive meaning.
2. I notice synchronicities and know they have an intuitive meaning.
3. I notice patterns and know they have an intuitive meaning.
4. I know my tells (impressions or feelings I get that may mean something different to others).
5. I realize that symbols can represent a tell if I decide ahead of time what they mean.

The more yes answers, the more you already utilize your psychic tells. The number of yes answers will increase as you develop and practice the methods in your handbook.

Terminology: Reading Signs and Symbols

Tell: A feeling, impression, or clair that means something unique to you but may mean something different to someone else.

Exercise: Symbol and Tell—Your Psychic Shorthand

This exercise aims to discover a pictorial symbol representing each of our clairs. Having a symbol helps us bypass our left brain to some extent to get to our right brain more quickly. Remember that our left brain (logic) is still needed when we develop our psychic handbook. Still, most of us have trouble balancing it and trusting that our right brain (intuition) is as trustworthy and credible as our left brain.

Steady your breathing. Go to a safe space in your mind. The concept of clairvoyance, clear seeing, enters your mind's eye. Allow your inner eye to see a symbol as you ask: If my clairvoyance had a symbol, what would that be? The first symbol that comes into your mind's eye is your symbol for clairvoyance. Now, allow that image to fade, or you might even erase it like a whiteboard. Now, let your inner ear hear a symbol as you ask: If my clairaudience had a symbol, what would that be? The first symbol that comes into your inner ear is your symbol for clairaudience. Now, allow that sound to fade, or you might even erase it like a whiteboard. Now, let your inner knowing realize a symbol as you ask: If my claircognizance had a symbol, what would that be? The first symbol that comes into your mind's eye is your symbol for claircognizance. Now, allow that image to fade, or you might even erase it like a whiteboard. Now, let your sense of touch feel a symbol as you ask: If my clairtangency had a symbol, what would that be? The first symbol that comes into your mind's eye is your symbol for clairtangency.

Journal Prompts: Symbol and Tell—Your Psychic Shorthand

I recommend you begin working on your symbol and tell journal now. You can start here and then transfer your entries to your personal handbook. Below are some words to get you started. Write down the ordinary meanings so that you recognize any potential biases. Then, write down what you choose to use or already know. It may help if you integrate the Three C's (colors, chakras, and clairs). Remember, you can assign your tell. I often make my tells the same because they are repeated in many modalities, such as dream interpretation, tea or coffee readings, charm readings, etc. For instance, I set the intention that a dark cloud means potential trouble whether I see it in a dream or tea leaf. It is much easier when I receive the word in one modality and it means the same to me when I receive it in another. Psychic knowingness does not have to be complicated. The easier you make it, the better psychic you will become. Some words mean different things in different cultures; therefore, you must always include your current, in-the-moment intuition, or you will stumble in your delivery. Some common symbols that may have dual meanings include, but are not limited to, numbers, colors, guns, and police.

Write your word, typical meaning, and your assigned meaning or tell for the following words: *alien, arrow, church, cross, gun, owl, police, rainbow, raven, red, snake.*

Avoid These Pitfalls

One of the biggest mistakes in relaying psychic messages is mistaking your experiential filter for a psychic message. Simplifying the message leads to accuracy. Instead of thinking you must solve the mystery, fix an issue, or tie things up with a beautiful bow, relay the message, and then close your mouth. That's right. Stop talking. Stop speculating. It is not your job to fix things or figure everything out. Just relay the message and stop. Notice if you use words such as *maybe, perhaps,* or *I think* when relaying a message. While you might use these words out of habit, check to make sure you are not speculating. Also, always keep in mind the perspective of your querent. Consider their culture and learning style.

Psychic Success

Getting a message hammering away at you out of your system is a relief. If you take the advice in this chapter and relay the information you are given instead of attempting to crack the case, you will feel very relieved. Once you learn that it is not your job to solve everyone's problems and that you are merely the conduit of information, being psychic will stop being as significant a burden. Don't get me wrong. People will still, as the saying goes, want to kill the messenger, but you will just relay the message professionally and then step away. You will find that querents will return for readings and consider you more credible.

CHAPTER 12

YOUR CHANNELING
AND MEDIUMSHIP

Just as there are many ways for people to demonstrate psychic abilities, there are also many ways that people go about mediumship. As with almost everything, unless a robust ethical opinion is involved, I always make it very clear that I am not claiming superiority over those who view mediumship differently than me. However, I do view mediumship quite differently than the prominent school of thought known as Spiritualism. Many claim that all mediums are psychics, but not all psychics are mediums. This oft-repeated phrase is grossly misleading. Mediumship is a form of tapping into psychic knowingness. The difference is the frequency you are tapping into, but more importantly, the expectation of the querent. My lifetime of experiences and my years of successfully practicing and teaching mediumship make me take this very seriously. Everything is energy. That energy never goes away, but it changes form. Once someone knows how to adjust to different forms or frequencies of energy, it becomes natural to communicate with beings at different frequencies.

A medium is simply a newspaper or telephone that delivers the news between an energetic being in a different frequency and the querent. The medium should never be in an ego state when delivering messages. Those who have lost loved ones hang on your every word. It is my experience that most beings in other frequencies come through most readily to those they trust to impart their message correctly.

Many define channeling as allowing another entity to take over your body. I do not let anything take over my body; I do not recommend it. Before I knew better, I did allow myself to be spoken through by other entities. It took a toll on my health, and again, even if you think you are protecting yourself, I would be careful with this type of channeling. What speaks through me is my higher self, which is connected to Source. That part of me is wiser than this earthbound version. I trust my higher self to know what should flow through me and what should not.

As you work through this chapter, remember that it is merely an introduction to mediumship. Still, if you begin with a solid ethical foundation, spirits will trust you with their information. Once they trust you, they will communicate with you.

Checkup: Your Mediumship Baseline

This checkup aims to ascertain if you communicate with the frequency of departed loved ones who are no longer in earthly, physical forms or other spirit beings.

1. I have seen or sensed ghosts since I was a child.
2. I have seen or communicated with departed loved ones.
3. I believe souls continue living once they depart their earthly bodies.
4. I am approached by spirits who want me to give them attention.
5. I have heard people talking to me when no one is around.

The more yes answers, the more you are already using mediumship abilities. Remember, this is a checkup for your benefit. It will only help you to the extent you are honest.

Terminology: Mediumship

Medium: A living person who communicates with other beings through frequency alignment.

Mediumship: Communication with other beings through frequency alignment. This communication can include any energy, such as a departed animal companion.

Frequency alignment: All energy oscillates (vibrates) at varying frequencies (rates). The rate of vibration comes into alignment when communicating with various types of spirit beings.

Channel: Something or someone who is the energy conduit (information or messages). The channel is the go-between and relays the message. Many erroneously claim channeling involves allowing another entity to take over your body to be the conduit. Some may allow such an occurrence, but it is incorrect to state that as the definition of a channel.

Channeling: Serving as a messenger or conduit of information (often between two varying frequencies).

Physical mediumship: A type of mediumship where the spirit world manipulates our physical world. For example, automatic writing, where the spirit world guides the hand, is a form of physical mediumship. This type of mediumship was popularized by the Fox sisters, who communicated with spirits through table rapping.

Mental mediumship: A type of mediumship where the spirit world manipulates the senses and clairs of the medium, which are then interpreted through the mind of the medium.

Mediumship gallery: A mediumship reading for a group of people.

Ways to Connect as a Medium

There are four primary ways to connect with energetic frequencies. For our purposes, let's call them loved ones, but they may be animals, nature spirits, or other types of energetic beings that are not in the earthly frequency. The four primary ways of communication are as follows:

1. The loved one has stepped forward and is showing themselves or speaking to the psychic medium. The psychic medium can see and talk to the loved one. There is direct communication. In this situation, the medium can honestly say, "I see/I am speaking to your loved one." If the querent is not familiar with my work, I will ask the loved one to give me a sign that will let the querent know I am indeed communicating with their loved one.

2. The psychic medium senses the loved one but is not directly connecting. While the information is coming from the loved one, here there is no direct communication. The key to understanding this scenario is that the psychic senses the loved one and gets impressions from them but cannot honestly say they are directly seeing or communicating with them. In this situation, the medium can honestly say, "I am sensing and receiving impressions or information from your loved one."

3. The medium receives a psychic message about the loved one that comes through just like any other intuitive reading. In other words, the psychic has intuitive impressions that are not coming from the loved one. This is the same as any other message, but the expectation of the querent is to receive a message from their loved one. In this scenario, the psychic can still deliver valuable information but should be honest that they are not receiving it from the loved one. In this situation, it is misleading for the medium to imply that they are directly communicating with the loved one. The medium can say, "Although I am not directly communicating with your loved one, here is information I am receiving." This honesty will often lead to the loved one actually trusting the medium and stepping forward.

4. The psychic is tapping into what the querent thinks about their loved one (telepathically), which happens in many readings. In this instance, there may be valuable and accurate information that the medium picks up on from the querent. However, it is best to let the querent know. This honesty will often lead to the loved one actually trusting the medium and stepping forward.

All these methods can provide valuable information to the querent; however, paying attention to how the information is received and letting the querent know is essential. Those who have lost loved ones are highly vulnerable and should never be led to believe you are seeing or talking to their loved ones if you are not. The most important thing is to remember that the messages you deliver are not about you as a medium. The messages are about the spirit being and their loved one in earthly form. Spirits will trust you more if you always remember this.

Exercise: Your Standard for Excellence

This exercise aims to consider the seriousness of mediumship messages and the expectations of those receiving them. Knowing your ground rules is essential; explaining them to those you deliver messages to is also important. For instance, you might tell the querent that you do or don't need a name. I always tell my clients that I would rather them not provide any information to me except a name. But I also explain that I may ask questions, not to "lead the witness" but to validate who I am picking up on, because when I read, many spirit beings rush forward and want to be heard.

One of the most important things you can do to become a great medium is to think of someone you know well who has passed. Let the relationship with that person guide how you would want mediumship handled. My standard is that of my great mama, who passed at 106 years old. I know how she comes to me, and I will not let anyone pretend they are talking to her if they aren't. Great Mama is my standard of excellence.

Journal Prompts: Your Standard for Excellence

1. Think of the person who is your model for excellence (mine is Great Mama). How would you expect a messenger to handle requesting, receiving, reading, and relaying information based on your standard for excellence?

2. Make a list of what is within your bounds and what is outside them. Remember, this is what you would want, so there are no right or wrong answers.

3. List ways your standard for excellence will help you maintain high standards when delivering messages about someone's loved one.

4. Realize that everyone will have different ways they want things handled. Not all mediumship readings are with loved ones. Often, you may be communicating with a less-desirable spirit. How would you want a medium to handle an unwelcome spirit? How would you handle an unwelcome spirit if a client told you they did not want to communicate with that spirit?

Eleven Mythconceptions and Expectations about Mediums and Mediumship

There are quite a few mythconceptions about mediumship. These can lead to a querent expecting a reading about a loved one or other spirit being to transpire in a certain manner, which may hinder the reading. For example, perhaps the querent thinks that a medium must be able to get a name in order for a mediumship reading to be legitimate. Some mediums may get names, but others may not. The mediums who get information that is clearly about the loved one in question might receive information in different ways than other mediums, but it is still clearly channeled. In fact, the medium might be spot on in the message, but the querent erroneously thinks the medium must know everything. I explain to my clients that information usually comes to me as rapid-fire bullet points. I do not fill in the blanks with any speculation or words of compassion unless that is the message I receive.

1. *Mediums must wait a fixed amount of time before connecting with a departed soul:* Many psychic mediums will not meet with a querent for a fixed amount of time after someone has passed. There are various reasons for this, such as the departed has not moved on to another frequency or it is not healthy for the querent. While I have seen many souls hang around until their memorial service, there is no set time period for when the soul is ready to communicate. They may visit a loved one right after they pass, or they may take some time. I believe it is usually more ethical to wait a while before meeting with a

querent. They are vulnerable and in a state of shock or grief. I have, however, made exceptions to the waiting period rule. Like most things in life, I have a general set of guidelines, but I take them on a case-by-case basis.

2. *A psychic medium's primary job is to prove there is an afterlife:* While some psychic mediums may practice mediumship to assure themselves and others that there is an afterlife, this is not why I practice mediumship. My job is to deliver messages from whatever frequency is communicating with me. It is not my job to prove or convince anyone of anything. I am the newspaper, the conduit, and the channel of information from a frequency that others might not tune in to as effortlessly.

3. *Mediums must know the departed's name or they are not real mediums:* Many querents go into readings with the idea that if the medium can figure out the name of someone in their life who is departed, then that medium is the real deal. While a medium who does get a name may be the real deal, this is only one indicator of a genuine medium. Some mediums are good with names, some with songs, or some with jobs. Different mediums receive different information, often from reading to reading. Sometimes, I will get a name and other times I do not. Mediumship is not a circus act. I regularly communicate with those who have passed. I like to get some sort of validation for the querent if they do not know me so that they can be open to the message. However, my job is to honestly impart the information I am given. I have observed many fraudulent readers get a big aha from a querent or audience just by saying a name and someone in the group responding that the name applies to their loved one.

4. *Mediums must know how the departed passed or they are not real mediums:* Many querents go into readings with the idea that if the medium can figure out how someone in their life departed, then that medium is the real deal. While a medium may receive a cause of death, this is only one indication of a genuine medium. Some mediums are good with names, some with songs, or some with means of death. Different mediums receive different information, often from reading to reading. I tend to pick up on suicides or foul play very quickly. I believe that is because those who have died by suicide know I will treat them and the querent with fairness. People do not commit suicide. The word *commit* has a negative connotation. Those who die by suicide are

not bad people just because they died by suicide. They do not have extra lessons to learn, as many will claim. Those who die by foul play probably appear to me because they also trust me. They tend to care more about the querent than they do about someone paying for a crime. They see things from a different perspective and hope the querent can also. There have been times I feel the departed one has withheld information from me, such as how they passed, in order for the loved one to focus on something else.

5. *If one detail is wrong, the entire reading is bunk:* While there is some amount of predestation if a soul has a blueprint for their life, there is still free will. Energy can and does change. I encourage those I read for to write down what comes out of my mouth. I may say a string of words that go together but make absolutely no sense to me. If I am not given an explanation as to what these things mean, I will not speculate. I will not fill in the blanks with statistics or safe assumptions. I will not even tell a querent that the departed one loves them unless that is the message I am told. There will be times that a detail may seem incorrect, but in my case, it is usually in my reading or interpretation of a detail that should have just been stated and then left alone.

6. *The psychic medium should know everything:* Psychic mediums do not know everything. I know enough that I often firmly tell the spirits around me to "Let me have my space!" I work criminal cases, I pick juries, I use remote viewing to locate missing people, but I do not and do not want to know everything. Once again, the energy could shift, and the reading could be wrong, or more often, the reader goes one step too far and assumes instead of delivering the message imparted.

7. *If the psychic medium asks any questions, they are fishing:* This is a big area of consideration because much of this depends on the psychic medium. Assuming we are speaking of someone who comes recommended, there are times when questions can get you where you are going a lot faster. Here is how it works with me: I do not like to know the names or any information about the querents before I meet with them. My assistant takes down names and numbers, and I am told when to show up. I want a clean reading. However, there are situations where time dictates that we get to the point quickly. In that case, I may ask for the first name of the departed and who they are to

the querent. When a psychic medium does this, it is not because they are fake; it is often because they want to get to the heart of the matter instead of jumping through hoops to be the star of the show. Most everyone who gets in for a reading with me knows I do not waste time and the reading is not about me. They want to cut to the chase. While there may be the rabbit-out-of-the-hat trick feeling at times, that is not why I am a psychic medium.

8. *If the psychic medium does not connect with the correct departed one, the medium is a fraud:* Many querents think they should not even tell the psychic medium who they want to get in touch with. Well, that is a big problem for me because I see and communicate with spirits every day. When the spirits know I'm open for business, they come running up to talk to me. So for the sake of time, it helps to let the psychic medium know who you want to hear from. However, there are times when that departed one may not come through. A psychic medium cannot just conjure up any spirit at any time, so it is best to have a person in mind but be open to the fact that someone else may come through.

9. *Psychic mediums research you before the reading or gallery:* Legitimate mediums do not research clients ahead of meeting with them. I do not do this with any of my clients. I even set the intention that I will forget what I told a client in any previous sessions. I call this *clean reading*. To be honest, clean readings are much simpler. The more pre-information I have, the more I may muck up a reading. Also, I have a lot of clients and am very busy, so I would not have time to research anyone even if I wanted to do so.

10. *If a psychic medium states generalities, they are a fraud:* Sometimes, information I receive from departed ones is mind blowing, but often it is boring as heck. There are times I receive information that seems very general—so general that I question what the point of this reading is. Am I giving my client value in this reading? But I continue to relay the general ho-hum message because that is what I am receiving. Oddly, these are typically the readings where the querent comes back to me and says, "You are never going to believe what happened. You know when you told me that my mom told me to take better care of myself, and later you told me to look at some old photos? You told me 'This is very broad and could apply to anyone, but I am supposed to tell you.' Well, I opened a drawer this morning and there were photos of when

my mom and I visited a spa. Thanks, it really meant a lot." Those are the times I say, "Thank your mom because that had nothing to do with me. Your mom knew how the message should be delivered."

11. *Psychic mediums can command spirits:* Psychic mediums do sense or see spirits, or at least I assume they do if they claim to be a psychic medium. I talk to spirits every day because they are everywhere. I am surprised when there are not spirit beings all around. It is more unusual not to see a ghost than it is to see one. Although I may ask spirits questions or ask them to leave me alone, I always treat them with respect. I engage before I sage. However, I cannot command spirits. If a querent comes to see me for a message and expects me to tell all the spirits to speak to me and in what order, that is actually a sign of someone who might be a fraud. There are many times I can talk to spirits and get them to cooperate, but there are also times the spirits are just not in the mood. Ghosts are people too!

Exercise: A Hypothetical Mediumship Gallery

This exercise aims to examine some mediumship methods that are frequently practiced. Consider the following scenarios or strategies used by many mediums (acknowledging straightaway that a variable can change every situation). Many of the methods listed may ultimately be accurate, but how do you feel about the means to impart the information? These scenarios are taken from my observation of many mediums and mediumship teachings by others over many years, combined with my personal experience of being a medium. I rarely employ any of these methods. Although I acknowledge that the information may be accurate, it is the means we are concerned with in this exercise.

1. *I See That Hand Method:* A medium tells an audience to raise their hands if a scenario applies to them and to keep their hands up until the scenario doesn't apply. An example of this is to tell the group to raise their hands if their loved one passed from cancer.

   Instead of asking a room full of people, or even one querent, to let you know when something applies or doesn't apply, request information that a loved one wants to impart to a querent. Otherwise, this is the epitome of fishing by process of elimination.

Determine which of the four ways you will receive the message and go straight to the person for whom the message is intended. Please note that in actuality, there may be topic clusters who unintentionally sit by one another in groups. Sometimes, they will all be in the same row or even seated diagonally. This is very interesting because the message might apply to all of them, but you will need to press the source of your information to be more specific.

2. *Frail and Heart Failure Method:* A medium makes a statement such as "The departed one needed a wheelchair." When no hands go up, they change it to a walker or state that the departed one was fragile near the end. They may go on to add that the loved one passed due to heart failure.

Ultimately, everyone passes of heart failure, and many times, someone is frail when they pass. So, while it might be accurate that someone was frail and passed from heart failure, it is not the most credible way to approach a connection between the querent and the passed loved one.

Many who get mediumship readings expect the medium to know the cause of death. It is vital to explain expectations regarding the reading. Why is the information coming through? Is the information given to let the querent trust the reader, or was there some question about the actual cause of death? The most important thing is to be honest with the querent.

3. *The Baby Who Never Fell to Earth Method:* A medium claims there was a baby that never made it into the world due to miscarriage. Then, the medium proceeds to tell the audience member who had a miscarriage that the baby has reincarnated as someone else. The odds are with a medium on this issue. Many people lose children due to miscarriage. The chances of having someone who has lost a child in the gallery are great. However, this should not be an opportunity for a spot-on moment. While this certainly is

something many querents want to hear about, telling the querent the baby will live for infinity and is about to be reincarnated is playing the odds and playing with emotions. If a mother really wants to know about a child, I give the mother the opportunity to tell me she would like to see if I can connect with her child. Opening this dialogue is not fishing. It is giving the mother an opportunity to know that I will not turn her pain into an aha, spot-on, it's-all-about-me moment. It is about the mother's grief over the loss of her child.

The medium must be ethical if someone is there seeking information about a lost child. Never play the odds to get a hit. Toying with emotions in mediumship readings is downright unethical. Be very careful telling a parent that their child has reincarnated. Even if you receive that information, do a risk/benefit analysis of telling the parent that information. Some querents will tell you they want brutal honesty when they actually may not be prepared to hear certain things.

4. *A Man and His Dog Method:* A medium claims a father has passed away. A dog is with him, and the father wants to know what happened to his shirts. While it is not unlikely that an animal is coming through, and those who pass may not be thrilled that you gave their things away, it is a high-probability read. If that is what the loved one wants delivered as a message, then okay. But do not use it as a high-probability guess to imply a connection. Ask the departed one if he has a message surrounding this high-probability read.

5. *Psychic Flattery Method:* When the medium is not connecting, they tell the querent how psychic the querent is. Many people who go to psychics enjoy being validated for their own abilities. This psychic flattery gets on my nerves. Many readers try to flatter querents with this statement. While it may be true, flattery regarding the psychic ability of the querent when the medium strikes out in other ways is, frankly, pathetic. Now, that you have read this, you may be shocked how many times you see it used by readers.

6. *Past-Life Punt Method:* The medium is not connecting, so they say the information must be from the departed loved one's past life. If the medium initially stated it was a past life, then the scenario would be different; however, this is just the medium punting and changing the play because they do not want to say okay and move on with the reading.

7. *Let's See What Will Stick Method:* The medium begins to give general advice that could apply to almost anyone while still having people keep their hands up if something applies to the departed one they want to hear from at the time. The medium throws out all types of scenarios to see what will fit. If readers are not licensed counselors or life coaches, they should refrain from interjecting their advice and limit their readings to the psychic information they receive. Get specific. These broad, sweeping statements are fishing.

8. *Tie It All Up with a Pretty Bow Method:* The medium starts speculating by putting all the pieces together with statements such as "Maybe your loved one is showing you flowers to show they loved you." As stated above, but definitely worth repeating, if readers are not licensed counselors or ordained ministers, they should refrain from interjecting their advice. They should limit their readings to the psychic information they receive. It is not your job to tie everything up with a perfect bow for the querent. Just deliver the information given.

9. *Blame the Departed One Method:* When the medium is wrong, they say, "I'm not being nosey, but your loved one is saying this." Blaming the departed one is one of the lowest tricks I've ever seen a psychic stoop to in all my professional years. The best mediums will acknowledge their limitations.

10. *Grandmother's Favorite Flower Method:* When discussing a grandmother, the medium brings up roses or some other flower scent. Roses representing grandmothers may have worked in the Victorian era, but grandmothers don't necessarily smell like or grow roses today. Yet mediums still use this. It is not inherently incorrect to say, but it is often just utilized to get a hit.

Journal Prompts: A Hypothetical Mediumship Gallery

As you go through this hypothetical mediumship session, consider how you would want to handle the reading or receive one for your standard. I have noted a few of my thoughts or how I would handle things differently, but journal your thoughts.

1. Have you seen psychic mediums use any of these methods? How did you respond to such techniques?
2. Which scenarios do you find unacceptable and why?
3. Which scenarios do you find acceptable as long as the method leads to some sort of message that helps the querent?
4. What are your thoughts on playing the odds?
5. How would you handle a group reading?
6. Do you think it is important to be honest with querents about whether or not you are actually communicating with their loved ones?

Avoid These Pitfalls

The hypothetical gallery covered many things to avoid. In a nutshell, be honest with those seeking mediumship connections. The lowest form of psychic is the one that takes advantage of people at their darkest moments. If something feels wrong, it probably is wrong. Learn to be comfortable with not always connecting with the departed. Learn to be okay if you have a few misses. Stop worrying about being right or wrong. Just be honest about the information you are receiving and how you are receiving it.

Psychic Success

You will know when your channel is working on all cylinders. I have a saying that I use when I feel I'm not connecting: "My channel is busted." Yes, it is a bit of a joke, but I will let people know when I am not connecting. The interesting thing is that the minute I say that, all of a sudden information starts flooding in. It is because I released my attachment to the outcome. Psychic success in mediumship is almost always about your ethics. If you are honestly connecting, people will know. If you are full of bologna, people will also know. There is no need to be nervous if you are honest with yourself, the querent, and the departed one.

PART 1
CONCLUSION

You did it! Or at the very least, you read about assembling your psychic handbook to meet your unique, intuitive psychic style. Thinking through who you are and who you want to become has helped you know what areas to focus on depending on where you are in your psychic development. Going through the clairs, chakras, and colors (auras) has helped you realize how utilizing the Three C's can make increasing your psychic awareness much more manageable. You also know to stay calm because this is your handbook. You do not have to precisely know which clair you are using when; however, you are aware that you do use them, and in many cases, they begin to flow together. This self-awareness has helped you understand what kind of psychic knowingness you naturally possess and how to develop it. You now realize the function of this handbook is to improve your capabilities and performance, ultimately making you a better psychic. You have a plan that leaves room for more creativity, leading to more remarkable psychic development. You are on your way to psychic success. Let's look at how divination and psychic knowingness have existed since time began. It is exciting and fun to look at ancient divination practices and see how to use them now. Refrain from feeling boxed into practice. You will change and evolve for different times and circumstances, much like practices evolve as the diviners evolve.

PART 2
DIVINATION EXERCISES FROM THE ANCIENT TO THE MODERN

This part of the book will break down some of the various types of divination and the modalities utilized throughout time. Divination is a way to fortune-tell. I call this *future-telling*, but divination also involves unearthing past and present hidden information. A *modality* is a process, technique, or method of doing something. In our case, a modality is the method we choose for our divination. The various types of divination are divided into categories for ease of use because many are similar. Most modality names will have the suffixes *-mancy*, *-scopy*, and *-logy*. In this book, the suffix *-mancy* means "prophecy," *-scopy* means "to observe," and *-logy* means "logic."

A little history is discussed, which is quite fascinating. Note that ancient usages are not meant to be all inclusive or teach the history of the times or culture. They are covered for several reasons: One is to remind us that divination has been utilized since the beginning of civilization; it is not New Age in any way. Another reason is to remind us that many of the practices utilized now were used in various ways by several, if not many, cultures. It is important to avoid appropriation from other cultures; however, it is also essential to recognize that many cultures integrated the customs of other cultures. Where the line of appropriation begins can be unclear in many divination practices; therefore, I propose to err on the side of always showing respect by acknowledging and honoring any cultural practice. Ancient divination methods are also included to remind us why we use divination. The ancients had basic concerns regarding food and survival. But just as we seek answers regarding spirituality, so too did the ancients. We use divination to answer questions of a practical or spiritual nature that help us in our daily lives.

You may note that some past civilizations used forms of divination to determine whether someone was a criminal or a witch. Divination was sometimes the only form of trial an accused received. Although you certainly won't use a form of divination for those purposes, exercises are included in part 2 to utilize these modalities today—modern exercises. Some of these exercises may seem far-fetched, but they are given as examples to teach you that you can use anything for divination.

Further, this book does not teach you everything about the various modalities. While learning and respecting ancient practices, I have reworked modes of divination for hundreds of intuitive classes. So, for example, while I might study and understand tarot on a professional level, I will also take liberties with the art of tarot, adjusting ways of using it in my intuitive classes (where we learn that we can use anything or nothing to develop our psychic knowingness). I encourage you to use the modern exercises as a starting point and use your handbook to develop your psychic associations further. When utilizing divination, it is imperative to set your intention. In other words, before you begin any form of divination, be clear in your mind what you are asking and what the signs indicate. You will find your accuracy is much greater if you do this every time you divine. Three things to consider are provided under each topic to help you get started in the reading or interpreting of the message. Clearly, there are more than three ways for interpretation, but as with everything in your handbook, eventually you will know that the interpretation is best when it is individual to you as a diviner. Practice and begin to trust yourself.

Category 1: Animals

Throughout time, there have been many forms of divination based on the characteristics of animals, and the study of different animals had various names depending on the animal. This form of divination falls under an umbrella category known as *zoomancy*. Although divination involving animals may vary significantly from country to country or region to region, what is certain is the extent to which we humans rely on the actions of animals for many things, ranging from sustenance to companionship. It is no wonder there are so many forms of divination involving animals and even more superstitions and omens that spring from those divinations. These messages were relied upon in daily life because animals were a way to tap into nature and its patterns, which were pivotal for early humankind.

Note that while ancient divination practices often involved the sacrifice of animals, those forms are deliberately excluded from this book. There are plenty of ways to divine with animals without harming them. Be sure to set your intention before observing animals for answers.

Ailuromancy (Cats and Prophecy)

Ailuromancy is also known as felidomancy because it involves the movement of cats. The ways and mannerisms of cats have been used in divination since ancient times. Bast is the goddess associated with cats who protected Egyptians and brought fun and play to them. Egyptians kept black cats in their homes for protection. Almost every move the cat made meant something to many diviners. How a cat jumped, landed, washed, looked, or followed instructions were all studied for messages. A cat sneezing might mean rain, while a cat washing itself might also mean rain. Black cats crossing your path were once considered bad luck in the United States, while they indicated good luck in the UK. One thing is certain: Cats have long been revered as mystical beings with messages to impart.[8]

Modern Exercise

If you have a cat or have access to cats you observe regularly, add the category ailuromancy or felidomancy to your handbook. You can always keep a photographic journal on your phone. Try to have a separate section for each cat you observe regularly. As you collect more and more data, you will associate specific actions of the cats with certain tells or predictions that you can make.

Things to Consider

+ If a cat has its ears back, someone is angry.
+ If a cat's tail is pointed straight up, someone is aware of the motives of someone else.
+ If a cat's tail is tucked, someone is frightened.

Alectromancy, Alectormancy, Alectryomancy (Cock/Rooster and Prophecy)

Ancient civilizations used many forms of divination to find treasure or identify criminals. Alectromancy was popular in Rome as a tool to identify thieves. Kernels of grain would be laid out in a circle at each letter of the alphabet, and a white rooster would be set in the middle. The seeds the rooster pecked at would form a word to identify the culprit. One Roman emperor used alectromancy to determine his successor. The rooster picked four kernels, T-H-E-O. The emperor had people murdered whose names began with Theo.

....

8. Raymond Buckland, *The Fortune-Telling Book: The Encyclopedia of Divination and Soothsaying* (Visible Ink Press, 2004), 11; Theresa Cheung, *The Element Encyclopedia of the Psychic World* (HarperElement, 2006), 12.

Unfortunately for the emperor, he missed Theodosius, who became the next emperor. If a simple yes-or-no question was asked, the diviner would place one pile of grain or corn to indicate yes and one to indicate no. The pile that the rooster went to first was the answer, or sometimes it would be the most pecked piles that suggested the answer.[9]

Modern Exercise

A pendulum is an ideal substitute for the rooster in this form of divination. Ask your question and then hold your pendulum over a chart of letters. You can draw this chart or use preexisting charts. Once you spell out a word or name, ask the pendulum if it is finished with the letters. Of course, if it is a yes or no you seek, have the pendulum indicate the answer: yes or no.

Things to Consider

+ If you are working with a pendulum for the first time, calibrate it by becoming familiar with the way it swings for a yes or no.
+ If you learn to feel the pull of the pendulum, you will notice the directional pull is more important than how big it swings.
+ If you work with pendulums consistently, you will trust the answers more.

Apantomancy (To Encounter and Prophecy)

Apantomancy is divination with whatever presents itself by chance encounter. The background or training of the one divining will determine the modality used. Another type of apantomancy is redundant happenstances of any sort. This includes observing animals and specific behaviors. Many times, the animal is a black cat or bird. An example is a black cat crossing the street or birds hitting glass windows. It also involves having different chance encounters with animals and then watching for synchronicity. For example, seeing three birds at the same place every day at the same time.[10]

....

9. Buckland. *The Fortune-Telling Book*, 13; Cheung, *The Element Encyclopedia*, 17; Clifford A. Pickover, *Dreaming the Future: The Fantastic Story of Prediction* (Prometheus Books, 2001), 81.

10. Buckland, *The Fortune-Telling Book*, 18; Cheung, *The Element Encyclopedia*, 26; Pickover, *Dreaming the Future*, 77.

Modern Exercise

Go for a walk and see what catches your attention. Repeat this walk at various times during one day or at the same time over multiple days. Note if you observe the same activity each time. For example, I see three blue jays together or three in a row when I need reassurance or a reminder that my guides protect me. Always remember to assign meaning to these occurrences. That way, you will know what they mean the next time you see them. It is your handbook; you can assign whatever meaning you want.

Things to Consider

- If you pay attention to things around you, signs and patterns will eventually emerge.
- If there are patterns or repetitions, make a note of them so that you can compare over time.
- If you want to personalize your divination, assign your own meaning to the activity you observe.

Arachnomancy (Spider and Prophecy)

This form of divination involves watching spiders and how they move or rearrange leaves. Many cultures believe in looking to the spider or the spider's web to determine news regarding weather and money. A spider making a web in the morning indicates money will come some time that day. If the spider is busy early in the evening, news will come before nighttime. In many cultures, it is believed that killing a spider will make it rain. Many cultures burn or cut symbols on pieces of paper or leaves. These papers are then placed in a box with a giant spider. The numbers or symbols moved by the spider are the lucky numbers or symbols. This practice is most notably used in Africa and is known as *ngam*, or spider divination. A giant black spider, similar in shape and size to a tarantula, lives in a nest in the earth, and a diviner interprets its actions. The diviner takes up to two hundred cards and places them in a pot that is closed on top but open where it covers the spider's nest. The following morning, after placing the cards in the pot with the spider, the diviner will interpret what the spider has done with the various cards.[11]

. . . .

11. Buckland, *The Fortune-Telling Book*, 9, 447, 477; Cheung, *The Element Encyclopedia*, 46; Pickover, *Dreaming the Future*, 84.

Modern Exercise

Spiderwebs are beautiful and exciting to watch. If you find a spiderweb, regardless of where the web is, take a moment to closely observe it without disrupting it. Look at the patterns to see what messages there are. If you see a spider or another insect on the web, determine what message they have for you. Look for things such as the type of insect and how the spider has trapped it. Add the location of the web into your reading. The proximity of the web to something such as a boat might also be taken into consideration.

Another easy exercise is to cut and lay out string in all different directions on a table or floor. Then, look for the message. It is fun to do this with silly string in a can. Spray the web onto a concrete surface or black card stock paper and divine a message. You could also use glue to make a pattern on the black card stock paper and then read it for a message.

Things to Consider

+ If the spider is not visible near the web, plans may be too complicated.
+ If the spider is on the web, it is time for patience.
+ If the spider has another insect in the web, victory over adversity is indicated.

Augury (Omens of Animals)

Augury was utilized in "Rome and Greece, as well as in Mexico and Peru" to predict the future.[12] Originally, it applied to the flight patterns of birds, but it expanded in meaning over the ages. Patterns and behaviors of different animals were studied for this type of divination. These were considered omens. While omens are often considered unlucky, there can be good and bad omens. Different animals had various names. Examples of augury span ailuromancy (cats) to entomancy (insects) to myomancy (mice).[13]

Modern Exercise

The types of augury listed above are found throughout part 2, this section, of the book. Augury is the umbrella category; therefore, the exercises are under each specific category. For a broad exercise, consider if you have ever used any types of augury. Reflect on that

. . . .
12. Buckland, *The Fortune-Telling Book*, 50.
13. Buckland, *The Fortune-Telling Book*, 51; Cheung, *The Element Encyclopedia*, 46; Pickover, *Dreaming the Future*, 30, 82.

experience. How did the type you used work out for you? Do you still utilize it? Perhaps just as importantly, are there any types of augury you don't want to use and why?

Things to Consider

+ If you are drawn to certain animals or have access to them, that type of augury might work well for you.
+ If you allow your creativity to flow when working with augury, it can be not only useful for divination but also quite fun. You can set your own intention as to what certain behaviors mean.
+ If there is a type of augury that is not enjoyable to you, then let it go. There are plenty of types of divination and absolutely no reason to force something you do not enjoy.

Auspicy and Avimancy (Flight Patterns and Birds)

Auspicy involved studying the flight patterns of birds for divination.[14]

Modern Exercise

Go outside in an open field. Lie down on a blanket and look up at the sky. Or you could sit in your car if you prefer. Watch the movements of the birds you see. Divine a message from the way they fly. Note the direction, the groups, the stragglers, and anything else you observe. Another fun way to watch birds is in the city. Sometimes, you will notice many birds grouped on a building or road light. Observe how long they stay together, what makes them fly away, and how they are grouped. I have even taken photos of birds perched on a pole while stopped at a streetlight. Later, I used the photograph to give me a message.

Things to Consider

+ If the birds all stay together, things are going to go easily with groups.
+ If the birds are mostly together but there are stragglers, maybe someone is being left out.
+ If the birds all seem to be separate, a new group of friends might be warranted.

....

14. Buckland, *The Fortune-Telling Book*, 51–52.

Batrachomancy (Frog and Prophecy)

Divination using frogs, toads, and newts is usually connected with water; therefore, much of the divination with these amphibians involved something with rain or the weather in general. In the Ozarks of the United States, the shifting of a bullfrog's skin from light to dark means rain will fall within a twelve-hour period. Since there were no weather channels in older times, much divination occurred around the need for rain for crops. If a frog, toad, or newt was seen, it was often interpreted as a sign of impending rain.

The next time someone tells you they don't believe in predicting the future, ask them kindly if they look at weather forecasts. We have utilized our powers of observation and intuition for ages to predict the weather and survive and thrive.[15]

Modern Exercise

Pick a modality to begin predicting the weather in and around your area. If you happen to see frogs, toads, newts, or other amphibians enough that you can use them for this exercise, then do so. Otherwise, pick something else to help you predict the weather. You could also get a bullfrog sound via a white noise app or download a song with bullfrog music. Listen to it a few times and set the intention for each sound. That way, you will know your tells to divine weather when you happen to hear the bullfrog sounds.

Things to Consider

- If you hear a bullfrog, nature is inviting you to narrow your focus instead of taking in the big picture.
- If you cannot hear any bullfrogs, you need a time of respite.
- If you hear many bullfrogs, there is a grateful energy in your environment.

Entomancy (Insect and Prophecy)

Divining based on the behavior of insects is fascinating. Like many animals, ancient divining based on insects falls closely to more of an omen or superstition, such as crickets, ladybugs, bees, and grasshoppers being a sign of good luck. At the same time, a beetle might indicate lousy luck. However, many ancients, such as the Greeks, used insects to predict the future. It is said that as an infant, Plato had a swarm of bees circle his cradle,

----

15. Buckland, *The Fortune-Telling Book*, 62, 81.

which then landed on his lips and made honey. This foretold his gift of intelligence and communication.[16]

Modern Exercise

When you notice an insect, try to divine what message it is imparting to you. Sometimes, you have time to sit and observe them, while on other occasions they press you to use your psychic knowingness instantly. Either way, you can receive a message even if you don't know much about the insect or its typical meaning to others. Try to get a message based on how it shows up in your life, its appearance, and its behavior. It is all right if you have preconceived notions or knowledge about the insect. Integrate the notions or expertise into the message you see by observing them. I notice dragonflies a lot. They are beautiful to me. Before I studied what a red, blue, green, or iridescent rainbow dragonfly meant to others, I received messages of what they meant to me individually and collectively. Because I downloaded my messages without anyone telling me what conclusions to reach, I am more connected to dragonflies and the messages they have for me than if I had researched them first. It is important to write down in your handbook what different insects mean to you before studying or researching their meaning. Remember to communicate with insects. They are often connected to the fairy realm.

Things to Consider

+ If you see a mosquito, you need to be more tolerant.
+ If you see a ladybug, you will have good luck.
+ If you see a beetle, you might have a run of bad luck.

Hippomancy (Horse and Prophecy)

In ancient times, Celts (associated with the horse goddess Epona) used this form of divination, and Germans were also involved in observing horses. The horse's color, the foot that the horse chose to step with first, if the horse stepped on something, and the dust it stirred up were all observed for different messages. Horses are highly psychic animals, along with cats and dogs.[17]

. . . .

16. Cheung, *The Element Encyclopedia*, 46, 190.
17. Buckland, *The Fortune-Telling Book*, 244; Cheung, *The Element Encyclopedia*, 46; Pickover, *Dreaming the Future*, 80.

Modern Exercise

Horses are highly psychic animals. I always found it ironic to think people are called "horse whisperers" when the horse is probably giving *us* information: human whisperers. A way to connect with horses is to interact with them. When riding or grooming your horse, pay close attention to the thoughts that enter your mind. These are probably from the horse. If you don't have access to horses, call on them like a guide and ask for guidance. You might even watch videos of horses roaming freely. Notice how you feel and what messages you receive.

Things to Consider

- If you feel the horse is nervous, trust the horse and be aware of your surroundings.
- If the horse is calm, soak in this beautiful healing energy.
- If the horse is agitated, give the horse its space. Pay attention to the energy around the horse and clear any stale or unwanted energy.

Ichthyomancy (Fish and Prophecy)

Haruspication is the act of divination using the entrails of animals slain in sacrifice. A branch of haruspication called ichthyomancy involves reading fish. Ancient Greeks and Scandinavians used this form of divination. In one form of the practice, the head or entrails of the fish were studied. The number of fish, location, color, and behavior were considered for the message. Further, whether the fish was in or out of the water was a consideration.[18]

Modern Exercise

For this exercise, you may need a field trip if you don't have an aquarium at home. Find an aquarium and pick a fish to study. Then, you can add another fish and see how it relates to the first fish. I was raised to fish by my grandmother, who lived for 106 years. When I go to our boat or dock, I constantly receive messages from my grandmother and the fish. I even received a warning when a lot of alligator gar were by our boat. If you are

....
18. Buckland, *The Fortune-Telling Book*, 241–42, 273; Cheung, *The Element Encyclopedia*, 46, 316; Pickover, *Dreaming the Future*, 84.

fishing for sustenance, as you clean the fish, study the parts of the fish for a message. Of course, always be grateful for any animal sacrifice for our sustenance.

Things to Consider

+ If you see a fish jump in the water, something is trying to get your attention, but is not meant for you to totally take on as a challenge.
+ If you catch a fish, you are being provided for. Show gratitude.
+ If a fish gets away, be aware of things within your grasp that might slip through your fingers if you aren't careful.

Myomancy (Mice/Rats and Prophecy)

Myomancy involves divining the movements, sounds, and destruction of rats and mice. They are usually considered a warning of something nasty or evil. A Roman emperor and a Roman commander were said to have resigned their reigns due to the alleged warnings of mice and rats.[19]

Modern Exercise

Watching mice in a maze or labyrinth is a good way to observe their behavior. Out of kindness, provide plenty of rewards along the path. Since we don't all have mice, watching a video of mice can act as a way to use this type of divination. One path could indicate a no answer to a question or a certain outcome, while the other would indicate a yes answer to a question and a different result. You can even use some type of maze game and assign different answers to different paths. If you happen to notice a swarm of rats running, you probably want to observe what they are running from and run yourself. Some omens are common sense.

Things to Consider

+ If the mouse is alone and seems lost, consider how you may be on a misguided path.
+ If the mice are all together and running away, trouble is brewing—run.
+ If the mouse seems interested in you, pay attention to the creatures around you.

. . . .

19. Buckland, *The Fortune-Telling Book*, 326; Cheung, *The Element Encyclopedia*, 46, 465; Pickover, *Dreaming the Future*, 80.

Ophiomancy, Ophidiomancy (Snake and Prophecy)

Ancient Egyptians believed a dream about a snake was good luck, but the Greeks considered it a sign of trouble regarding sickness or enemies. The divination of snakes included observing the snake's color, type, and behavior. If a snake was coiled and did not seem agitated, the message was to have more patience and that a threat is not as bad as you thought.[20]

Modern Exercise

You will receive intuitive messages if you see a snake or dream about one. You might already have your own ideas of ways to interpret the message. Many people think of snakes as evil. I suggest clearing your mind of your biases and instead reading with a clean third eye. (See part 1, the Clean Third Eye exercise on page 61.) Create a long snake out of pieces of paper. Divide it into sections and put words, phrases, colors, or even tarot cards in the different sections. Roll a die to see where you land on the snake for a reading. You could also read the shed skin of a snake.

Things to Consider

+ If you dream about a snake that scares you, beware of a traitor in your midst.
+ If you dream of a snake underwater, watch for things that sneak up on you when you least expect them.
+ If you see or dream of a snake shedding its skin, it is time to shed some old habits.

Zoomancy (Animals and Prophecy)

This form of divination is a catchall or umbrella category for divination with animals.[21]

Modern Exercise

Pick an animal that you want to study and divine. Once you have devised your system of interpreting their signs, move on to another animal. The animal might blend into a power animal that helps guide you like spirit guides mentioned in chapter 5.

. . . .

20. Buckland, *The Fortune-Telling Book*, 351; Cheung, *The Element Encyclopedia*, 46, 502; Pickover, *Dreaming the Future*. 86.
21. Buckland, *The Fortune-Telling Book*, 351; Cheung, *The Element Encyclopedia*, 799; Pickover, *Dreaming the Future*, 87.

Things to Consider

+ If you need encouragement, pick an animal you are drawn to.
+ If you want to recognize lessons, pick an animal that scares or repulses you.
+ If an animal picks you by appearing in dreams or seems to come to your attention for three days in a row, this animal has great messages for you.

Category 2: Bodies of Water

Water is an ideal conduit for intuitive information. Whether it is your shower or a natural body of water, the more you utilize the water element, the more intuitive messages you will receive—especially those involving emotions.

Bletonism or Bletonomancy (Water Current and Prophecy)

Water divining, called *bletonism* or *bletonomancy*, was named after a well-known French diviner named Bleton. This form of water divining included finding underground water springs and currents.[22] (See also Dowsing and Rhabdomancy below.)

Modern Exercise

Go to a body of water and watch the water's movement. This body of water can be as simple as a puddle formed in the street from an afternoon rain. Based on the movement of the water, formulate a reading. You can also read what you see reflected in the water.

Things to Consider

+ If the water is still and feels peaceful, then the message is one of calm emotions. If it feels stagnant, the message is one of something old, unused, or neglected.
+ If the water is flowing, unencumbered movement and freedom is indicated.
+ If the water is rough, hard times may be on the horizon.

. . . .
22. Buckland, *The Fortune-Telling Book*, 71; Pickover, *Dreaming the Future*, 171.

Category 3: Body Movements

Observing the way people move has long given diviners information for intuitive messages.

Ambulomancy (Walking and Prophecy)

Divination based on observing the way one walks, such as the length, speed, or number of steps of the walk.[23]

Modern Exercise

Go to a crowded area and find a comfortable place to sit. Take your journal with you to record your findings. Begin by noting interesting things you observe about how people walk. Over time, begin to see if you notice patterns. Once you have learned your tells, you are ready to give a message based on how someone walks. Ask a friend to walk and see what message you receive.

Things to Consider

+ If someone walks with their head down and leans forward, they do not want to be bothered and are often insecure.
+ If someone looks around while walking, they are taking in the world. Next, figure out why. Are they enjoying themselves or being protective?
+ If someone takes little steps, they are cautionary in their movements.

Gyromancy (Spinning and Prophecy)

Gyromancy is a type of divination where someone spins around in a circle until they get dizzy. The circle can be pre-labeled with letters, words, numbers, or the houses of astrology. The person might fall multiple times to spell out a word. Another type of gyromancy is that of the whirling dervishes. They spin until they go into a trance, as whirling blurs the line between the physical and metaphysical.[24]

. . . .

23. Buckland, *The Fortune-Telling Book*, 15.
24. Buckland, *The Fortune-Telling Book*, 235; Cheung, *The Element Encyclopedia*, 274; Pickover, *Dreaming the Future*, 172.

Modern Exercise

Label a large circle on the ground with letters, numbers, colors, or astrological houses. Have a volunteer spin around until they are dizzy. Note where they are in relation to your labels.

Things to Consider

+ If a person is spinning, notice how long they spin before getting dizzy—
  the longer they spin, the longer the message may take to come to pass.
+ If the person stops or falls within the boundary of your area or circle, then note what they stopped or landed near.
+ If they spin outside the area or circle, there may not be an answer now.

Category 4: Body or Physical Appearances

Divination using the body or physical appearance is readily available without having to use another tool to receive or interpret the message.

Cartopedy (Foot and Prophecy)

Cartopedy, a form of somatomancy (body divination), is divination using the foot (like using the hands in palmistry). In ancient times, cartopedists were consulted regarding the feet of a potential spouse.[25]

Modern Exercise

Get a piece of paper and trace your bare foot. Think of the foot in sections, like the entire body with chakras. The toes are the crown chakra; the heel is the root chakra. Now, look at your foot and see where there are marks. You could also sense or feel where the foot is sore.

. . . .
25. Pickover, *Dreaming the Future*, 71.

Things to Consider

+ If there is a callous on the heel, this may indicate an overactive root chakra.
+ If the toes are smooth and without blemish, this may indicate a balanced crown chakra.
+ If the arch is flat (flat footed), this may indicate an underactive solar plexus chakra.

Dactylomancy (Finger and Prophecy)

This is divination by rings, and there are various methods. One is placing different types of metal rings on the fingernails. There is not much known about this method, but the rings probably corresponded to planets. Another form was to use a table with letters and the rings like pendulums to spell out words. They would also hold a ring over a bowl of water or wine and use it like a pendulum.[26]

Modern Exercise

Pick a subject and ask to look at their hands. Note on which fingers they have rings and what size the rings are. Are the rings meant to draw attention to the individual? Are the rings small and dainty or large and ostentatious? Now, look at the finger the ring is on to determine which planet is associated with the ring and finger (see Palmistry).

Things to Consider

+ If someone has a ring on their middle (Saturn) finger, it may indicate someone who is firm with their boundaries.
+ If someone has a ring on their ring (Apollo) finger, it may indicate someone who likes to be in the spotlight.
+ If someone has a ring on their pinky (Mercury) finger, it may indicate someone who is good at communication.

. . . .
26. Buckland, *The Fortune-Telling Book*, 172; Cheung, *The Element Encyclopedia*, 143; Pickover, *Dreaming the Future*, 198.

Iridology (Iris and Study)

Iridology is close to oculomancy. They both involve divination based on the eyes. Iridology is known to use the iris as the source of information. The iris is the colored part of the eye. It is believed that the iris points to every organ in the human body. Oculomancy involves looking deep into the eyes and using the reflection to see messages.[27]

Modern Exercise

Print out photos of people. Try to enlarge the eyes before printing. Focus your attention on the eyes and give a reading based on the color and shape of the eyes.

Things to Consider

+ If someone has light-colored eyes, such as blue or green, it may indicate someone who can see things clearly. Green and blue eyes may also indicate mystery and intelligence.
+ If someone has larger, dark eyes, it may indicate someone trustworthy and kind.
+ If you look at and compare many eyes, you will rapidly advance. As you advance, begin pulling in your own findings for reading shapes and unique features.

Labiomancy, Cledonomancy, Cledonismancy (Lips and Prophecy)

Labiomancy involves the movement of lips. The focus is more on the movement of the lips than the actual words. Cledonismancy involves words uttered upon meeting.[28]

Modern Exercise

Put on noise-canceling headphones and have one or more people say things to you. Read one person at a time or combine them all for a message. You can integrate how they move their mouths and lips into what they are saying. You can also listen to words spoken randomly. Write down what you hear. Then, turn your attention elsewhere and write down what you hear. It may be one word or several. Do this for about five minutes or until you have a fair variety of words or phrases. Now, put them all together for your

---

27. Buckland, *The Fortune-Telling Book*, 339; Cheung, *The Element Encyclopedia*, 498; Pickover, *Dreaming the Future*, 75.
28. Buckland, *The Fortune-Telling Book*, 130, 289; Cheung, *The Element Encyclopedia*, 118; Pickover, *Dreaming the Future*, 190.

message. This type of divination is close to cledonomancy. You may even begin a day writing down chance remarks and then interpret all of them at the end of the day. Notice if any of the messages are repetitive.

Things to Consider

+ If you have one word or phrase that is repeated many times, this is a strong message that should not be ignored no matter how silly it may seem.
+ If it seems like there was no rhyme or reason to any of the words gathered, find the message in the chaos and cacophony.
+ If you hear your name, take this as a direct sign from a guide as a wakeup call.

Palmistry (Palm and Engaging In)

One of the oldest forms of divination. Palmistry may have originated in China around 3000 BCE. Still, Indian scriptures also provide evidence of the practice this early. Aristotle wrote a book on palmistry for Alexander the Great. Chinese palmistry involves two primary techniques: the Five Element or Five Phase System and the Eight Trigram System (which follows the concept of *bagua* in feng shui). There is also Indian palmistry, which places great importance on signs and symbols found on the hands, such as a fish representing wealth or a tree representing success.[29]

Modern Exercise

Take a look at the palms of your hands. Your nondominant hand represents what you came into this life with, and your dominant hand represents how your life is now. Notice the length of your fingers compared to the length of your palm. Observe whether you have full or plump mounts on either or both hands. Do you notice fine lines anywhere? What shape are your fingertips? Take note of any specific markings or symbols on your palms and fingers.

....
29. Buckland, *The Fortune-Telling Book*, 359–63; Cheung, *The Element Encyclopedia*, 520–22; Pickover, *Dreaming the Future*, 63–67, 75.

Things to Consider

+ If the Mount of Venus (the section of the palm by the thumb) is hard and not well rounded, it may indicate that you are not fulfilled sexually or are not taking care of your body.
+ If the palm of your hand is relatively longer than your fingers, it indicates that you have a fire hand and are a passionate person.
+ If you notice a square on the Mount of Jupiter (the section of the palm under the pointer finger), it could indicate that you are a natural leader or teacher.

Physiognomancy, Physiognomy (Facial Features)

Physiognomancy involves observing faces for divination. The facial shapes and appearances were divided into seven planets. For example, solar or Sun faces were round and happy, and Venus faces were perfect and symmetrical.[30]

Modern Exercise

Based on your knowledge of the celestial bodies, decide what features someone with that face might have. Tackle them one at a time and then begin to compare various faces: Sun (action energy), Moon (shadow work), Venus (love), Saturn (lessons), Mars (drive), Mercury (communication), and Jupiter (leadership). Keep a journal of your divination method, including photos of individuals. You could also see how filters change the message, if at all.

Things to Consider

+ If someone's face looks like Venus, this may indicate someone is a loving person or in love with the idea of love. However, they may be sad and fickle.
+ If someone's face reminds you of Mars, it indicates someone who is strong, courageous, headstrong, and action oriented.
+ If someone's face reminds you of Mercury, they are young, playful, mental workers, and communicative.

. . . .

30. Buckland, *The Fortune-Telling Book*, 371; Cheung, *The Element Encyclopedia*, 545–46; Pickover, *Dreaming the Future*, 76.

Category 5: Bones

Bone reading is an ancient practice involving reading the bones of various animals. The Shang Dynasty of China used this ancient form of divination shortly after the time of Moses. The diviners wrote on the bones and then heated them until they cracked, and then gave the message. Today, bones are still read, but often they are cast and then read based on shapes and patterns formed. Bone reading also involved bone throwing. Certain bones would have specific meanings.[31]

Ashagalomancy, Astragalomancy, Astragyromancy (Joint and Prophecy)

This is a form of bone divination where the knucklebones of hooved animals, such as goats or sheep, are used like dice. Knucklebone divination might be the oldest game known worldwide to humankind.[32]

Modern Exercise

The dice exercise on page 208 serves as an effective and fun modern exercise.

Things to Consider

Utilize the Things to Consider section from the dice exercise on page 209.

Osteomancy (Bone and Prophecy)

Osteomancy, also known as bone throwing, is one of the oldest forms of divination. It is highly intuitive and personalized since the collected bone sets are individual and unique. Diviners read by tossing a bunch of bones, including animal bones and horns, exoskeletons, sticks and bark, stones, and shells of snails and sea animals.[33]

Modern Exercise

A modern-day set can include household items and trinkets—anything meaningful to you. Collect bleached bones or order them from a reputable supplier. Decide what you want to divine from these bones and what each bone represents. Consider marking the

. . . .

31. Cheung, The *Element of Encyclopedia*, 80; Pickover, *Dreaming the Future*, 67.
32. Buckland, *The Fortune-Telling Book*, 25–26; Pickover, *Dreaming the Future*, 133.
33. Buckland, *The Fortune-Telling Book*, 354.

bones so that you will know their meaning. Cast or throw the bones and see how they land. After assigning meaning to your set, the bones are cast and interpreted by reading their relative positions. Notice any groupings, patterns, or outliers (a bone off your casting cloth or a distance away from the other bones).

Things to Consider
+ If a group of bones land together, these can be read together.
+ If there is a bone by itself, where is it? Is it leaving the story or coming into the story?
+ If a bone goes off the cloth, will you consider it in play, or should it be noted that it is being ignored?

Category 6: Books

Books are an easy way to get a message. Cultures have used books for ages to receive messages. Many sacred texts were and still are used.

Stichomancy (Verse and Prophecy)

Stichomancy means divination from random passages in books. It is a method in which the seeker randomly opens a book, then chooses a random passage on the page (usually by pointing with eyes closed) to receive a message from the spirit world. It is a great option when you need an answer immediately and don't have access to other tools. You can also set a book on its spine and let it fall open to a random page.[34]

Modern Exercise

Think of a question. Pick up a book you feel drawn to and open it to a random page. Then, close your eyes and run your fingers down the page, and where your finger stops, read the passage or phrase for your message.

Things to Consider
+ Consider everything on the page—it could be a drawing, a heading, one word, or a paragraph. Let the message flow and don't second-guess it.

....
34. Buckland, *The Fortune-Telling Book*, 450; Pickover, *Dreaming the Future*, 150–51, 365.

+ Mark the passage with a date. Chances are, this will come up again.
+ Pull another book and go to the same page and see if you get synchronicity in the message.

Bibliomancy (Book and Prophecy)

Bibliomancy started as picking verses randomly in a holy book but later came to mean any book. The diviner randomly opens the book, and the message is where the reader's eyes fall.[35]

Modern Exercise

Pick out a Bible or other book. Randomly open the book to a page and note the first word or phrase you see. I use this form of divination when I sign my books. The person chooses a page number. I then circle that page number for the message unique to them.

Things to Consider

+ If you are unsure how to begin, consider everything on the page—it could be a drawing, a heading, one word, or a paragraph. Let the message flow and don't second-guess it.
+ If you can write in the book, mark the passage with a date. Chances are, this will come up again.
+ If you want to layer the reading, pull another book and go to the same page and see if you get synchronicity in the message or something to add to the original message.

Dictiomancy (Dictionary and Prophecy)

Dictiomancy is divining insight via dictionary entries. The message is received by opening a dictionary to a random page.[36]

. . . .
35. Buckland, *The Fortune-Telling Book*, 65–66; Cheung, *The Element Encyclopedia*, 70; Pickover, *Dreaming the Future*, 146, 241.
36. Cheung, *The Element Encyclopedia*, 157.

Modern Exercise

Use the method for bibliomancy. Open the dictionary to a random page and note what word you see first. You can use a digital format of this type of divination by scrolling randomly to a digital page and then noting the first word you see.

Things to Consider

+ If you know the meaning of the word, ask yourself what it is telling you.
+ If you do not know the meaning of the word, write it down with the definition. Learn to use the word because it is now going to be part of your vernacular. Think of a spelling bee when using a dictionary for divination. Ask yourself where the word originated and what the root words are, and even look to see how it is used in a sentence.
+ If the word is one that provokes strong positive or negative emotions, explore the emotions of the word.

I Ching (Consulting the Ancient Chinese Book of Changes)

I Ching is a five-thousand-year-old divination system believed to have been invented by Fu Hsi, a legendary emperor of China. Initially, the diviner cast a bundle of yarrow sticks. Later, coins became a more popular tool. Hexagrams were built according to a coin toss. Then, the *Book of Changes* was consulted for the interpretation.[37]

Modern Exercise

For this modern exercise, Benebell Wen, the author of *I Ching, The Oracle: A Practical Guide to The Book of Changes*, has kindly provided instructions for a divination session.

> This is a beginner-level approach to a question and answer with the *Book of Changes*. For this exercise, we'll be working with a nontraditional divinatory method, though one inspired by twelfth-century ritual techniques.
>
> The day before the divination, thoroughly wash and sanitize a coin of your choice, then place it in a bed of salt overnight to consecrate it. You may consider lighting incense or a candle to set the space, but these are entirely optional.

. . . .

37. Buckland, *The Fortune-Telling Book*, 249–50; Cheung, *The Element Encyclopedia*, 315–16; Pickover, *Dreaming the Future*, 121–27.

When you're ready, hold the consecrated coin in hand and visualize an orb of white light illuminating at the crown of your head. This is your own inner light. Visualize the light now extending upward toward the heavens in a pillar, connecting you to Heaven.

Whisper, "I come before you with a question." Then, present your question.

Toss the single coin and note whether it is heads or tails. If it is heads, you have cast a yang line, drawn as a solid line. If it is tails, you have cast a yin line, drawn as a broken line. This is the bottommost line of your six-line hexagram.

Toss the coin a second time and draw the corresponding yin or yang line above the first. Toss the coin a third time and draw the corresponding yin or yang line above the second. Continue for a total of six coin tosses until you have cast a six-line hexagram. This is similar to a "page number" of a sacred text.

Turn to your favorite *Book of Changes* reference or, alternatively, to online resources to look up which hexagram you've divined. The response from Heaven is not necessarily going to come in the form of a grammatically structured sentence, but rather as an essence. The essence of this hexagram is the answer to your question.

Things to Consider

+ If you think this is difficult, it is. I Ching is a complicated system. Realize that it requires study.
+ If you really want to become proficient in this form of divination, realize that reading about it needs to be combined with the practical application of the tools.
+ If you become frustrated, be patient with yourself.

Rhapsodomancy (Verses and Prophecy)

Rhapsodomancy involves consulting a book of poetry or using song verses (can be done with the radio or a song playlist).[38]

Modern Exercise

Get lyrics of a song and write them on multiple pieces of paper (perhaps one line on each sheet of paper), shake them together inside a container, and draw one out for a message.

....
38. Buckland, *The Fortune-Telling Book*, 406; Cheung, *The Element Encyclopedia*, 610; Pickover, *Dreaming the Future*, 150.

Concentrate on your question to receive a message. You can also use the radio or titles of songs to receive a message.

Things to Consider

+ If you hear a lyric repeated word for word, take this as a strong indicator of a direct message.
+ If you hear something that means the same but is stated differently, do not dismiss it. Be sure to explore the message further and journal about it. Consider the nuances of the different-yet-similar messages.
+ If nothing seems to go together to form a message, pick one random lyric and write it down next to one line of poetry. Combine the two and see what message comes.

Stoicheomancy (Stoic and Prophecy)

Stoicheomancy, a branch of bibliomancy, is practiced by opening books written by Homer or Virgil to a random page and reading the passage to divine a message. Homer's writings, like *The Iliad* and *The Odyssey*, were considered by the Greeks to be sacred like the Bible or the Quran. However, Rome preferred Virgil's *The Aeneid*.[39]

Modern Exercise

Use *The Iliad*, *The Odyssey*, or *The Aeneid* for your stoicheomancy.

Things to Consider

+ If you know the stories, integrate them into your reading.
+ If you do not know the stories, do not worry about it; just intuit the message.
+ If you feel compelled to read more, read above and below where your eyes fell on the page.

. . . .
39. Buckland, *The Fortune-Telling Book*, 450–51.

Category 7: Burn, Fire, Smoke, and Ash

Observing fire and how objects burn has long been used for divination. There are many different methods for these types of readings.

Anthracomancy (Charcoal and Prophecy)

Anthracomancy, closely related to scrying, is divination by coals. *Anthrax*, in Greek, means "charcoal." There is a type of charcoal called *anthracite* that burns without producing a lot of smoke. Gazing into these smoldering coals makes for great divining. As they burn, they take on many shapes and then form into entirely different shapes.[40]

Modern Exercise

Roast a marshmallow over coal and then give a reading based on how the marshmallow heats up. Read the marshmallow, fire, and the ashes.

Things to Consider

- If the marshmallow lights up and cooks evenly and quickly, this implies an easy road ahead.
- If the marshmallow takes a while to light up but eventually roasts nicely, then this implies patience is needed.
- If the marshmallow falls off into the fire, this indicates trouble or obstacles ahead.

Botanomancy or Botomancy (Plant and Prophecy)

Botanomancy (a form of pyromancy) is divination with plants, such as the burning of various branches and herbs, most commonly vervain and briar. Diviners would carve messages into the branches and then burn them. The intuitive interpretation came by listening to the crackling sound when they burned and divining information from it. Information can also be gathered by reading the smoke.[41]

. . . .

40. Buckland, *The Fortune-Telling Book*, 17.
41. Buckland, *The Fortune-Telling Book*, 71–72; Cheung, *The Element Encyclopedia*, 84; Pickover, *Dreaming the Future*, 88.

Modern Exercise

Collect some branches or herbs. Start with only one type until you learn your tells. Place the branches or herbs into the fire and listen to the sounds they make as they burn.

Things to Consider

- If the branches or herbs make a lot of noise when they burn, it indicates action taking place.
- If the branches or herbs make little noise when they burn, this indicates little to no change.
- If the branches or herbs fail to light, this can indicate a solid resistance to any desire for help or interference.

Candles

Candle readings are based on the way a candle burns. The flame, smoke, ash, wax, and burn time may all be included in the reading.[42]

Modern Exercise

Light a candle. (Tapered candles work well.) Let your eyes gently fall on the burning flame. Watch how the candle burns. Notice the flame and the smoke. Later, you can even get a message from the patterns the wax makes. This is called *caromancy* (wax and prophecy).

Things to Consider

- If the flame is intense, the answer is favorable.
- If the flame is weak, the answer is not favorable.
- If the flame keeps going out for no apparent reason, danger is a possibility.

- - - - - - - - - - - - - - - - -

42. Buckland, *The Fortune-Telling Book*, 83–85; Cheung, *The Element Encyclopedia*, 97–98; Pickover, *Dreaming the Future*, 182.

Capnomancy, Captromancy (Fire/Smoke and Prophecy)

Capnomancy is the broad category of reading the smoke from fire. The smoke can be interpreted in many ways based on the intention set by the diviner. Often, herbs might be tossed into the fire to add another layer to the reading.[43]

Modern Exercise

Light a candle or start a safe fire in a cauldron or fireplace. Watch the smoke to give a message. As you advance, practice tossing various nontoxic herbs into the fire to provide more life to the smoke you interpret.

Things to Consider

+ If the smoke is weak, the subject of the question is growing weak, or the answer is no.
+ If the smoke is spiraling, changes or new beginnings are indicated.
+ If the smoke is in a zigzag formation, obstacles are on the horizon.

Causinomancy (Burn and Prophecy)

Causinomancy is a form of divination that involves interpreting messages by placing objects in a fire to see how quickly they burn. Sometimes, the ashes were also used to complete the reading.[44]

Modern Exercise

Start a safe fire in a cauldron or fireplace. Then, put a stick or some other safe object in the fire to see if it burns quickly or slowly.

Things to Consider

+ If the item burns quickly, things will move quickly. This can be positive or negative, depending on your intent.

. . . .

43. Buckland, *The Fortune-Telling Book*, 287; Pickover, *Dreaming the Future*, 85.
44. Buckland, *The Fortune-Telling Book*, 95; Pickover, *Dreaming the Future*, 182.

+ If the item burns slowly, things will move slowly. Depending on your intent, this can be positive or negative.
+ If you see the ashes make formations or shapes, you can read those also.

Ceromancy (Wax and Prophecy)

Ceromancy involves heating wax in a brass bowl until it turns to liquid. The liquid is then poured into another container of cold water to divine the wax's shape.[45]

Modern Exercise

Tip a candle over a water-filled bowl. Allow the wax to drip into the water. Then, read your message based on the shapes and patterns of the wax. You can also touch the cooled wax to see if you receive a message. Colored candles will also add another layer to your reading.

Things to Consider

+ If the wax all clumps together, you can read that as one big issue, or you may want to melt your wax again.
+ If the wax forms clusters, observe how many are present and where they are related.
+ If you see pictures or symbols in the wax, read and relay those.

Daphnomancy (Laurel and Prophecy)

Daphnomancy is divination by burning laurel branches (bay leaves) and reading how they burn. If the wreaths crackled as they burned, it was a good sign, while silence was a bad sign. How fast the wreaths burned was also considered.[46]

Modern Exercise

This exercise is good for determining if something is positive or negative. You can write your question on the bay leaf. Bay leaves are historically associated with victory. Place a

45. Buckland, *The Fortune-Telling Book*, 106; Cheung, *The Element Encyclopedia*, 102; Pickover, *Dreaming the Future*, 187.
46. Buckland, *The Fortune-Telling Book*, 174; Pickover, *Dreaming the Future*, 190.

bay leaf into a contained and safe fire. Watch how it burns, but more importantly, listen to how it burns.

Things to Consider
+ If the bay leaf burns quickly, this may represent a swift victory.
+ If the bay leaf burns slowly, this may result in a loss.
+ If the bay leaf makes a lot of noise, this may represent something that is demanding the querent's attention.

Knissomancy (Vapor and Prophecy)
Knissomancy (also known as libanomancy) is divination based on incense. Most ritualistic ceremonies involve some incense. The smoke is observed for a message.[47]

Modern Exercise
Light a stick of incense such as frankincense. Observe the smoke characteristics from the incense for your message.

Things to Consider
+ If the incense smoke is thick, it may indicate heaviness or difficulty seeing one's way through to a resolution.
+ If the incense smoke is thin or wispy, this may represent a situation that is either weak or easy.
+ If the incense produces little to no smoke, it may indicate no activity or a delay. If the smoke is suddenly extinguished, danger may be indicated.

Lampadomancy (Light and Prophecy)
Divination by flame from an oil lamp. The smoke, color, wick, flickering, and anything that could be observed would be considered in the reading.[48]

. . . .

47. Buckland, *The Fortune-Telling Book*, 287; Cheung, *The Element Encyclopedia*, 368.
48. Buckland, *The Fortune-Telling Book*, 290; Cheung, *The Element Encyclopedia*, 378; Pickover, *Dreaming the Future*, 193–94.

Modern Exercise

Light a tiki torch. Observe the smoke, color, wick, flickering, and anything else that you would like considered in the reading. The type of oil used might have played a part in this; however, this can also be said of candles that we read today. Some wicks and candle wax are made to burn cleaner than others. As in every reading, it falls on the diviner to consider these things if they feel they are essential to the reading.

Things to Consider

+ If the smoke appears heavy, this may indicate strength and that the fire is doing its work.
+ If there isn't much smoke, this may indicate weakness and the fire is not working.
+ If a specific color or colors appear, interpret them using the chakras or the aura colors.

Libanomancy (Frankincense and Prophecy)

Libanomancy is divination based on reading the smoke or ash from incense. Most ritualistic ceremonies involve some incense. With libanomancy, the diviner observes and reads the smoke or ash from the incense. (See also knissomancy.)

Modern Exercise

While libanomancy involves reading smoke or ash, we will consider the ash reading in this modern exercise. Place a stick of incense on an incense holder. Once it has burned itself out, read the ashes that remain.

Things to Consider

+ If the ash is curling upward, it is a good sign.
+ If the ash is curling downward, it is an unfortunate sign.
+ If sparks are produced, good news will come soon.

Category 8: Cards

Divination using various forms of cards is a broad topic that can fill books. Here, we will touch on some of the systems associated with card divination. For deeper study, see the additional resources in the back of this book.

Cartomancy (Paper and Prophecy)

Cartomancy is an ancient practice of divining with tarot cards or regular playing cards. The practice of reading with tarot cards is also referred to as *taromancy*. With playing cards, there are four suits—hearts, clubs, diamonds, and spades. Hearts represent emotions and love. Clubs represent communication and achieving goals. Diamonds represent everyday matters, including finances and work. Spades represent obstacles and challenges. In tarot, there are four suits known as *pips*.[49] (See tarot for tarot cartomancy.)

Modern Exercise

Get a deck of playing cards. The diamonds represent finances, the clubs represent communication and goal achievement, the hearts represent emotions and relationships, and the spades represent essential matters including obstacles and challenges. While shuffling the cards, ask a question. Then, randomly choose a predetermined number of cards or whatever comes to mind as you begin. Notice what number is on the card and which suit it is. Aces represent new beginnings, twos represent choices, threes represent harmony, fours represent stability, fives represent change, sixes represent growth, sevens represent that time is of the essence, eights represent change, nines represent surprises, and tens represent travel.

Things to Consider

+ If you interpret the number differently than described above, go with your intuition.
+ If you have multiple cards with seemingly conflicting meanings, such as harmony (three) and change (five), consider how harmony and change could be interrelated.
+ If you have three cards, all of which are one suit, this may indicate a strong emphasis in that area.

. . . .
49. Buckland, *The Fortune-Telling Book*, 87–94; Cheung, *The Element Encyclopedia*, 99; Pickover, *Dreaming the Future*, 149.

Oracle Decks

Oracle decks consist of cards that usually have an image, word(s), or both on them. Unlike tarot or Lenormand cards, oracle cards do not adhere to any fixed system of reading or meaning. A guidebook is often included with the deck that explains the art or images and some possible interpretations.

Modern Exercise

Think of a question or request a general message. If you do not have oracle cards, you can get a coffee table book, magazine, or random photograph online or even go to a museum to view the artwork as a large oracle card. This helps you learn to use oracle cards in almost any environment. Receive the message by letting impressions come into your mind's eye. Read or interpret the image and relay the reading to the querent.

Things to Consider

+ If your mind goes blank, simply describe what you see on the card.
+ If you are overloaded with messages, let your eye fall to one image on the card to begin.
+ If you disagree with a word written on the card, you may choose not to integrate it into the reading and relaying of your message or you may dig deeper to see if there is more to the message than at first glance. You can cover up the word, read the message without the word, add the word into your initial message, or relay the entire message to the querent.

Taromancy

Taromancy is the practice of reading with tarot cards. There are seventy-eight cards: twenty-two major arcana cards and fifty-six minor arcana cards (fourteen cups, fourteen swords, fourteen wands, and fourteen pentacles). The twenty-two major arcana cards represent archetypes and significant life occurrences. The fifty-six minor arcana represent daily matters, are numbered ace through ten, and have four court cards in each suit. A page, knight, queen, and king typically represent the court cards. The cups represent emotions, relationships, and love. The wands represent action, vitality, and creative projects. The pentacles represent everyday matters, including wealth and health. The swords represent communication, conflict, and logic. (See also Cartomancy.)

Modern Exercise

Start with the traditional deck of Rider-Waite-Smith tarot cards. Ask a question while shuffling the cards. Draw three cards representing the past, present, and future. Read the cards based on your knowledge of the cards and your intuition. Some great books on tarot are listed in the resource section at the end of this book.

Things to Consider

+ If all three cards are major arcana, this indicates significant life decisions or events.
+ If all three cards are of the same suit, such as cups, this emphasizes emotions and relationships.
+ If all three cards have the same number, this is a great way to incorporate numerology. (See also Numerology.)

Kipper Cards

Kipper cards are a thirty-six-card fortune-telling deck from nineteenth-century Germany. Each card shows a situation in which the reader can find themselves and quickly identify and interpret the future.[50]

Modern Exercise

Cut out or print out photos to represent the Kipper cards. Pick situational photos. Put the photos on paper like a comic book to fit a situation.

Things to Consider

+ If people are in the cards, note which direction they are facing. Left is the past, forward is the present, and right is the future.
+ If there are cards that predominantly relate to emotions, consider where they are positioned in relation to the other cards.
+ If the cards are predominately places, consider whether these are actual places versus metaphorical.

. . . .
50. Toni Puhle, *The Card Geek's Guide to Kipper Cards* (pub. by author, 2017), 2.

Lenormand

Marie-Anne Adelaide Lenormand of France learned many different divination modalities before creating her Lenormand cards. She was a prolific diviner and was said to have predicted Napoleon's rise to the throne of France. The original Lenormand decks consisted of thirty-six cards, but ironically, she never used them. A number, picture, and title were depicted on each card. The number on the card could also tie into playing cards. The numbers included ace through king (1–14) in each of the four suits.[51] (See cartomancy and numerology.)

Modern Day Exercise

There are many varieties of Lenormand cards today. Get thirty-six blank index cards and number the cards 1–36. Then, write the following words on each card:

1. Rider—Nine of Hearts
2. Clover—Six of Diamonds
3. Ship—Ten of Spades
4. House—King of Hearts
5. Tree—Seven of Hearts
6. Clouds—King of Clubs
7. Snake—Queen of Clubs
8. Coffin—Nine of Diamonds
9. Bouquet—Queen of Spades
10. Scythe—Jack of Diamonds
11. Whip—Jack of Clubs
12. Birds—Seven of Diamonds
13. Child—Jack of Spades
14. Fox—Nine of Clubs
15. Bear—Ten of Clubs
16. Star—Six of Hearts
17. Stork—Queen of Hearts
18. Dog—Ten of Hearts

. . . .

51. Alexandre Musruck, *The Art of Lenormand Reading: Decoding Powerful Messages* (Schiffer Publishing, 2018), 133–46.

19. Tower—Six of Spades
20. Garden—Eight of Spades
21. Mountain—Eight of Clubs
22. Crossroad—Queen of Diamonds
23. Mice—Seven of Clubs
24. Heart—Jack of Hearts
25. Ring—Ace of Clubs
26. Book—Ten of Diamonds
27. Letter—Seven of Spades
28. Man—Ace of Hearts
29. Woman—Ace of Spades
30. Lily—King of Spades
31. Sun—Ace of Diamonds
32. Moon—Eight of Hearts
33. Key—Eight of Diamonds
34. Fish—King of Diamonds
35. Anchor—Nine of Spades
36. Cross—Six of Clubs

Alternatively, use a synonym for the title if you are inclined. Then, draw or find a corresponding image to cut out and put on your Lenormand set. Also, add the corresponding playing card affiliated with each title. Making the cards and practicing with them instills the system in the minds of many who learn kinesthetically. Alternatively, you could buy a deck of playing cards and write the word on the corresponding card.

Things to Consider

- If you are familiar with tarot, note that the cards do not necessarily mean the same as in Lenormand.
- If you draw two cards, the first might represent a noun (person, place, or thing) and the second might represent an adjective (describes or modifies the noun).
- If you want to progress to reading yes-or-no questions, you need to know the cards' meanings; some are positive, some are negative, and some are neutral. Then, draw an uneven number of cards, such as three, and ascertain whether

there are more positive or negative cards. Alternatively, if a playing card is inset on each of your Lenormand cards, determine whether there are more black or red playing cards. If there are more red cards, your answer would be yes. If there are more black cards, your answer would be no.

Category 9: Casting

Casting, tossing, bouncing, or throwing items has long been used for divination. This category can be made into some very interesting modern exercises.

Astragalomancy, Cleromancy, and Cubomancy (Vertebrae and Prophecy)

Divination with dice that have letters or numbers was quite popular in the past. In ancient times, especially in Mesopotamia, diviners used knucklebones, which may be the oldest game known to humankind. Eventually, different types of dice with various numbers of sides were used all over the world. The Dalai Lama uses dice to make important decisions. There were varying ways to read with dice. One such method was to draw a circle and throw the dice in the circle to see where they landed. Any dice that rolled outside of the circle were not counted in the message. The numbers on the remaining dice were added together and numerology was used for the reading. Another option was to use preset questions with preset answers that corresponded to the numbers.[52]

Following are some suggested number meanings of dice totals when three are thrown. Any die going out of bounds is not counted:

1. A positive answer to the question asked.
2. A negative answer to the question asked.
3. Good fortune is indicated.
4. Difficulties are indicated.
5. A positive new relationship is indicated.
6. Show gratitude for someone you may be taking for granted.
7. Someone near, who is not to be trusted, may betray you.
8. Be careful not to become the scapegoat for things that are not your fault.
9. Successful relationships are indicated.

. . . .
52. Buckland, *The Fortune-Telling Book*, 25–26, 153; Pickover, *Dreaming the Future*, 133.

10. Success and new opportunities are indicated.

11. A separation is indicated.

12. Good news is indicated.

13. Do not proceed. Something better will arise.

14. A positive new friendship that could evolve into more than friendship.

15. Follow the rules.

16. An unplanned trip is indicated.

17. Be willing to pivot.

18. Your wish will be granted.

Modern Exercise

Start with one die. Roll it onto a sheet of paper where you have written words, colors, numbers, or anything to which you want an answer. If, for instance, you want to see what color of car suits you best, draw colors on your paper, then roll the die onto the paper. If it lands off the paper, then it could mean you should not get a new car at this time. If it lands on the paper, what color did it land on and what is the number on the die? Let's say it landed on blue with the number two. You might have two choices of blue cars that you will decide between. Another alternative is that you might need to wait two months before buying the blue car. It is all about setting your intention as to what the numbers mean before rolling the die.

Things to Consider

- If you use numbers, decide on the meaning of each number, then apply them to all your readings. Consistency helps in reading and relaying messages.
- If you use letters, set your intention before rolling as to what the letters will represent.
- If you use colors, remember to keep it simple using the Three C's. Never change your original intention. Stick to the interpretation even though it might seem like the reading is flip-flopped in some way and needs rearranging.

Charm Casting (Charms)

Casting or throwing things has long been used for divination. In the case of charm casting, you use charms as your tool. Professional diviner Carrie Paris notes, "There are several ways to cast and read charms and I always say that your way is the best way. Charm casting is also one of the best user-friendly divining tools we have, and this is partly because most casting kits aren't tied to an established esoteric system. In other words, any tchotchke, small bric-a-brac or miscellaneous item can be used when we assign meaning to them."[53]

Modern Exercise

You can easily get sets of charms online, or perhaps you have collected them. Toss a small handful, perhaps three to five, on a scarf, table, the ground, or any flat surface. If you have preset boundaries, such as a scarf or piece of velvet, you can decide before you toss or cast the charms what certain sections of the boundaries mean. Once you predetermine how you are going to read where the charms fall, toss three to five charms on the cloth. Then, integrate the meanings of the charms with their placement on the cloth.

Things to Consider

- If the charm goes out of bounds, then perhaps that means no or not now, or it could mean that the particular charm is not relevant to the situation.
- If the charms fall all together or in a cluster, it may indicate those charms should be read together.
- If a charm is removed from the others, it may indicate something that is from the past or the future that is affecting the situation. (To the left is the past; to the right is the future.)

Dominomancy (Domino and Prophecy)

Divination using the numbers on dominoes. They are read much like you read dice, and you can also use them to read for multiple querents at a time. There are different ways to

---

53. Buckland, *The Fortune-Telling Book*, 45–46; Cheung, *The Element Encyclopedia*, 110; Carrie Paris, email interview, June 6, 2022.

divine with dominoes, including single-tile draws or spreads similar to tarot, such as the past-present-future spread.[54]

The general interpretations of the individual suit values are as follows (make sure you read both halves of the domino):

- 0: The querent (person) asking the question
- 1: Travel
- 2: Relatives, loved ones, and close friends
- 3: Love
- 4: Money
- 5: Work and career
- 6: Fortune and luck

Modern Exercise

Lay domino tiles face down and shuffle. Randomly draw one or as many tiles as you have questions. Read the tiles left to right and look up interpretations. There are preset meanings to the number combinations, but you can also create your own system.

Here are some general interpretations of the individual tiles. You can look up the rest or make up your own.

- 0–0: Trouble or serious problems will strike unexpectedly.
- 1–2: A visit from, or a journey with, an old friend.
- 2–3: An outstanding debt will be honored.
- 3–4: A happy affair, marriage, or love union.
- 4–5: Good fortune awaits in the near future.
- 5–6: A change of employment or a good day with someone close.
- 6–6: A happy and fortunate future.

....

54. Buckland, *The Fortune-Telling Book*, 185–88; Raymond Buckland, *The Buckland Gypsies' Domino Divination Deck* (Llewellyn Publications, 1999).

Things to Consider

+ If you are overthinking it, set it aside for a while.
+ If you are familiar with numerology, integrate it into your readings.
+ If you want to totally channel the meanings, do so. The intention you set and practice with is what will matter in the reading.

Favomancy (Bean and Prophecy)

Favomancy is a form of divination that was used in Russia and Bosnia. I learned this divination method while visiting my grandmother's farm. It involves beans and interpreting the patterns into which the beans fall when cast. Ask your question, cast the beans, and read and relay the information you see.

Modern Exercise

Gather three light-colored beans. With paint or a marker, color one side of each bean. Establish your own system for interpreting patterns.

Things to Consider

+ If there is one dark side up, this could indicate a positive outcome.
+ If there are two dark sides up, this could indicate a neutral outcome.
+ If there are three dark sides up, this could indicate a negative outcome.

Runecasting (Secret, Mystery)

Runes are ancient Proto-Germanic sigils that were thought to possess divination properties. There are different types of runes, such as Germanic Futhark or Elder Futhark, and Witch's Runes. Runes typically have sets of twenty-four to twenty-five small stones or even crystals with symbols inscribed on them. Runes can stand alone as a symbol or letter, or they can be placed together to spell out a word.[55]

. . . .

55. Buckland, *The Fortune-Telling Book*, 416–17; Cheung. *The Element Encyclopedia*, 618–19; Pickover, *Dreaming the Future*, 155–57, 178, 412–13.

Modern Exercise

Concentrate on a question, reach into a container of runes, and pull three runes. Read them to answer a question or issue. You can also turn the runes face down and intuitively draw three and read them based on your knowledge of reading runes. A few basics of runes to consider from the Elder Futhark:

ᚠ (Fehu): Cattle or moveable wealth—wealth and abundance

ᚢ (Uruz): Ox—strength, energy, and good health

ᚦ (Thurisaz): Mallet, giant—associated with Thor because it looks like Thor's hammer (Mjolnir), chaos, pain, strife, and defense

ᚨ (Ansuz): Message—associated with Odin and his wisdom, communication, insight, and answers

ᚱ (Raidho): Journey, wheel—travel, movement, proactive, and your control of life

ᚲ (Kenaz): Ulcer or torch—visions, creativity, transformation, enlightenment, and insight

ᚷ (Gebo): Gift—love, harmony, friendship, joy, luck, and fortune

ᚹ (Wunjo): Joy or pleasure—joy, pleasure, good times, closeness to Divine, belonging, success

ᚺ (Hagalaz): Hail—destruction, confusion, miscommunication, change, uncontrolled forces

ᚾ (Naudhiz): Need or distress—necessity, anxiety, restrictions, change, survival, and patience needed

ᛁ (Isaz): Ice—blockages, frustrations, need for inward reflection, cycle, conclusion, growth

ᛃ (Jera): Year, time, and harvest—hard work, patience, and abundance

ᛇ (Eihwaz): Yew tree—protection, magic, transition, life's cycle, connection

ᛈ (Perthro): Destiny—mystery, chance, play, and spiritual evolution

ᛉ (Algiz): Protection or guard—protection, instincts, safety, and comfort in surroundings

ᛊ (Sowilo): Sun—optimism, vitality, good fortune, and energy

↑ (Tiwaz): God of war pre-Odin—warrior, victory, success, and self-sacrifice

ᛒ (Berkana): Birch tree—fertility, springtime, growth, regeneration, and new beginnings

ᛗ (Ehwaz): Horse—momentum, progress, harmony, trust, and partnerships

ᛗ (Mannaz): Mankind—humanity, compassion, cooperation, innocence, and assistance

ᚱ (Laguz): Water—water rituals, voyages, confusion, intuitive guidance, and inner awareness

◇ (Ingwaz): Fertility god—peace, rest, and nature connection

ᛞ (Dagaz): Day—transformation, hope, release, happiness, and certainty

ᛟ (Othila): Homeland—family, safety, increase, and abundance

Things to Consider

+ If you put the runes in a line, it may indicate past, present, and future or the timeline of a story.
+ If you cast the runes and two are together and one is by itself, it may indicate the two are to be read together and the outlier may be a distant influence on the situation.
+ If you cast the runes and one or more are upside down, it may indicate that these are things yet to be revealed or are hidden from the querent.

Category 10: Celestial Bodies

For ages, humankind has looked to the skies for answers and messages. This is an extremely broad topic, so please see the additional resources at the back of this book if you want to learn more about these fascinating forms of divination.

Astrology (Celestial)

Astrology is an ancient system of divination still in use today. It considers where the planets were positioned when you were born to determine different aspects of your life. Many cultures throughout time have studied the stars: Babylonia, China, India, North

America, South America, Tibet, and more.[56] I highly recommend you study astrology. My favorite astrologers are Monte Farber and Theresa Reed. Their content is listed in the additional resources section at the end of this book. The reason I recommend these teachers is because they break down astrology so that it is easier to learn. Although they are highly trained and scholarly, they can teach to every level of student.

The Houses of Astrology:
1. Self
2. Value and possessions
3. Communication
4. Family and home
5. Pleasure
6. Health
7. Partnerships
8. Transformation
9. Purpose
10. Social status
11. Friendships
12. The house of the unconscious

Dates for Zodiac Sun Signs:
- **Aries:** March 21–April 19, the ram, cardinal, fire, ruled by Mars in the first house.
  - *Pros:* adventurous, ambitious, leader
  - *Cons:* impulsive, impatient, self-oriented[57]
- **Taurus:** April 20–May 20, the bull, earth, fixed, ruled by Venus in the second house.
  - *Pros:* determined, reliable, practical
  - *Cons:* stubborn, possessive, resentful

· · · · · · · · · · · · · · · · ·

56. Buckland, *The Fortune-Telling Book*, 29–31; Cheung, *The Element Encyclopedia*, 38–43; Pickover, *Dreaming the Future*, 104–108.
57. Keep in mind that cons are often the extreme of pros and vice versa. This applies to all signs.

- **Gemini:** May 21–June 20, the twins, air, mutable, ruled by Mercury in the third house.
  - *Pros:* versatile, witty, intelligent
  - *Cons:* scattered, superficial, changeable
- **Cancer:** June 21–July 22, the crab, water, cardinal, ruled by the Moon in the fourth house.
  - *Pros:* compassionate, nurturing, intuitive
  - *Cons:* moody, clingy, overemotional
- **Leo:** July 23–August 22, the lion, fire, fixed, ruled by the Sun in the fifth house.
  - *Pros:* loyal, creative, attention seeking
  - *Cons:* lazy, egocentric, demanding
- **Virgo:** August 23–September 22, the virgin, earth, mutable, ruled by Mercury in the sixth house.
  - *Pros:* meticulous, practical, skilled
  - *Cons:* worrier, overthinker, perfectionist
- **Libra:** September 23–October 22, scales, air, cardinal, ruled by Venus in the seventh house.
  - *Pros:* diplomatic, easygoing, partner oriented
  - *Cons:* flirtatious, indecisive, gullible
- **Scorpio:** October 23–November 21, the scorpion, water, fixed, ruled by Pluto in the eighth house.
  - *Pros:* determined, passionate, magnetic
  - *Cons:* resentful, jealous, secretive
- **Sagittarius:** November 22–December 21, the archer, fire, mutable, ruled by Jupiter in the ninth house.
  - *Pros:* optimistic, straightforward, honest
  - *Cons:* careless, tactless, overly philosophical
- **Capricorn:** December 22–January 19, the goat, earth, cardinal, ruled by Saturn in the tenth house.
  - *Pros:* realistic, tenacious, ambitious
  - *Cons:* pessimistic, rigid, miserly

- **Aquarius:** January 20–February 18, the water bearer, air, fixed, ruled by Uranus in the eleventh house.
    - *Pros:* humanitarian, inventive, eccentric
    - *Cons:* unpredictable, detached, unemotional
- **Pisces:** February 19–March 20, the fish, water, mutable, ruled by Neptune in the twelfth house.
    - *Pros:* intuitive, compassionate, selfless
    - *Cons:* escapist, weak-willed, unfocused

Modern Exercise

I highly recommend an independent study of this divination method. Some great books are listed in the resources. The best thing to remember is to not get overwhelmed. It is very easy to access a free app on the internet. TimePassages is one such app that is a great starting place. To get the most accurate astrological information, know your date, county, country, and exact time of birth. If you don't relate to your Sun sign, try reading your Moon sign and rising or ascending sign. When looking at your chart, notice there are twelve parts, as noted in the houses listed above.

Things to Consider

- If the planets are spread out somewhat evenly throughout the chart, this could indicate someone who can operate in a balanced manner and has many interests in life. However, they may seem somewhat scattered.
- If the majority of the planets fall above the horizon (houses 7–12), this may indicate a person who is an extrovert. If the majority of the planets fall below the horizon (houses 1–6), it may indicate someone who is an introvert.
- If the majority of the planets fall to the left of the vertical line (slices 10–12 and 1–3), this may indicate a person more comfortable with being self-sufficient, independent, and the initiator of actions meant to improve, strengthen, and defend their position in life. If the majority of the planets fall to the right of the vertical line (slices 4–9), this may indicate a person more comfortable with teamwork, learning from the experiences of others, and allowing things to happen at their own pace and in their own time.

Category 11: Colormancy

As mentioned in part 1 of this book, understanding colors as they relate to aura, colors and chakras, and colors as they relate to moods is one of the best ways to improve your psychic knowingness.

Modern Exercise

See exercises in part 1 of this book.

Things to Consider

See corresponding Things to Consider under the exercises in part 1 of this book.

Category 12: Crystals

Crystals are both beautiful and fascinating. Many people ask for different ways to use them. Using crystals for divination is not only enjoyable but also leads to accurate information.

Crystallomancy

Crystals have been used for ages for their various properties, such as protection and healing. Crystals were also placed in prehistoric tombs in some cultures.[58]

Modern Exercise

Choose seven crystals that will easily fit in the palm of your hand. Choose one color for each of the seven primary chakras: red, orange, yellow, green, blue, indigo, and violet. Cast them on a flat surface. The surface should be labeled with the chakras. Observe where the various crystals land. Does the green land near the heart chakra, or did it even land in bounds? Begin explaining what you observe, and this will begin to turn into a reading. There are many ways you can divine with crystals. You may know the meaning of the crystal, but even if you don't, you can look at the shape and color of the crystal and determine a reading based on that information alone.

. . . .
58. Buckland, *The Fortune-Telling Book*, 151; Pickover, *Dreaming the Future*, 193.

Things to Consider

+ If the majority of the crystals fall in a particular house (see category 10), this would indicate an emphasis in this area.
+ If you note which crystals land in certain houses, you can get a lot of information just from that observation. For example, a rose quartz in the fourth house would indicate love for family and home.
+ If there are patterns or clusters, take note of them in conjunction with the crystals in the group.

Lithomancy (Stone and Prophecy)

Lithomancy is reading crystals. There is not a recorded history on lithomancy, but there are several known ways to read crystals. One way is to place a black cloth on a flat surface and see what color reflection the crystals cast on the cloth. Another method is to cast thirteen stones associated with astrology and matters of life. Then, you interpret where they land on the cloth (you could use a round cloth such as an astrology chart). It is important to set your intention ahead of time regarding what the stones mean and what each side of the cloth means.

The traditional thirteen lithomancy stones of the British Isles include love, magic, fortune, home, life, news, Mercury, Venus, Mars, Jupiter, Saturn, Sun, and Moon. You can choose which stones to use, but try to keep them similar in size and shape. My personal collection includes love/rose quartz, magic/labradorite, fortune/green aventurine, home/tiger's eye, life/carnelian, news/Picasso jasper, Mercury/amazonite, Venus/jade, Mars/bloodstone, Jupiter/amethyst, Saturn/jet, Sun/sunstone, and Moon/moonstone.[59]

Modern Exercise

Get a cloth or roll of butcher paper. Draw a large circle and then divide it into the twelve houses of astrology. Label the house numbers, and perhaps put a little about what each house stands for in its respective area. You can also buy these cloths premade for a reasonable price. Choose thirteen crystals to cast. Hold the crystals in the palm of your hand and then drop them onto the cloth. You can do all kinds of readings with the astrology houses. Look for where they land, compare the house meaning to the crystal

....
59. Buckland, *The Fortune-Telling Book*, 301; Cheung, *The Element Encyclopedia*, 401; Pickover, *Dreaming the Future*, 136.

meaning, check to see if they are in clusters or spread out more evenly. You can also compare the casting to your own chart or that of the querent's.

Things to Consider

+ Look at the astrological house meanings in category 10 above. If the majority of the crystals fall in a particular house, this would indicate an emphasis in this area.
+ Note which crystals land in certain houses. If a rose quartz fell in the fourth house, it would indicate love for family and home.
+ Observe patterns such as clusters and the meaning of the crystals in those clusters.

Spheromancy (Sphere and Prophecy)

Spheromancy is a form of crystal ball reading. In the sixteenth century, Queen Elizabeth I sought messages from Dr. John Dee. Dee received his information by working with his associate and medium Edward Kelley. Kelley went into a semi-trance and divined what he saw in the crystal ball.[60]

Modern Exercise

Hold a crystal ball in your hand so that you can see into the ball. Focus on your question if you have one. Soften your eyes as you gaze at the crystal. Turn the crystal slowly in your hand and observe what you see. Take your time and let any of your clairs wash over you. Say or write down anything that comes to mind. Everything can be a message.

Things to Consider

+ If you see something that forms a shape, such as a face, see what message comes to you.
+ If you want to utilize the sphere to its full advantage, turn the sphere in all different directions while requesting information.
+ If you want to see into the ball easily, it is best to use a clear quartz as the crystal ball.

. . . .

60. Buckland, *The Fortune-Telling Book*, 151–52, 446–47; Cheung, *The Element Encyclopedia*, 135; Pickover, *Dreaming the Future*, 194–96.

Category 13: Dowsing and Scrying

This section is about discovering information through specific practices that feature tools such as sticks and mirrors.

Dowsing

Dowsing is a form of divination using a stick or twig shaped like a fork, a rod, or a pendulum to locate or find things. (See part 2, chapter 1 for more information on pendulums.) Dowsing was originally used to find water, minerals, oil, and—you guessed it—criminals. Martin Luther declared the rods devil's work; hence the term *water witching* was used. Rods or pendulums can be used to locate anything and to answer questions.[61]

Modern Exercise

Have someone hide an item outside or inside, or you can hide it for someone. Using a forked stick, copper rods, or a pendulum, begin to ask to be led to the item. When you feel a small tug, follow the direction. You can even ask if you are getting warmer, and the tool will give you a clear yes or no, especially if you have calibrated the tool ahead of time. Calibrate your pendulum by seeing if it swings vertically or horizontally when you ask it to show you yes or no. You can also dictate what each direction means.

Things to Consider

- If the rods are crossing, you may have arrived at what you were trying to find.
- If the rods or pendulum are moving, follow the direction.
- If the rods or pendulum are not moving, this may be the area you are meant to explore.

Catoptromancy and Enoptromancy (Mirror and Prophecy)

Catoptromancy is divination with a mirror and was practiced in ancient Rome and Egypt. Later, young girls would look in a mirror at the moon's reflection and count how long before a cloud or a bird passed by the moon. The longer the wait for something to pass

....

61. Buckland, *The Fortune-Telling Book*, 188–89; Cheung, *The Element Encyclopedia*, 163–65; Pickover, *Dreaming the Future*, 198.

by the moon, the longer the girls were said to have to wait for marriage. Looking into a mirror lit by moonlight would also reveal the face of a lover.[62]

Modern Exercise

There are lots of misconceptions and fear-inducing distractions related to mirrors. It is often alleged that a mirror is a portal. Well, let's get this straight—big deal, every one of us is a portal. A mirror is no more a portal than you are. Sit in front of a mirror and see if you recognize yourself. Do a short breathing meditation while softly gazing into the mirror. Are you connected with the shell of a body staring back at you? From a very young age, I felt a separation from my true self and my body.

Things to Consider

+ If you look in the mirror and see a stranger, remember you are in a temporary costume of sorts.
+ If you look in the mirror and are critical of what you see, the message may mean that you need to work in this area for self-growth.
+ If you look in the mirror and sense other energies staring back at you, this could indicate ancestors or spirit guides trying to communicate with you.

Category 14: Dreams

The category of dreams is broad. We will not cover everything about dreams, but they need to be explored because we spend much of our life sleeping. If we begin to pay attention to our dreams, we are potentially tapping into a source of great information about our unconscious self. While there are many books that define what certain dreams mean, you are the best source for the meaning. I find it more important to journal about my dreams than to rely on others for meaning. The more you track your dreams, the more you will understand their meanings and usefulness in your waking hours.

Oneiromancy (Dreams and Prophecy)

Over five thousand years ago, the Mesopotamians studied dreams. Clearly, the ancients realized the messages that dreams can impart. Dreams have continued to influence us,

....

62. Buckland, *The Fortune-Telling Book*, 94–95; Pickover, *Dreaming the Future*, 192.

whether we realize it or not. In an average lifetime, twenty-five years are spent asleep, with thousands and thousands of dreams. Sigmund Freud called dreams "the royal road to a knowledge of the unconscious."[63] With so much time spent asleep and dreaming, it only makes sense that our dreams should be tracked for meaning. Most dreams occur during rapid eye movement (REM) sleep and are usually in color. It is unusual to dream in smells or taste due to the REM brainwave states of theta and high-frequency gamma.

With practice, you will begin to notice patterns in your dreams that are almost like your tells. Although you may be tempted to look up what your dreams mean, first try to see if there is a pattern to your dreams that seems to convey a message to you. Your dreams are significant, so begin to write your dreams down in your handbook. Write down every detail you recall even if it seems insignificant. Try and associate the dream with some phase of your life. Make sure you note how the dream makes you feel.[64]

Modern Exercise

It is particularly important to keep a dream journal and pen by your bed if you want to begin studying dreams. Practice reading (interpreting) a few dream symbols: bridge, chair, door, ladder, rainbow, snake, and toothache.

Things to Consider

+ If you want to interpret your own dreams, a journal by your bed helps you to not dismiss or forget details. Consider color, animals, sound, and overall environment. Are you floating or grounded? Are you participating or observing?
+ If you have reoccurring dreams, you are not alone. The nine most common dreams are being attacked or chased, being late, being naked, loved ones dying, falling, flying, school, losing your teeth, and sex. These may indicate current fears or past traumas that are trying to get your attention.
+ If a dream wakes you up, note how the dream made you feel.

. . . .

63. Sigmund Freud, *The Interpretation of Dreams*, ed. and trans. James Strachey (Avon Books, 1965), 647.
64. Buckland, *The Fortune-Telling Book*, 344–47; Cheung, *The Element Encyclopedia*, 167–71; Pickover, *Dreaming the Future*, 90–91.

Category 15: Food and Baking

Since food is necessary to sustain life, it is no surprise that various types of divination involve using food.

Aleuromancy (Flour and Divination)

Aleuromancy is named for the Greek word for flour. This was the predecessor to fortune cookies. Messages would be written and baked into small cakes. Another alternative was to see the shapes left after the water and flour mixture was emptied from a bowl.[65]

Modern Exercise

Take small slips of paper and write messages on them. They can be affirmations or messages that answer questions. Wrap cookie dough around them and bake them. You can find numerous recipes and instructions for making online. Notify the person eating the cookie that there is a message inside. You could also take what remains in the bowl and read those shapes.

Things to Consider

+ If all of the messages are positive affirmations, begin to collect them.
+ If there are words of warning in the messages, know that you can change the form of energy and course correct.
+ If you put a collection of messages together, you can mix and rearrange the words and see what randomly comes together for a new reading.

Alomancy and Halomancy (Salt and Prophecy)

Alomancy involves tossing or casting salt into the air and observing how it falls and the shapes that are made. Like many other types of divination, the salt may also be placed in a bowl of shallow water and watched to see how it disintegrates.[66]

. . . .

65. Buckland, *The Fortune-Telling Book*, 14; Cheung, *The Element Encyclopedia*, 17; Pickover, *Dreaming the Future*, 185.
66. Buckland, *The Fortune-Telling Book*, 14; Cheung, *The Element Encyclopedia*, 17; Pickover, *Dreaming the Future*, 182, 185.

Modern Exercise

Simply place salt into a shallow bowl of water and observe how it disintegrates. You can also look and see how the salt behaves in the water and draw conclusions from that. Another way to divine with salt is to not use water but to toss or sprinkle the salt onto a glue sheet. Then, interpret the patterns, symbols, and images.

Things to Consider

- If the salt disintegrates quickly, it means that things will happen more quickly.
- If it disintegrates slowly, it means that things will happen more slowly.
- If it sticks to the sides, it may not be ready for action.

Alphitomancy (Barley and Prophecy)

Barley or wheat was made into a cake, and the diviner watched the person eating the cake to determine if they were guilty. A sign of guilt was a horrible stomachache. However, the Greeks also used them as offerings for harvest.[67]

Modern Exercise

Bake or buy cakes in three different flavors. Each flavor should have a preset meaning assigned to it. Read based on how much they eat and if they like it.

Things to Consider

- If the querent prefers a lemon cake, the results may be somewhat bitter and hard to accept.
- If the querent prefers a sugar cake, the results may be positive, but be aware that they may be too good to be true.
- If the querent prefers a simple pound cake, this may indicate a more neutral answer.

. . . .
67. Buckland, *The Fortune-Telling Book*, 14; Pickover, *Dreaming the Future*, 186.

Cromniomancy and Cromnyomancy (Onion Sprouts and Prophecy)

In ancient times, names were written on onions, and the onions were placed on an altar on Christmas Day. The first one that sprouted after being planted on Twelfth Night indicated the person of interest. This could be used for many reasons, including people guilty of a crime or deciding who to marry (when someone had a choice). They also put them on the table at Christmas Eve with the name on the onion. The one that sprouted first afterward was the person with the best health.[68]

Modern Exercise

Purchase or grow some green onions. Write different words or numbers on the onions. Let the sitter randomly draw an onion for the answer to their question. You could also see which onion sprouted first and read what message you had written on that onion. You could replace the onions with any root vegetable.

Things to Consider

- If you want to keep it simple, just write on one onion.
- If so inclined, you can write a different message on several onions.
- If the onions have symbols on them, decide how they apply to what is going on in the querent's life.

Category 16: Fabrics

There is not a lot of published information on divination with fabrics; however, I think there's a lot of potential in this category. I discuss my family's beliefs below. This is a chance for you to develop your own system.

Fabric Divination

Lore from my family is that when trading, people would pick their fabrics and receive or give messages based on the fabric.

---

68. Buckland, *The Fortune-Telling Book*, 144–45; Cheung, *The Element Encyclopedia*, 135–36; Pickover, *Dreaming the Future*, 186.

Modern Exercise

Randomly pick several precut swatches of fabric, ribbon, suede, or leather strips. Based on the color, pattern, texture, and any other interesting information, give a fabric reading.

Things to Consider

+ If the fabrics chosen are consistent in color, pattern, or texture, sticking to a path is indicated. The fabrics will reveal whether this path is considered good or bad.
+ If the textures are smooth, an easy path is indicated.
+ If the textures are rough, a more difficult path is indicated.

Category 17: Flowers

Flowers are very high vibration. Their auras are evident and bright, as shown by Kirlian photography. It is no mistake that we give flowers to those who are ill or in the hospital. Roses have a particularly high vibration. Divination with flowers goes back for ages due to their availability, beauty, and high vibration.

Anthomancy (Flowers and Prophecy)

Divination with flowers, where flowers and their colors have different meanings. Flowers are high vibration, like crystals. They have long been displayed on altars or in temples as tributes to deities. Flowers respond to sympathetic or hostile environments.[69]

Modern Exercise

Assemble a bouquet of a variety of colors. Randomly choose a flower. Give a reading based on the color of the flower chosen. This ties into the Three C's of readings—your clairs, chakras, and colors provide depth to the reading. If you know what the flower is, you can use your knowledge of any associations with that flower in your readings. However, you do not need to know anything about the flower to give a reading. Begin to state what comes to mind as you look at the flower. Another method is to see how petals of a flower move in water. What patterns or lack thereof are made?

. . . .
69. Buckland, *The Fortune-Telling Book*, 16–17; Pickover, *Dreaming the Future*, 87.

Things to Consider

+ If the flowers smell fresh, a new beginning is indicated.
+ If the flowers are bright and cheerful, a positive outcome is indicated.
+ If there are lots of thorns, there may be difficulty ahead.

Floromancy (Flowers and Prophecy)

There are various types of flower divination. Many of us might have picked a daisy and plucked the petals, asking, "They love me; they love me not." The day you find a flower carries a message also. In general, all the days but Thursday and Saturday are fortunate days to find a flower. Floromancy is also connected to the idea that flowers have emotions. They are living beings after all.[70]

Modern Exercise

Take note of the first flower you find or see in the spring. Tie it to the day of the week you found the flower.

Things to Consider

+ If the flower is found on Tuesday, efforts will be rewarded.
+ If the flower is found on Thursday, exercise caution and vigilance.
+ If the flower is found on Sunday, exceptional luck is indicated.

Category 18: Liquids

As we have seen in this book, many methods of divining came about by what was available or on hand to use. Due to their availability, there are many types of liquid divination.

Cottabomancy (Wine and Prophecy)

Cottabomancy was derived from a drinking game the Greeks played. They flung wine sediment from their glasses toward a target. They would ask a question and listen for a sound or where the sediment landed. Cottabomancy also utilized brass bowls filled with

. . . .
70. Buckland, *The Fortune-Telling Book*, 206–07; Cheung, *The Element Encyclopedia*, 216.

wine, water, or ink. The diviner stared into the liquid in the bowl until they went into a trancelike state. They then delivered any messages they received.[71]

Modern Exercise

Pour wine into a vessel (traditionally a brass bowl), then swirl. Look at the wine residue in the bowl and observe to see what the shapes, bubbles, residue, and foam are communicating.

Things to Consider

- If the wine bubbles or clumps together, this could be a group dynamic either for you or against you.
- If the wine foams, it may be hard to get to the truth.
- If the wine leaves residue, there is unfinished business.

Leconomancy (Oil and Prophecy)

Leconomancy is a form of divination using oil in water to scry.[72]

Modern Exercise

Fill a shallow, clear bowl with any type of liquid. You can swirl the liquid if necessary. Observe how the liquid behaves. This form of divination can be layered by dropping in herbs to see how they affect the water and if they form patterns or even form shapes or letters. Essential oils are ideal to use here. If you know the oil's properties, you can study how it interacts with other elements in the bowl for another layer of information. Put the water in the bowl first and then add drops of oil.

Things to Consider

- If the oils clump together, consider the type of oil it is. It could mean everything is coming together in a positive way, or something is forming to get your attention and work against you.

. . . .

71. C. Riley Augé, *Field Manual for the Archaeology of Ritual, Religion, and Magic* (Berghahn Books, 2022), 26; Fitzedward Hall, *Modern English* (Scribner, Armstrong & Co., 1873), 37.
72. Buckland, *The Fortune-Telling Book*, 293; Cheung, *The Element Encyclopedia*, 384–85; Pickover, *Dreaming the Future*, 188.

+ If the essential oils form a pattern, read the pattern.
+ If you know the property of the oil, it should be added to your reading.

Hydromancy (Water and Prophecy)

Typical characteristics taken into account when reading with water were speed, color, and ripples. You could drop a stone in the water and see how many rings formed. The seas, rivers, and fountains were also studied for their movements and colors. The unfortunate side of hydromancy is that it was used to reveal whether someone was a witch. It was a no-win situation because if they sank or drowned, they were innocent, but if they floated, they were guilty of witchcraft.[73]

Modern Exercise

Practice skipping a rock into a lake, river, or stream. If the rock sinks, the answer to your question may be that the situation was too hard and difficult. If it skips along the surface of the water, count the number of times it skips. Then, divine what the number of skips represents and then watch the ripples. The farther out the ring of ripples goes, the more likely that your issue is causing problems for others as well. You are not alone in your concern because there is a ripple effect. However, if there are few ripples and they do not extend far from the rock, then the situation or obstacle will not include anyone else.

Things to Consider

+ If the rock sinks, maybe the issue has resolved itself. It is up to you whether you will bring it back again.
+ If the ripples go out wide, the issue is causing a problem for others.
+ If there are only a few ripples, not many are affected.

....
73. Buckland, *The Fortune-Telling Book*, 246–48; Cheung, *The Element Encyclopedia*, 306–07; Pickover, *Dreaming the Future*, 187.

Category 19: Numbers

Numbers hold energetic frequencies just like everything does, and numbers have been utilized for ages to divine information. There are different types of numerology and different interpretations of what numbers mean. I recommend picking a method and sticking with it for use in divination.

Arithmancy (Numbers and Prophecy)

Arithmancy is an early type of numerology by use of numbers, typically derived from letters and names. Many historians believe that it began with Pythagoras, who believed he could divine the future with numbers. Numbers were assigned to letters and then used to predict the future, once tallied. The victory of Achilles over Hector in the Trojan war was predicted with arithmancy. There are many different numerology systems. To begin, find one and work with it. You can always build on it and add to the complexity later.[74]

Modern Exercise

There are a number of numerology systems, but perhaps the simplest form is to use the following chart to calculate your life path number using your date of birth. Your life path number is your purpose for being on earth and is much like the Sun sign in astrology. It reveals your strengths, weaknesses, and what drives and inspires you. For example, Tina Turner was born on November 26, 1939. To calculate her life path number, add:

November (11) + Date (26) + Year (1939)

$= 1 + 1 = 2$

$= 2 + 6 = 8$

$= 1 + 9 + 3 + 9 = 22$, then $2 + 2 = 4$

$= 2 + 8 + 4 = 14$, then $1 + 4 = 5 =$ life path number

It is interesting to note there are various ways to group the numbers in order to add them. With the straight-across method, the double-digit number indicates an important

....

74. Buckland, *The Fortune-Telling Book*, 24, 334–39; Cheung, *The Element Encyclopedia*, 31, 490; Pickover, *Dreaming the Future*, 169.

turning-point age in your life. Example: $1 + 1 + 2 + 6 + 1 + 9 + 3 + 9 = 32$ (turning point age) and $3 + 2 = 5$ (life path number).

It is also relatively simple to determine your destiny number, which is your road map or compass to your goals. Your personality number is how you show up in the world, much like a Sun sign in astrology. Your soul number describes how you inwardly react to things, much like a Moon sign. To calculate these, you use your name in the chart as follows:

1 2 3 4 5 6 7 8 9

A B C D E F G H I

J K L M N O P Q R

S T U V W X Y Z

1 = A, J, S

2 = B, K, T

3 = C, L, U

4 = D, M, V

5 = E, N, W

6 = F, O, X

7 = G, P, Y[75]

8 = H, Q, Z

9 = I, R

To calculate your destiny number, simply take the name for whatever or whomever you want to receive information about and plug in the numbers for each letter. For example, Tina Turner's numbers are $2 + 9 + 5 + 1 + 2 + 3 + 9 + 5 + 5 + 9 = 50$, then $5 + 0 = 5$

Reduce the number to a number from 1 to 9. Then, based on the meanings of the numbers 1–9 you will have a pretty good idea of the information regarding that name. In the case of Tina Turner, her destiny number was 5. The number 5 means she was adventurous, adaptable, and courageous, known as the Adventurer.

. . . .

75. The letter Y is a vowel if the word does not have any other vowels. It is also a vowel if it is the last letter in a word or syllable. Otherwise, it is a consonant.

There are many meanings assigned to the numbers, but this is a starting point. Pick a set of meanings that resonate with you and use them consistently in interpreting and delivering your message.

Possible Numerology Meanings
- 1: The Leader: Ambitious, creative, independent, new beginnings
- 2: The Peacemaker: Compassionate, sensitive, imaginative, balanced, generous
- 3: The Creator: Material minded, seeker, intelligent, creative, ambitious
- 4: The Coordinator: Intuitive, eccentric, organized, practical, truthful
- 5: The Adventurer: Active, analytical, inquisitive, adaptable, courageous
- 6: The Humanist: Sociable, peacemaker, diplomatic, generous, healer
- 7: The Seeker: Psychic, mysterious, generous, wise, spiritual, esoteric
- 8: The Analyst: Organized, responsible, nostalgic, eccentric, leader
- 9: The Philanthropist: Emotional, loyal, possessive, humanitarian, optimistic
- 11: The Master Messenger (master number, so don't reduce): idealistic, philosophical[76]
- 22: The Master Builder (master number, so don't reduce): hardworking, industrious
- 33: The Master Teacher (master number, so don't reduce): spiritual, leader
- 44: The Infinite Creator (very rare master number, so don't reduce): miraculous intervention

You can also calculate your personality number. A personality number is much like a Sun sign in astrology. It is how you show up in the world. Your personality number is calculated using the consonants in your name. TNTRNR = 2 + 5 + 2 + 9 + 5 + 9 = 32, then 3 + 2 = 5. Tina Turner's destiny number was the same as her life path number (the Adventurer, 5: adventuresome, adaptable, and courageous).

To calculate your soul number, add all of the vowels in your name. A soul number is how you inwardly react to things. It is much like a Moon sign in astrology. Continuing with the Tina Turner example, IAUE = 9 + 1 + 3 + 5 = 18, then 1 + 8 = 9, Turner had

....

76. Master numbers have double the energy of their single-digit counterparts. The master number 11, for instance, is an amplified 2.

a soul number of 9. She inwardly reacted to things in a humanitarian, optimistic, and emotional way.

Things to Consider:
* If you are interested in using numerology, pick one interpretation of number meanings.
* If you are ever curious as to which name to use, often it is best to go with the legal name.
* If the person had extreme pivotal points in their life, it is interesting to see how their turning point number compares with events happening during that time period.

Fractomancy (Fractal and Prophecy)
Fractals are extremely intricate, ever-changing patterns that reveal details when magnified many times with mathematical formulas. These computer-generated fractals are then interpreted by the diviner.[77]

Modern Exercise
Put several geometric patterns onto the screensaver of your computer. Let them all swirl together, and then read what you see. You can pause it or fall into a hypnotic state while they're swirling.

Things to Consider
* If there is a symmetrical pattern, this could indicate a yes.
* If there is an ugly pattern, this could indicate a no.
* If there is no real pattern, this could indicate uncertainty.

. . . .
77. Pickover, *Dreaming the Future*, 171.

Category 20: Powder, Sand, and Earth

Like many ancient categories of divination, this category covers natural elements that were readily available for divination.

Abacomancy, Amathomancy (Dust and Prophecy)

Amathomancy involves tossing or casting sand, dirt, or even ashes on a surface of some sort and reading what patterns or symbols emerge. The dust is read much like tea leaf patterns in tasseography.[78] Jackson Pollock was known for using this method in paintings he used to foretell the future.[79]

Modern Exercise

Pick a substance such as sand, flour, paint, etc. to use. Then, toss a handful or a paintbrush splash onto a shallow surface. Look for the patterns. Then, give your reading.

Things to Consider

+ If there is a clear picture that forms, integrate that into your reading.
+ If all of the substance seems to migrate to one area, what does that area represent?
+ If there are thick areas and thin areas, interpret what those mean. For example, thick may mean harder to navigate or a stronger foundation.

Geomancy (Earth and Prophecy)

Geomancy means foresight by earth. This form of reading was widespread through the seventeenth century because of the Silk Road, which allowed merchants to introduce various forms of divination to other parts of the world. Earliest styles of divination involved reading cracks in the ground, throwing handfuls of earth onto the ground, striking the sand with a stick to create random patterns, or randomly drawing a few stones, seeds, or roots and recording the odd or even numbers of dots generated. Performing this four times generates one of sixteen binary tetragrams—the geomantic tableaux—each with associated meanings and astrological correspondences.[80]

. . . .

78. Buckland, *The Fortune-Telling Book*, 1; Cheung, *The Element Encyclopedia*, 5–6.
79. Steven W. Naifeh, Gregory White Smith, *Jackson Pollock: An American Saga* (Clarkson N. Potter, 1989).
80. Buckland, *The Fortune-Telling Book*, 220–25; Cheung, *The Element Encyclopedia*, 239; Pickover, *Dreaming the Future*, 201–205.

Modern Exercise

Pour sand onto a shallow plate or cookie sheet. Read how the sand lands on the plate or sheet. To layer this reading, add different-colored sand or drop a pebble or crystal on the sand.

Things to Consider

+ If the sand covers the entire sheet, things are evenly distributed and there is balance.
+ If the sand all falls in one area, perhaps some rethinking of priorities is indicated.
+ If sand falls off the area, perhaps things are consuming your energy that are out of your control.

Category 21: Sacred Relics and Statues

Sacred relics and statues were used by ancient peoples for worship, but also to impart signs or messages to those who put great meaning into the relic or statue. Sculptures and paintings were used to feel close to a deity, saint, or revered one. Many people believed messages were sent by the deity through their likeness.

Iconomancy (Likeness or Image and Prophecy)

Iconomancy is divination using a religious image. An *icon* is a likeness, image, statue, or photo of a religious figure. The diviner receives information or the gift of divining directly from the deity.[81]

Modern Exercise

Find a church where they have religious statues or paintings. Walk through the church quietly when no service is being held. See which statue catches your attention. Then, watch the icon to see if you can get a message. If you can't get into a church, you can use a small figurine or photo in a magazine to represent the larger figurines who provide and impart messages to those who are respectful of the rules of the chapel or sanctuary.

. . . .
81. Buckland, *The Fortune-Telling Book*, 273.

Things to Consider

+ If an image seems to be smiling at you, benevolence may be coming your way.
+ If the image seems to be sad, some obstacles may be coming your way.
+ If the image seems upset, malevolence may be coming your way.

Idolomancy (Image and Prophecy)

Divination using a sculptured figure, not a painting. The diviner receives information directly from the deity. As with many other types of divination methods, this involves an actual statue.[82] One time I was at a chapel at a mission. I had received bad news, and I was lighting a candle for a friend, and unfortunately, I said a cuss word. There was a statue of a nun. She looked at me, shook her head, and then bowed it. For a short moment, I was able to interact with a nun only to get her upset with me. Nuns aside, I did love that chapel.

Modern Exercise

Decide on a deity you want to communicate with and mold clay into the figure. While molding, ask the deity the questions concerning you.

Things to Consider

+ If the clay does not want to mold into any shape, perhaps the deity does not want to work with this situation.
+ If the clay molds easily, take this as a sign the deity is willing to work with you.
+ If a symbol comes through in the mold, use this symbol to communicate with the deity.

. . . .

82. Buckland, *The Fortune-Telling Book*, 273.

Category 22: Sharp Objects

Sharp objects such as needles, knives, arrows, and hatchets were often used in the past for divination. The ancients used what was available to them, and sharp objects were some such objects.

Acultomancy (Needle and Prophecy)

Acultomancy stems from the earlier Latin acutomancy (which referred to needles). In this method, you drop needles into a bowl and then slowly pour in water and see what happens to the needles. What shapes or clusters are formed? The needles were also dropped into a shallow pan of flour or powder to see what designs were formed.[83]

Modern Exercise

Gather needles, pushpins, popsicle sticks, or toothpicks. Add an extra layer of information by using different colors of pushpins or toothpicks. You can write numbers, symbols, letters, or words on whatever you choose to substitute as needles. You can use whatever amount you want, but historically sixteen or twenty-one was the number used. Place them in some sort of bag or container so that you can mix or shake up the materials chosen. Cast the materials on the ground or into a shallow bowl of water, flour, or sand. You can also use a sheet pan. If using water, it is best to cast or drop the needles first and then slowly add the water. Set the intention of what the needles, colors, or numbers represent. Look at how the needles land.

You can also use needles or other sharp objects with a piece of paper to answer questions. For example, if you can't decide between three different colors of cars, you could draw a circle on a sheet of paper and randomly write the colors within the circle. Then, close your eyes and spin the paper around and stick the sharp object through the paper. The color the needle pierces or lands closest to is your answer. You can also tie a needle on a string and use it as a pendulum.

Things to Consider

+ If the needles cross other needles, then you might have an enemy working against you.

. . . .
83. Buckland, *The Fortune-Telling Book*, 3–4.

+ If there is more than one needle crossing, there is more than one enemy.
+ If no needles are crossing, you are strong and protected.

Aichmomancy (Spearhead and Prophecy)

Aichmomancy is much like needle divination, except instead of needles, knives or spears are usually thrown and then the patterns or shapes are read. There is also a method where the spear is spun in the sand to see what it points to for the message, much like modern-day spin the bottle.

Modern Exercise

Use a butter knife to see where it points when you spin it. As always, set your intention ahead of time and be clear about your question. Spin the butter knife and see where the tip points. The objects under consideration could be letters, words, numbers, or even items placed in a circle encompassing the knife.

Things to Consider

+ If using letters, words, or numbers, reset the butter knife so as not to start at the same point every time.
+ If you can't think of a question, spin the butter knife and let the person it points to ask the question.
+ If the butter knife keeps pointing in the same direction, but between two people or subjects, narrow it down to those two.

Axinomancy (Axe and Prophecy)

Axinomancy was used in the old days to determine if someone had committed a criminal act. Axes were used in different ways, including searching for treasure by placing an agate on a heated axe to see if it fell. Another method was to see which direction the handle pointed when an axe, hatchet, or saw was thrown into a tree or onto the ground. The handle would point the way to the criminal. Interestingly, a prophecy of the ruin of Jerusalem was predicted with axinomancy.[84]

. . . .

84. Buckland, *The Fortune-Telling Book*, 59–60; Cheung, *The Element Encyclopedia*, 52; Pickover, *Dreaming the Future*, 133.

Modern Exercise

Get a package of rubber bands. They aren't sharp but are a safe way to practice this method of divining. Hold one rubber band, pull it back, and let it fly. Repeat with several more rubber bands. Look and see where and how they landed. Then, give your reading. If you used wide rubber bands, you could write messages on them. You can even buy different-colored rubber bands. You can also use arrows with messages on them to see which goes the farthest and which one fizzles and doesn't fly at all. Instead of arrows, you could use Nerf darts or toys with the messages written on them.

Things to Consider

+ If all the rubber bands are one color, read the message written on the rubber band that soared the longest distance. Also, look at the one that went the shortest distance because it may be something that needs work.
+ If different-colored rubber bands are used, assign meanings to them. For instance, blue may represent a need to calmly speak, red may represent a need to assertively speak, and yellow may represent a need to keep your mouth shut.
+ If you use arrows or plastic noodles, see if any similar messages are grouped together.

Belomancy, Bolomancy (Arrow/Dart and Prophecy)

Arrows have been used for divination purposes since the time of the Chaldeans. Like many leaders in ancient times, the king of Babylon relied on divination. Arrows would have messages written on them, then they were fired off. With belomancy, sharp objects may be thrown or catapulted from a device such as a bow.[85]

Modern Exercise

Draw a circle or use a Velcro or real dartboard. Assign words or numbers to the various spaces on the board. Throw darts or whatever sharp object you are using at the board. Read where they land.

....

85. Buckland, *The Fortune-Telling Book*, 62–63; Pickover, *Dreaming the Future*, 133.

Things to Consider

+ If the messages land in the same area, how many are there and what do the messages have in common?
+ If the messages don't seem to take off, perhaps reframe the question.
+ If intentions are not clearly stated, know that it may lead to more confusion.

Category 23: Shells

Shells are easy to gather in certain areas, which makes them ideal for divination use. Sometimes, meanings are assigned to certain types of shells. Whether you use a predetermined system for reading shells or simply use intuition, shells are popular for divination.

Conchomancy (Mussel and Prophecy)

Seashell divination is fortune-telling by reading seashells. It is used in the Santeria and Yoruba practices. In the Santeria practice, seashell divination is known as *Diloggun*. In *Ifa*, practiced by the Yoruba people, 16 shells (16 is considered magical) are used in a reading for 256 possible combinations. The shells are dropped on a cloth or a board, and then interpreted by number of mouth-up or mouth-down shells. Please note that while many shell divination systems are open to anyone to practice, Diloggun and Ifa are closed practices.[86]

Modern Exercise

When you go to the ocean, walk along the beach and collect seashells. Think about what you are going through or experiencing when you find a seashell to add to your collection. Perhaps you have begun a relationship, and the shell you find will represent new beginnings in relationships. Assign your own meaning based on color and structure. You can also place a seashell on your ear and analyze the sound.

Things to Consider

+ If you find or cast a conch shell, a new beginning may be indicated.
+ If you find or cast a snail shell, travel is indicated.
+ If you find or cast a cowrie shell, a matter involving money is indicated.

....
86. Buckland, *The Fortune-Telling Book*, 137–38; Pickover, *Dreaming the Future*, 67–69.

Category 24: Sounds

The use of sounds is an affordable and popular divination method. Anything that makes noise can be used for this category.

Chalcomancy (Copper or Cup and Prophecy)

Chalcomancy involves striking gongs, chalices, or metal bowls with special mallets to get messages while listening to the sounds and tones.[87]

Modern Exercise

A singing bowl is the ideal instrument for this modern exercise. Think of your request, then write down two possible answers on separate sheets of paper. Place each piece of paper face down on a table and mix the answers. Set the singing bowl on top of the papers so that the papers are completely covered under the bowl. Strike the bowl with a mallet in multiple directions until one of the answers comes out. (Remember to always strike the bowl in the correct manner.)

Things to Consider

+ If the slips of paper both come out together at the same time, read them as one answer.
+ If the tone of the bowl is harsh or unpleasant, there may be challenges with the outcome.
+ If it requires more than five strikes for the piece of paper to come out, there is another option that needs exploration.

Gastromancy (Belly and Prophecy)

Prophecy based on guttural sounds. In the past, it was a popular after-dinner pastime. The participants believed that voices in the belly were voices of the nonliving and could predict the future.[88]

. . . .

87. Rosemary Ellen Guiley, *The Encyclopedia of Magic and Alchemy* (Facts on File, 2006), 27; Henry Carrington Bolton, *The Counting-Out Rhymes of Children: Their Antiquity, Origin, and Wide Distribution: A Study in Folk-lore* (D. Appleton & Co., 1888), 29.
88. Buckland, *The Fortune-Telling Book*, 217–18; Cheung, *The Element Encyclopedia*, 237; Pickover, *Dreaming the Future*, 190.

Modern Exercise

Listening to the growl of our stomachs is an interesting modern exercise to work with our Three C's (clairaudience, the solar plexus chakra, and the color yellow). The more you use the Three C's, the easier intuitive messages often flow. It is important to stretch yourself in exercising your psychic muscles. If you grow comfortable with a psychic group, this is a fun exercise that may yield intuitive messages. It is perfectly acceptable to have fun when practicing your intuition. In fact, I highly recommend it.

Things to Consider

+ If the stomach is making no noise whatsoever, the solar plexus is most likely underactive.
+ If the stomach is making normal sounds (the digestive system is working), the solar plexus is most likely balanced.
+ If the stomach is loudly growling, the solar plexus is most likely overactive.

Category 25: Spoken Language

Language is another readily available and affordable category of divination.

Clamancy (Cry Out and Prophecy)

This kind of divination involves voices, sounds, random shouts, and cries (particularly at night, and also in crowds).[89]

Modern Exercise

Visit the woods, a crowded area, or your own yard. Focus on your question and listen to random noises as clues or answers to what you are seeking.

Things to Consider

+ If the sound is quiet and subtle, it may indicate a subtle but significant event.
+ If the sound is loud and obvious, it may indicate an event that is impossible to miss that turns your life upside down.

. . . .
89. Buckland, *The Fortune-Telling Book*, 130.

+ If there is a blend of sounds all at once, it may indicate a lot of things happening at once in your life.

Cledomancy or Cledonomancy (*Rumor and Prophecy*)

Cledonomancy involves divining a message from offhand or unexpected remarks that are made.[90]

Modern Exercise

Think of a question or prompt when around crowds of people. Then, listen for words or phrases. Write them down as answers to your questions. Alternatively, the cumulative words or phrases you hear may combine to provide the message that you receive.

Things to Consider

+ If the messages have a theme, this may indicate a wakeup call.
+ If the messages are all seemingly random, this may indicate a need to find a consistent thread in your life.
+ If it is hard to catch any words or phrases, this may indicate it is not time for you to know the information.

Category 26: Trees and Plants

The category of trees and plants has been used for ages for divination. As we have seen, anything that is a readily available resource can be used to receive a message.

Botanomancy (*Plant and Prophecy*)

Botanomancy is a general term for divination that uses any plant or plant part. Botanomancy was an ancient Druid practice of divination. Questions were carved on tree branches, and then the branches were burned. The fire, smoke, and crackling sounds were examined and read by the diviner.[91]

. . . .

90. Buckland, *The Fortune-Telling Book*, 130; Cheung, *The Element Encyclopedia*, 118; Pickover, *Dreaming the Future*, 190.
91. Buckland, *The Fortune-Telling Book*, 71–72; Cheung, *The Element Encyclopedia*, 84; Pickover, *Dreaming the Future*, 88.

Modern Exercise

Think of your question. Ask your question and cast your plant material into the fire. Listen to the sound and observe the smoke and any patterns to reveal your answer.

Things to Consider

- If the chosen material crackles, a positive outcome is indicated. If it makes a hissing sound, an unfavorable result is indicated.
- If there is a lot of smoke, look for images or patterns in the smoke. If there is no smoke, there are things hidden or unrevealed regarding the question.
- If the plant material curls up as it burns, the situation needs close attention. If the material quickly disintegrates, try to stop giving any more energy or attention to the situation because it has already been decided on your behalf.

Daphnomancy (Laurel Branch and Prophecy)

Divination based upon the use of laurel branches. This form of divination was probably practiced by the Druids.[92]

Modern Exercise

Write a question on a bay leaf. Then, observe and interpret the smoke as you burn it in a bowl.

Things to Consider

- If the bay leaf burns quickly, a favorable, fast response is indicated.
- If the bay leaf burns slowly, an unfavorable, delayed response is indicated.
- If the bay leaf does not seem to burn or puts out the flame, more intention and energy needs to be given to the situation.

. . . .

92. Buckland, *The Fortune-Telling Book*, 174; Cheung, *The Element Encyclopedia*, 144; Pickover, *Dreaming the Future*, 190.

Dendromancy (Oak, Yew, or Mistletoe Trees and Prophecy)

With dendromancy, different tree types or mistletoe were examined. A few modern-day scholars think that this form of divination was based upon the interpretation of the shapes and direction of smoke rising from burning mistletoe and oak.[93]

Modern Exercise

Collect a tree limb. Make your request and then break the branch for your message.

Things to Consider

+ If the branch breaks easily, a favorable outcome is indicated.
+ If the branch won't break, an unfavorable outcome is indicated.
+ If the branch doesn't have leaves, lack or stagnant prosperity is indicated. However, if a branch with leaves is chosen, prosperity is on the horizon.

Sycomancy (Fig Leaf and Prophecy)

Sycomancy involved writing questions on fig leaves and letting them dry. The speed at which they dried was noted. If a leaf dried fast, it indicated a bad omen. It was a positive omen if the leaf dried slowly. There are many species of fig trees, and many revere them as the Tree of Knowledge.[94]

Modern Exercise

Write messages on several slips of paper and roll them up. The paper represents a twist on using the fig leaves. Be sure to include a blank slip to indicate no answer, not now, maybe, or up to you/not listed. Place them in a strainer and hold it over steam. The slip that unrolls first is your answer.

Things to Consider

+ If several unroll at the same time, read them together to get the answer.
+ If the slip takes a long time to unroll, this may indicate a delay in the event occurring.
+ If the slip unrolls quickly, this may indicate a quick answer or result.

. . . .

93. Buckland, *The Fortune-Telling Book*, 178–79; Pickover, *Dreaming the Future*, 182.
94. Buckland, *The Fortune-Telling Book*, 456; Pickover, *Dreaming the Future*, 151.

Category 27: Weather

Divining by observing the weather was essential to survival in ancient times. The ancients used various types of weather to predict how their crops would fair.

Aeromancy (Air or Atmospheric Conditions)

Aeromancy is an umbrella term for many types of divination involving the weather, including, but not limited to, cloud divination, wind divination, thunder divination, lightning divination, and star divination. If anyone ever tells you it is wrong to foretell the future, perhaps ask them if they observe the clouds to predict whether it will rain. Aeromancy was one of the seven Renaissance magical arts forbidden by canon (Catholic) law. The other six were necromancy, geomancy, hydromancy, pyromancy, chiromancy (palmistry), and spatulamancy.[95]

Anemoscopy, Austromancy (Wind and Prophecy)

Anemoscopy is divination by observing wind characteristics. Wind readings rely upon intensity, sound, and direction.[96]

Modern Exercise

Go outside and note the cardinal directions. Formulate a question in your mind while facing east. Then, toss dirt or seeds and observe how and where they fall for your answer.

Things to Consider

+ If the wind blows to the north or the west, the answer to your question will be negative.
+ If the wind blows to the south or the east, the answer to your question will be positive.
+ If you toss dirt or seeds, use the direction considerations for your reading.

. . . .

95. Buckland, *The Fortune-Telling Book*, 4–6; Cheung, *The Element Encyclopedia*, 8; Pickover, *Dreaming the Future*, 183–84; Richard Kieckhefer, *Forbidden Rites: A Necromancer's Manual of the Fifteenth Century* (Pennsylvania State University Press, 1998), 32–33.
96. Buckland, *The Fortune-Telling Book*, 57; Pickover, *Dreaming the Future*, 184.

Brontomancy, Ceraunomancy, Ceraunoscopy (*Thunder and Prophecy, Thunder, Lightning Observation*)

Brontomancy was the use of thunder for divination. The observation included direction, length, intensity, distance from the diviner, and distance from other thunderbolts. Whether lightning accompanied it was also considered when interpreting the thunder. In Rome, when lightning was observed by the augur, all public business was cancelled.[97]

Modern Exercise

This modern exercise is much like the ancient practice. Listen to thunder, taking note of the direction, length, intensity, distance from the observer, and distance from other thunderbolts.

Things to Consider

- If the sound of thunder comes from the left, it is negative, and if it comes from the right, it is positive.
- If the sound is long and booming, it indicates more danger.
- If lightning accompanies the thunder, it is a strong message that should not be ignored.

Ceraunoscopy, Ceraunomancy (*Lightning and Prophecy*)

Ceraunoscopy is the ability to divine by observing the shape, type, intensity, color, and direction of lightning. The Greeks associated lightning with male deities. Pliny the Elder noted that lightning in the day hours was fiery bolts thrown by the god Jupiter, while night lightning was from Neptune. Seneca made it clear that to correctly divine the lightning, you had to know the divisions of the heavens: If the lightning indicated your allies (east), it was known as *pars familiaris*, but if it was in the area of your enemy (west), it was known as *pars hostilis*.[98]

97. Buckland, *The Fortune-Telling Book*, 77, 102–103; Cheung, *The Element Encyclopedia*, 135–36; Pickover, *Dreaming the Future*, 184.
98. Buckland, *The Fortune-Telling Book*, 103–104; Pickover, *Dreaming the Future*, 184.

Modern Exercise

The modern exercise is much like the ancient practice. Observe lightning, taking note of the direction, length, intensity, distance from the observer, and distance from other lightning bolts.

Things to Consider

+ If the lightning is horizontal, it indicates an unfavorable outcome. However, if the lightning is vertical, it indicates a favorable outcome.
+ If the lightning appears close, a swift outcome is indicated. On the other hand, if the lightning appears in the distance, a delay is indicated.
+ If there are multiple lightning bolts occurring simultaneously, this adds emphasis to the outcome and indicates multiple potential outcomes.

Nephalomancy (Clouds and Prophecy)

Cloud reading involves reading clouds based on the shape, color, movement, and any other factors that the diviner might observe.[99]

Modern Exercise

Go outside and place a blanket on the ground. Lie down on the blanket and look up at the clouds. You might see a shape take form in the clouds, or the clouds may represent a mood based on their color. Dark clouds represent a negative answer, while white clouds indicate a positive answer. Clouds high in the sky are indicative of spiritual matters, while clouds low in the sky represent more earthly matters.

Things to Consider

+ If the clouds are moving quickly, then change will rapidly occur.
+ If the clouds are moving across the sky, this might indicate travel.
+ If the clouds are moving slowly or not at all, things are becoming stale or stagnant.

. . . .
99. Cheung, *The Element Encyclopedia*, 118; Pickover, *Dreaming the Future*, 120, 183.

Category 28: Writing

Writing was widely used for divination. The key to this form of divination is to get yourself relaxed so that the messages easily flow through you instead of from you.

Automatic Writing and Drawing

Automatic writing is a type of writing that takes place when someone is in a relaxed state and allows their unconscious brain to write, or some say another spirit does the writing for them. Whatever the case, there are messages received for individuals or groups of people. The same idea is used for drawing.[100]

Modern Exercise

Hold your pen or pencil in your nondominant hand with a piece of paper in front of you. Direct your attention away from the page as you distract yourself by talking to someone, listening to music, or watching a television show. Allow your nondominant hand to start moving and writing or drawing freely.

Things to Consider

+ If the writing cannot be read, look for any pattern that emerges.
+ If there is only one word that is legible, this word is probably very important.
+ If there are lots of similar words, this adds emphasis to the message of those words.

. . . .
100. Buckland, *The Fortune-Telling Book*, 57–59; Cheung, *The Element Encyclopedia*, 33, 48–49; Pickover, *Dreaming the Future*, 169–70.

PART 2
CONCLUSION

You have finished a lot of work and hopefully had some aha moments and fun along the way. Remember that ancient usages are not meant to be all inclusive or teach the history of the times or culture. The ancient methods summarized help remind us that divination has been utilized since the beginning of civilization; it is not New Age in any way. The ancients had daily concerns regarding food and survival. Divination modalities meet us where we are. Use the ancient and modern methods as you feel inclined. Remember that practice makes psychic. You are well on your way, but it never hurts to learn how to bring it all together. Part 3 will help you layer modalities in informational, experiential, and fun ways.

PART 3
PRACTICE MAKES PSYCHIC: EXERCISES TO SHARPEN YOUR PSYCHIC SENSES

I love mixing modalities, creating new spins on existing modalities, and layering modalities. In part 3, I integrate many years' worth of extremely interesting exercises I either mixed, created, or layered. Like a chef creating a perfect meal, you will now have an opportunity to mix and layer all your favorite divination practices. But first let's go over some fundamental things to remember when using your psychic abilities to relay messages. These terms and subsequent exercises will help you tune in more to your querents and deliver more accurate messages.

Terminology: Reading

Readings: Messages that are received through divination that are delivered by the reader to the querent.

Reader: The one receiving the psychic information or message, interpreting it, and delivering it to the querent.

Querent: The one asking the question or receiving the message (also known as the sitter or client).

Checklist of Dos When Working with Querents

+ Ask the querent if they have a question or if they want a general reading.

+ Set your intention. This is personal to you as the reader. I ask that the reading be for the highest and best good of the querent. You may want to call upon a guide or deity. Some readers will do this out loud. That is up to you, but I do it silently because I do not like to make a show of it. The only time I set an intention out loud is when I feel that it is something the querent expects or needs.

+ A lot is made of how questions are framed. A querent should not be corrected, nor is it necessary to correct the form of their questions. Many will say not to ask yes-or-no questions, but I find they are excellent questions, especially when followed up with more information.

+ The main thing is that you have the question clear in your mind and you are clear about what is represented with the modality you are using. For example, let's first use tarot cards: If you are asked, "Should I buy a red or blue car?" decide clearly in your mind what the cards will represent. Do not simply start throwing cards down. I use a flowchart method. It is a spread of sorts, which is typically the only spread I need to use for great accuracy. (The next exercise explains my flowchart method.)

+ Do not become too dependent on clarifier information (such as pulling another card). If you are clear with your intention, it is rare when using most modalities that you will need clarifiers. It isn't unheard of, but rarer than how often many people use them. The issue is usually that the reader was not initially clear with their intention of what each card would represent.

Checklist of Don'ts When Working with Querents

+ The querent says, "I think you are correct, but in the opposite order," and the reader agrees. No! If you set the intention that the first card, rock, charm, etc. represents a certain person and the second represents another person, never flip-flop them to be correct in the short run. Stick to your reading, assuming you set your intention correctly.

- Do not adjust the reading and relaying of your message based on the response of the querent. This does not mean you should never change your tone, for example, if you see that the querent is becoming emotional. However, you should not lie about the message.
- A true psychic will have no need to rely on how the querent looks or acts. Read using your intuition and tools, not your observation of body language. While some readers observe the body language of the querent, I set an intention to disregard body language in my reading of a message. If I do include body language, I consider that a body language reading.
- Do not read based on statistics or common knowledge. Just because someone has broken up with someone else nine times does not mean they will a tenth time. I have given many readings where other readers have totally misread situations because they played the odds.
- Do not give advice. Unless you are a psychologist, you are not providing counseling to the querent. You are giving them an intuitive message.
- Don't tie everything up with a neat little bow. This is a huge temptation for readers: talking too much. Perhaps you clearly receive the message of a white picket fence and a couple waving goodbye to another couple. However, this is the only information you receive from your clair repertoire. A huge mistake many readers make is speculating beyond that message. It goes something like this: Reader: "I see a white picket fence and a couple waving goodbye to another couple." Querent: "Okay." Reader: "It seems like you will be getting a new house and have a happy home." Meanwhile, the querent was thinking, "This reader was great because she described my grandparents' house." In law we call this *one question too many*. A lawyer does not know when to shut their mouth and pass the witness. Likewise, sometimes you will need to know when to shut your mouth because the message was relayed. It is not your job to put all the pieces together.
- Never assume. Do not assume sexuality, do not assume political beliefs, do not assume the client is telling the truth, do not assume the client is mentally stable, do not assume the client is hearing everything you say—do not assume anything.

Exercise: Flowchart Readings

The purpose of this exercise is to start with certain scenarios and, like a flowchart, follow the path of the answers received. This can be done with almost any modality that helps you divine. The flowchart method I have devised is why I believe my messages are so accurate and I have so many return clients. For this example, we will use charms.

Equipment: A variety of different charms (or whatever modality you want to use)

Instructions:
Request the answer to a question. This may be a yes or no, or multiple choices if the querent is seeking direction. (Example: Which color car should I purchase?)

The reader then asks the querent to get the choices straight in their head as choice A, choice B, or choice C. The querent should not tell the reader which letter represents which choice, but they must be sure to keep them straight in their mind. (Example: The querent decides choice A is red, choice B is black, and choice C is white.)

The reader then draws a charm to represent each choice. (Example: Choice A is a dagger, choice B is a musical note, and choice C is a dog.)

The reader then reads (interprets) the message. A good way to phrase it is "What will it look like if the querent chooses A, what will it look like if the querent chooses B, and what will it look like if the querent chooses C?" The reader might relay a message like this: "If you go with choice A, it seems a little dangerous. A dagger is used for stabbing and is typically associated with aggression; therefore, choice A does not seem like the best choice. Choice B is going to have a good sound system, or you will enjoy the time in your car if you choose B. A musical note represents music or singing, and this feels positive. If you go with choice C, it will probably be a car of utility and fun. It will be dependable. In the literal sense, it might be a car that you feel comfortable having your dog ride in with you."

At this point, you can rule out choice A. If you want more information, continue with your flowchart reading. Pull another charm to place under choice B and choice C. Let's assume you draw a pencil charm for choice B and a stop sign for choice C. Choice B is a pencil, which is used for writing, but it is not a pen. You may want to go with choice B, but make sure you get all the information before you sign on the dotted line. Choice C seems to tell us to stop in our flowchart reading and not go with this choice.

Exercise: Divination Stations

The purpose of this exercise is to set up a variety of divination stations where participants can try out various modalities and sharpen their clairs in the process. This exercise is entertaining and makes a great activity at parties or in classes.

Instructions for Setup

Set up the number of stations you choose to have with plenty of room at each table to accommodate the activity. For instance, if the readings will represent a calendar year, set up twelve stations.

Number each station and place index cards, pens, and any other necessary items at each station. It is also helpful to have a timer at each station.

Any instructions for the station should be simple, laminated, and affixed to each station's table.

Participants

It is suggested that two participants go to each station at a time. Give the participants simple instructions affixed to a brown or white legal-size envelope. The participants keep the envelope with them throughout the exercise and then take it as a keepsake when finished.

They can write their name on the envelope and keep any messages or other things they receive at the stations inside the envelope.

Tell them to find an empty station and find a partner if they don't already have one. They do not have to go to all the stations or go in order. Emphasize that this is a fun way to connect.

The message will be written on an index card for the querent to keep. Make sure the reader always signs their name after the message. It is easiest if participants are reading in pairs at each station.

Examples of Divination Stations

As stated above, divination stations are areas where participants can try out various modalities and sharpen their clairs in the process. The following examples are stations I have utilized for years at classes and events. Each exercise is entertaining and makes a great activity at parties or in classes.

Ribbon or Lace Readings

These were used when people would buy their fabric; they would also get a reading. If the fabric was lace, the reading might be performed by looking through the lace (veil) at the querent. This exercise utilizes psychometry and clairtangency.

Needed at station: Precut ribbon, fabric, and lace materials, a bucket for the fabric, index cards, pens, stapler, and timer

Instructions:
Decide who will read first and who will be the querent first. The querent randomly chooses one or two pieces of fabric and hands them to the reader.

The reader grabs an index card and pen. Once handed the fabric, the reader hits the timer for two minutes. The reader then gives a message based on the look, feel, color, texture, etc. of the fabric. The reader can say the message out loud or write it on the index card. (If the reader doesn't want to write the message down, let the querent write down notes of the message on an index card.) The reader then staples the fabric to the index card and hands it to the querent.

Set the timer for two minutes, and the querent gives feedback to the reader. This should be honest feedback delivered in a kind manner.

The index card with the message and fabric stapled to it is placed in the querent's envelope. Then, the two participants switch, and the reader becomes the querent.

Song Shuffle Readings

This is associated with clairaudience. Music is a powerful tool to stimulate your clairaudience. The musical notes and lyrics combine for more specificity in the reading.

Needed at station: Index cards, pens, and timer

Instructions:

Decide who will read first and who will be the querent first. The querent pulls out their phone and goes to their playlist and randomly chooses a song via shuffle. Randomly go to a portion of the song and play it out loud for the reader to hear.

The reader grabs an index card and pen. Once the querent is ready to hit play on the music, the reader hits the timer for two minutes. The reader then gives a message based on the beat, tone, lyrics, feeling, etc. of the music. The reader can say the message out loud or write it on the index card. (If the reader doesn't want to write the message down, let the querent write down notes of the message on an index card.) Be sure to write down the name of the song.

Set the timer for two minutes, and the querent gives feedback to the reader. This should be honest feedback delivered in a kind manner.

The index card with the message and song name is placed in the querent's envelope. Then, the two participants switch, and the reader becomes the querent.

Jolly Rancher or Starburst Readings

These are associated with clairgustance and clairolfactory. Although clairgustance and clairolfactory are different, taste and smell are often sensed and intuited together. Also, the clairs are not actually eating something or smelling it, but the exercise helps you develop the clairs.

Needed at station: Jolly Ranchers, Starbursts, or any individually wrapped candy, bucket for candy, index cards, pens, and timer

Instructions:

Decide who will read first and who will be the querent first. The querent randomly draws a Jolly Rancher or Starburst from the bucket.

The reader grabs an index card and pen. Once the querent receives the Jolly Rancher, the reader hits the timer for two minutes. The reader then gives a message based on the color, scent, name, and intuited taste of the Jolly Rancher. The reader can say the message out loud or write it on the index card. (If the reader doesn't want to write the message down, let the querent write down notes of the message on an index card.)

Set the timer for two minutes, and the querent gives feedback to the reader. This should be honest feedback delivered in a kind manner.

The index card with the message and Jolly Rancher is placed in the querent's envelope. Then, the two participants switch, and the reader becomes the querent.

Bibliomancy or Stichomancy Reading

These exercises involving books are always fun and can be as simple or as complex as the participants want to make them.

Needed at station: A selection of books with the number of pages in each book taped to the cover, index cards, pens, and timer

Instructions:

Decide who will read first and who will be the querent first. The reader asks the querent to select a book. The querent selects the book and hands it to the reader. The reader looks at the number of pages affixed to the cover and asks the querent to choose a page in that range.

The reader grabs an index card and pen. Once given the page number, the reader hits the timer for two minutes. The reader then turns to the selected page and gives a message based on where their eye falls on the page. The reader can say the message out loud or write it on the index card. (If the reader doesn't want to write the message down, let the querent write down notes of the message on an index card.)

Set the timer for two minutes, and the querent gives feedback to the reader. This should be honest feedback delivered in a kind manner.

The index card with the message, book name, and page number is placed in the querent's envelope. Then, the two participants switch, and the reader becomes the querent.

Make Your Own Oracle Card Reading
People love to create their own oracle cards. This station is not only fun because both the reader and querent are actively involved, but it also leads to great readings due to the energy put into the card while making it.

Needed at station: Cut card stock for drawing an oracle card, markers, stickers, index cards, pens, and timer

Instructions:
Decide who will read first and who will be the querent first. Each participant spends two or three minutes making a mini oracle card. Make sure to set the timer because some will draw forever and others very quickly.

The reader grabs an index card and pen. Once given the querent's oracle card, the reader hits the timer for two minutes. The reader then looks at the oracle card made by the querent and gives a message based on what they see or what comes into their mind. The reader can say the message out loud or write it on the index card. (If the reader doesn't want to write the message down, let the querent write down notes of the message on an index card.)

Set the timer for two minutes, and the querent gives feedback to the reader. This should be honest feedback delivered in a kind manner.

The index card with the message and the oracle card drawn by the querent are placed in the querent's envelope. Then, the two participants switch, and the reader becomes the querent.

Essential Oil Reading
This station utilizes the sense of smell or clairolfactory. One thing to keep in mind at this station, and certain others with scent or taste, is any allergies. Otherwise, this station is fun and helps each party train their outer sense of smell so that eventually they can count on their inner sense of smell. It is important to remember that our sense of smell evokes some of our strongest emotions and memories.

Needed at station: A selection of essential oils, index cards, pens, and timer

Instructions:
Decide who will read first and who will be the querent first. The reader asks the querent to randomly select an essential oil. The querent selects the oil and hands it to the reader.

The reader grabs an index card and pen. Once given the oil, the reader hits the timer for two minutes. The reader then smells the oil, looks at the bottle, etc. The reader can say the message out loud or write it on the index card. (If the reader doesn't want to write the message down, let the querent write down notes of the message on an index card.)

Set the timer for two minutes, and the querent gives feedback to the reader. This should be honest feedback delivered in a kind manner.

The index card with the message and oil name is placed in the querent's envelope. Then, the two participants switch, and the reader becomes the querent.

Inkblot Reading
Although this station can be a bit messy, once you figure out what liquid (ink, glue, or paint) you want to use, it is very helpful for practicing intuitive messages.

Needed at station: Liquid glue, ink, or paint, precut black card construction paper, index cards, pens, stapler, and timer

Instructions:
Decide who will read first and who will be the querent first.

Each participant spends two or three minutes placing liquid glue, ink, or paint on one side of their construction paper and then folding it to make the inkblot design.

The reader grabs an index card and pen. Once given the querent's inkblot card, the reader hits the timer for two minutes. The reader then looks at the inkblot made by the querent and gives a message based on what they see or what comes into their mind. The reader can say the message out loud or write it on the index card. (If the reader doesn't want to write the message down, let the querent write down notes of the message on an index card.)

Set the timer for two minutes, and the querent gives feedback to the reader. This should be honest feedback delivered in a kind manner.

The index card with the message and the inkblot by the querent are stapled together and placed in the querent's envelope. Of course, the inkblot may need to dry!

Then, the two participants switch, and the reader becomes the querent.

Charm and Curio Reading

This is a crowd favorite for home gatherings, parties, or classes. I encourage everyone to collect charms and curios. I have many boxes because I have collected them since I was young. If you do not have any, just walk around and gather small trinkets such as buttons, pen tops, pebbles, bottle caps, small soaps, or anything you can find to put into your curio treasure chest.

Needed at station: Charms and curios, a box or bucket for the charms and curios, index cards, pens, and timer

Instructions:

Decide who will read first and who will be the querent first. The querent randomly chooses one or two charms or curios and hands them to the reader.

The reader grabs an index card and pen. Once handed the charms, the reader hits the timer for two minutes. The reader then gives a message based on what the charm is, what the charm is used for, and any message the reader receives. The reader can say the message out loud or write it on the index card. (If the reader doesn't want to write the message down, let the querent write down notes of the message on an index card.) The reader then hands the index card message and the charms or curios to the querent.

Set the timer for two minutes, and the querent gives feedback to the reader. This should be honest feedback delivered in a kind manner.

The index card with the message and charm or curio is placed in the querent's envelope. Then, the two participants switch, and the reader becomes the querent.

Globe Readings

Globe, map, or atlas readings are useful for finding out where someone might travel and for past-life readings. I have even used them to ask what type of crystal I should use based on where it is found in the world. Be creative and use this for all sorts of divination.

Needed at station: One globe, past-life oracle cards, index cards, pens, and timer

Instructions:

Decide who will read first and who will be the querent first. The querent asks about a past or future life on earth. The querent then spins the globe and randomly points without hesitation to a location.

The reader grabs an index card and pen and hits the timer for two minutes. The reader then gives a message based on where the globe landed. The reader may also have the querent draw a few oracle cards. The reader can say the message out loud or write it on the index card. (If the reader doesn't want to write the message down, let the querent write down notes of the message on an index card.)

Set the timer for two minutes, and the querent gives feedback to the reader. This should be honest feedback delivered in a kind manner.

The index card with the message, globe location, and names of the oracle cards (or the actual oracle cards) is placed in the querent's envelope. Then, the two participants switch, and the reader becomes the querent.

Pendulum Palooza Readings

This exercise is meant to help you practice using pendulums with an easy-to-read chart book assembled by Roger Welch and me.

Needed at station: *Pendulum Palooza* chart book or charts from the internet, a few pendulums, index cards, pens, and timer.[101]

---

101. Michelle Welch and Roger Welch, *Pendulum Palooza* (pub. by author, 2018).

Instructions:

Decide who will read first and who will be the querent first. The querent chooses what chart is to be used from the book or whatever charts are available at the station.

The reader grabs a pendulum, index card, and pen. Then, the reader hits the timer for two minutes. The reader uses the pendulum on the chosen chart and gives a message based on the result. The reader can say the message out loud or write it on the index card. (If the reader doesn't want to write the message down, let the querent write down notes of the message on an index card.)

Set the timer for two minutes, and the querent gives feedback to the reader. This should be honest feedback delivered in a kind manner.

The index card with the message and chart result is placed in the querent's envelope. Then, the two participants switch, and the reader becomes the querent.

Exercise: The Envelope Game

The purpose of this exercise is that everyone gets readings, and everyone practices giving readings with different modalities. This exercise stretches all of your clairs in a fun and interactive way.

Equipment: Legal-size brown envelopes, typing paper or note cards, pens, tarot cards or oracle cards, participants' phones with music, essential oils, flowers, photos of food or actual food, ribbons, charms, slips of paper with random phrases or words, staplers, staples, paper clips, and a checklist on the front of the envelope with each station listed so they can be checked off and initialed once someone has read at that station for that envelope. Bonus: tarot card for each modality.

Have different modalities set up at different stations. These can be one to a small table or more to a table with consideration for the number of participants who will gather around the table.

Clairvoyance: Tarot or oracle card

Clairaudience: Song

Clairolfactory: Oil

Clairgustance: Food photos or real food

Clairtangency: Ribbon

Claircognizance: Charms

Claireloquence: Random phrases

Clairsentience: Psychometry item

Instructions:

Prenumber the front of each envelope ahead of time, then pass the envelopes out randomly.

Everyone gets an envelope and writes their name inside where it can't be seen. While doing this, you are infusing the envelope with your energy. Holding the envelope in your hands also infuses your energy into the envelope.

The envelopes are handed to the moderator. They are then scrambled and randomly handed out with a divination station assignment.

Everyone goes to their divination station assignment. Each person places the envelope at the station to their right and rotates to the station to their left. In other words, you do not want to keep writing messages on the same envelope at the same station. It is more interesting to read for various people and for each person to receive readings from a variety of people instead of just one or two. Further, do not try to find out whose envelope you have. This is not the goal of the exercise. It is especially interesting when you have given yourself a reading without realizing it.

Remember to have an equal number of people at various stations to begin readings. If at the clairvoyance station, draw a tarot or oracle card. Spend one to two minutes writing a message for the owner of the envelope on the provided index card. Sign your name. Clip together the card and your written card and then place both in the envelope. Check off the clairvoyance box on the front of the envelope.

If at the clairaudience station, go to your music playlist, hit shuffle, and shuffle until you feel like hitting stop. This is the song you will receive a message from for your querent. Write down the name of the song and a one-to-two-minute message on the paper provided. Remember to sign your message, then place it in the envelope. Check off the clairaudience box on the front of the envelope.

If at the clairolfactory station, draw a scent and smell it. Write down the name of the scent, then based on this smell, write a one-to-two-minute message for the owner of the envelope. Sign it and place your reading in their envelope. Check off the clairolfactory box on the front of the envelope.

If at the clairgustance station, randomly select a picture of food or sample of food. Write a one-to-two-minute reading based on your clairgustance. Make sure you sign your reading, clip the photo and message together (unless you sampled the food), and place it in the envelope. Check off clairgustance on the front of the envelope.

If at the clairtangency station, draw a few ribbons. Feel the texture of the ribbons and then write down a one-to-two-minute reading for the owner of the envelope. Be sure to sign your name. Staple the ribbons to the index card and place them in the envelope. Be sure to check off the clairtangency box on the front of the envelope.

If at the claircognizance station, choose a charm as a message for the owner of the envelope. Write your one-to-two-minute message. Sign it and place it and the charm in the envelope. Be sure to check off the claircognizance box on the front of the envelope.

If at the claireloquence station, choose a few words or phrases that were placed in a container at the table ahead of time. See how the words or phrases fit together for a message. Write your one-to-two-minute message. Sign it and staple the words to the index card. Place them in the envelope. (If by chance magnetized words are provided, follow the instructions of the moderator as to whether you will give away the words or put them back in the container at the station.) Be sure to check off the claireloquence box on the front of the envelope.

If at the clairsentience station, pick up the psychometry item. Set your intention that this item will give a message to the person whose envelope you have, even though the item is not owned by them. Write your one-to-two-minute message. Sign it and place your signed index card in the envelope. Leave the psychometry item at the station. Be sure to check off the clairsentience box on the front of the envelope.

All envelopes will then be handed back to their owners, and they will be able to read all their messages.

Note: This same exercise can be modified to use different prompts that don't necessarily tie into the clairs. For example, using different modalities at each station to do a reading for six months in the future. Another option would be prompts involving words, and then the next station writes sentences to go with those words without knowing what the words are. For instance, 1. Dog, 2. Piano, 3. Football. Then, the next reader might write these sentences: 1. You will find love soon. 2. Return to a lost passion. 3. Take time to connect. The querent would then see if there were any connections between these words and sentences written and channeled randomly between the two readers.

In this case, the querent would see that two totally different readers gave them the message: 1. Dog—You will find love soon, 2. Piano—Return to a lost passion, and 3. Football—Take time to connect. If there is time to share, the querent might disclose that they have been lonely and would love an animal companion, that they used to love playing piano but stopped at some point in their busy life, and they used to connect with their father by watching football. These readings and validations are always powerful.

Exercise: Twelve Days for Twelve Months of Magical Manifestation

The purpose of this exercise is to layer twelve modalities together in one exercise and to utilize various clairs. You can do this exercise by yourself or with a group. The bonus is that a great yearly reading is given to the querent.

Do not worry if it is not the new year; you can start the exercise at any month. I call these forecast readings. I have had clients come to me year after year for these readings. Some of my most profound accuracies are in writing on their calendar sheets.

Instructions:

Gather all materials and set everything up ahead of time, especially if you are doing this for a class or group. This is great for an individual reading but extremely fun and filled with many aha moments when used in a class or festive setting. If this is for a group, make sure to set up various stations or tables to allow plenty of room.

Clipboards are a must for ease of writing. Then, have fun doing this just like the envelope game. And make sure you have enough for each modality, such as charms, so that you can have a random selection. Remember to have a sheet with twelve boxes for writing the message. This serves as your calendar for writing messages.

January: Ribbon Reading (saved from holiday packages)

Gather ribbons or yarn of various colors and textures beforehand. Cut them into approximately two-inch strips, then place at the table or area marked as January.

When doing the exercise, randomly draw one or two ribbons, then read the ribbon based on the color, texture, decorations, and any impressions received. Write a brief summary of your reading on the calendar sheet. Then, place the ribbon in the pouch or envelope attached to the calendar sheet.

February: Chocolate

Beforehand, get a box of chocolates (or individually wrapped and assorted chocolates).

When ready to begin, randomly choose a chocolate and taste it. Read the chocolate based on the color, texture, smell, taste, and any impressions received. Write a brief summary of your reading on the calendar sheet. Also include the name of the chocolate, if known, on the calendar sheet.

March: Charms and Curios

Prior to this activity, gather a variety of small charms or curios.

When ready to begin, randomly choose a charm or curio. Read the charm or curio based on what it is, what it is used for or does, what it symbolizes, and any further impressions received. Write a brief description of the charm or curio and a brief summary of your reading on the calendar. If you would like to gift the charm or curio to the querent, place it in the pouch; otherwise, write it down.

April: Nature Sign

For this activity, gather a variety of items from nature.

To start, randomly choose a nature sign. Read the nature sign based on what it is, what it is used for, what it comes from, what it is associated with, what it symbolizes, and any further impressions received. Write a brief summary of your reading on the calendar. If you would like to gift the nature sign to the querent, place it in the pouch; otherwise, write it down.

May: Flowers

Before this activity, gather a variety of flowers.

First, randomly choose a flower. Read the flower based on how it smells. Then, write a brief summary of your reading on the calendar sheet. If you would like to gift the flower to the person whose envelope you have, place it in the pouch. If you don't gift the flower, write a brief summary of the flower along with your message.

June: Oracle

Gather a deck of oracle cards prior to starting this activity.

To begin, randomly choose a card and read it. Write a brief summary of your reading on the calendar sheet. If you would like to gift the card, place it in the pouch; otherwise, make sure you describe the card.

July: Essential Oil

For this, you'll need to gather a variety of essential oils and some popsicle sticks or paper strips.

First, randomly choose an essential oil. Then, place a small drop on a thin popsicle stick or piece of paper. Read the essential oil based on impressions received from the scent. Make sure to write a brief summary of your reading on the calendar. Place the stick in the pouch or envelope.

August: Music

Prepare your source of music and a playlist prior to the exercise. Then, decide if the reader can pick a specific song from the list or hit shuffle and get a random song to read.

When ready to begin, read the song based on what you hear and feel, as well as any other impressions. Write a brief note on the calendar. Write down the name of the song on the pouch or envelope if one was randomly chosen.

September: Crystals

Gather a variety of crystals beforehand.

To begin, randomly choose a crystal. Read the crystal based on color, vibration, shape, pictures you see in the stone, chakra associations, knowledge of crystals, and any other impressions. Write a brief note with your message on the calendar. If you would like to gift the crystal to the querent, place it in the pouch or envelope; otherwise, write it down.

October: Candle Wax Readings

Gather a variety of colors of candles, and either use card stock as a base or prepare water for the wax to drip into.

First, randomly choose a small chime candle. Light and burn it until wax drips onto durable paper (like card stock) or into water.

Read the candle based on the color chosen and the way the wax melts onto the card stock or in the water. Write a brief note with your message on the calendar. If you used card stock, place it in the pouch or envelope; otherwise, write it down.

November: Tarot

Set out a tarot deck prior to the exercise.

When ready to begin, randomly choose a card and read it. Then, write a brief note with your message on the calendar. If you would like to gift the card to the querent, place it in the pouch; otherwise, write it down.

December: Holiday Wrap

Gather a variety of gift wrap and cut into 4 × 4-inch squares beforehand.

To start, randomly choose a piece of gift wrap. Read the gift wrap based on texture, color, design, and any other impressions you receive. Then, write a brief note with your message on the calendar. Place the holiday wrap in the pouch or envelope of the querent.

Exercise: Intuitive Gift Exchange

The purpose of this exercise is to utilize all of your clairs and practice what you have learned while putting together your handbook. It is also a great way to take gift exchanges to a whole other level of fun.

An advanced version of this game is to add psychometry and write your intuitively garnered descriptive words of what is inside the bag in addition to writing your messages. Your original messages are not meant to describe the item (psychometry), but instead to request, receive, read, and relay a message of why the querent got this gift. Adding on the psychometry is more about describing what the gift is versus a message as to why the querent received it.

Equipment: Gift under whatever dollar amount you decide, brown paper bag (the key is that for this gift exchange you do not want anyone to see who brought the gift), pens, paper or index cards, staples, and stapler

Instructions:

First, make sure each gift is placed in a brown paper sack, with the name of the giver hidden by the folded-down and stapled edge of the bag. All the gifts are placed on a table or in the center of the circle. It is important that no one knows who brought what gift because this might influence the reading they give.

Randomly choose gifts. Realize that you may choose your own since they are all in brown paper bags. Then, everyone passes their brown bag to the left.

Everyone writes a message on their bag for the person who will ultimately end up with it. Make sure to sign your name.

If time allows, pass the bags to the left again, and everyone writes a message on the bag intended for whoever will ultimately receive it.

Place bags on a table or in the middle of the circle and play the gift exchange game by the house rules. In other words, however the moderator usually does gift exchanges, follow those instructions.

Each time someone gets a gift, they should read their messages out loud and then open the gift.

Exercise: Psychic Musical Chairs

The purpose of this exercise is to get a group of people comfortable with one another so that they then become more comfortable reading for others and overcome their attachment to being right. It is a fun way to overcome inhibitions and let your intuition shine. And it can be a practice exercise for gallery readings.

Equipment: Chairs, music, pens, paper

Instructions:
Place chairs equal to the number of people in the group minus one. If there are ten people, put nine chairs in a circle.

Have the moderator or teacher start the music. Participants begin to walk around the circle while the music plays.

When the music stops, the participants sit in the chair closest to them. Someone will not get a chair.

The one that did not get the chair will now give an intuitive message for the person that is closest to them or the one who got the last chair. The message is delivered out loud in front of all those sitting in the circle. The message should only be about one to three minutes long. It should be the first thing that comes into the reader's head.

After the reading, do not remove another chair. The one who read gets back in the circle and you begin again.

Exercise: Mapping Out Past, Present, Future, or Parallel Lives

The purpose of this exercise is to utilize a globe or flat map of the world to use the law of attraction to help fire up your psychic downloads regarding where you or someone you are reading for may have lived a past, present, future, or parallel life. Of course, the globe or map will not include older civilizations and will be limited initially to the time the map was made. However, when interpreting the message, you may realize that you are in the area, but it was called something else.

Equipment: Globe or flat map and pendulum

Instructions:
If using a globe, you or the querent will spin the globe. The querent closes their eyes and spins the globe. Then, they point to a place on the globe. The reader then gives a past, present, future, or parallel life reading about the location and the querent.

If using a map, put it on a table and spin it around so the querent doesn't know what direction is facing where. The querent can point to a spot and cast charms or crystals on the map to add layers for reading. The reader then gives a past, present, future, or parallel life reading about the location and the querent. If charms, crystals, or other tools were added for layering, the reader integrates them into the reading.

Exercise: Tarot Yarn of Connection

I presented this exercise at Masters of Tarot, which was led by tarot expert Mary K. Greer at Omega in upstate New York. The presentation received positive feedback, and everyone seemed to bond over the exercise. The purpose of this exercise is that perhaps now more than ever it is important to understand how much we are all connected. You, while creating a psychic handbook, are in a unique position to create a safe space to explore this oneness and examine the footprint you are leaving behind. Tarot bonding encourages participants to open up to one another. It demonstrates concepts such as universal consciousness, the Collective, Source, we are all energy, and we are all one. This exercise is designed to help any level of tarot reader become more familiar with the cards and also inspires us to dive deeper into a situation, providing illumination to something we think we already understand.

Equipment: Yarn or string, three-different colored sets of index cards that are prenumbered with questions already on them (see questions in instructions), old tarot cards or some you pick up on sale or swap, stapler, staples, paper clips, and pen.

The purpose of this exercise is that it unifies a group by getting individuals to open up to one another. It also helps large groups become more inclusive, which is great for any conference or retreat! And it demonstrates concepts such as universal consciousness, the Collective, Source, we are all energy, and we are all one.

This exercise will help any level of tarot reader to become more familiar with the cards and go deeper with them. It encourages participants to realize the tarot can be used to dive deeper into a situation, providing illumination to something one may think they already understand. Plus, participants will be encouraged, with the help of the tarot, to take a look at the footprint they are leaving on earth.

General instructions:

Get three different-colored index cards that are prenumbered and have these three prenumbered questions written on them. I use printed mailing labels for large groups.

1. What is a struggle you survived or overcame that you use or could use to help others?
2. What is your greatest accomplishment, and how does it make the world a better place?
3. What is something specific that you want to do for this world? (The footprint you want to leave.)

Then, randomly draw a piece of yarn that has three tarot cards affixed to it (left, middle, right). You can assemble the tarot cards on the string ahead of time. Look at your index cards and pair the index cards with the three tarot cards. The tarot cards are left to right. The left tarot card goes with index card one, the middle tarot card goes with index card two, and the card on the right goes with index card three. Paper clip the corresponding index cards to the front side of the tarot cards.

Spend time making your own connections regarding these cards. Remove the paper clip to write your message on the index card. When finished with that card, simply paper clip it back, but now leave the front side of the tarot card showing.

Instructions for the group:

Next, sit in chairs in a circle, preferably next to someone you don't know. Everyone will hold up their yarn and make a connected circle, demonstrating the oneness of all.

Now, it's discussion time. Turn to the person on your right. Each one will discuss how index cards one and three, respectively, correlate to the tarot cards and how the cards of each tie together. What are similarities? How can the strength of one help the obstacle of the other? What are some aha synchronicities in the duality? Then, turn to the person on your left and repeat.

Look at the preprinted number on the back of the middle card. Go to that chair number and meet with the person who has the next number. Discuss your middle cards in the same way as the other discussions you've just had. Or if time is short, meet that person for follow-up later.

Lastly, everyone shares any interesting messages or aha moments with the rest of the group. Validation and feedback is important to developing your psychic knowingness. Keep your yarn with tarot and index cards as a memory of what you experienced.

Exercise: The Music Shuffle

The purpose of this exercise is to develop your clairaudience. It also ties in clairsentience. This exercise can be done as an individual or with a group.

Equipment: Each querent's phone with their music playlist, pen, and paper or index cards

Write down the name of two songs with some of the lyrics. The first should be an uplifting song that you consider your happy song. The second song should be more of a ballad or a slower song. It might make you a little melancholy, yet you still love the song. A third song will be chosen randomly when you receive your reading by shuffling your playlist and using whatever song shows up when you are told to stop or after about ten seconds.

An excerpt of the first song will be played, and everyone will write intuitive messages for the upbeat song on a piece of paper or separate index cards to be given to the querent. If you are in a group, always make sure as the reader that you sign your name after your message.

An excerpt of the second song will be played, and everyone will write intuitive messages for the ballad song on a piece of paper or separate index cards to be given to the querent. If you are in a group, always make sure as the reader that you sign your name after your message.

An excerpt of the random song will be played, and everyone will write intuitive messages for that song on a piece of paper or separate index cards to be given to the querent. If you are in a group, always make sure as the reader that you sign your name after your message. If you do this reading as an individual (for yourself) simply modify the directions to fit reading for yourself.

Exercise: Inkblot Readings

The purpose of this exercise is to practice your clairvoyance by reading the shapes formed by inkblots or paint.

Equipment: Ink (but can get messy), latex paint (not as messy), or white glue, and black card stock paper

Instructions:
Fold the card stock paper in half, then have the querent pick a color of ink or paint if so desired. Otherwise, just use what is provided. Ask the querent to put about five to seven drops of ink or paint on one side of the card stock.

Then, the reader carefully folds the card stock in half and waits a few minutes. After that, the reader opens the card stock paper up and gives a message based on the image made by the inkblot or paint pattern.

Exercise: Stained Glass Readings

The purpose of this game is to allow creativity and then read the messages that seem to appear from the page.

Equipment: Small stained-glass objects, or paper and crayons or markers

Instructions:
If you have access to some small pieces of stained glass, utilize those for the querent to hold and ask a question. If there is no access to stained glass, simply ask the querent to color in a shape with colors they choose. Give them a limited amount of time.

The reader then gives a message based on color, shape, feelings, or any other clair that they pick up from the stained glass or drawing.

Exercise: Remote Viewing Readings

The purpose of this exercise is to practice a type of reading called *remote viewing*. First remote viewing will be explained, and then an exercise for practicing will be given. Remote viewing is a great way to practice clairvoyance, precognition, and postcognition if you follow the instructions for how to do it the proper way.

Equipment: Target to view, optional projector and screen for larger groups, brown envelopes, photos, paper or index cards, pen, and a website such as Higgypop for targets to view

Instructions:
Remote viewing is a specific type of reading where the viewer or reader is given a target to view or about which to provide information. The reader is often given no information or clues as to what or who they are viewing. They are typically isolated and asked to write down any descriptions in addition to verbally describing what they receive on the target. The reader may tap into physical descriptions and also feelings.

Allegedly the government and Central Intelligence Agency have used remote viewing in the past to help give advantages in world-stage situations or to help in cases.

The moderator picks how they want to carry out the exercise. I have primarily utilized two methods. I either use websites that are geared to learning remote viewing, or I make copies of photographs and put them in envelopes. (However, I do not teach the material on the websites because they usually overexplain remote viewing, making it more complicated than it has to be.)

The first method is to go to the websites of organizations that teach remote viewing. They have numbered targets that they suggest the reader focus on before writing, sketching, or even molding the description. There are also several websites where you can find targets (photos) online to practice. One website I use in class is Intuitive Specialists, but there are others.

It is said that you do not have to be psychic to remote view. While I agree that there are certain steps that are taught and practiced, I have seen in classes through the years that those who are more psychic are sometimes more adept at remote viewing. On the other hand, I also find those who follow my simple instructions are the ones who advance the quickest no matter how much experience they have, or think they have, as psychics. As I have emphasized all through this book, just like with most things, there are some who are naturally psychic and there are others who have to work much harder at it. There are also some who are better at some modalities than others. Whether it is true that anyone can remote view, it is very clear to me after teaching that the student who follows some very basic instructions will certainly advance more quickly than others.

The number one thing that makes the reader better every single time is to describe, describe, describe instead of guessing the overall object. If those wanting to learn remote viewing follow this one suggestion, they will advance much more quickly.

The second method I utilize to practice remote viewing is to ask people to put photos in brown envelopes. Alternatively, the teacher or moderator can do this ahead of time for the exercise. There should only be one photo per envelope. The individual or class is then asked to remote view the target in the envelope. The same steps as above apply. I often use a projector to show the image afterward so that everyone can talk about their descriptions.

This is extremely important in any intuitive exercise: Have the reader find some connection they made. In my classes, we never use phrases such as "I am horrible at this" or "I totally blew that one." The key is to find the thing or things where you did make a connection. Contrary to popular belief, this is not contriving a hit, but instead learning to make connections. It develops your psychic knowingness.

Remote viewing takes time and practice. Be patient and practice.

Exercise: Postcard or Greeting Card Readings

The purpose of this exercise is to demonstrate that you can use anything for readings. While it is exciting to purchase oracle cards, sometimes they aren't available, or perhaps someone can't afford them. Instead, maybe you have collected postcards or greeting cards. If the cards are collected or saved over a length of time, there is also an aspect of psychometry in this exercise because there certainly may be some strong energy held in collected cards.

Equipment: Postcards or greeting cards, pen, and paper or index cards

Instructions:
Shuffle the collected cards. If it is just you, draw one card. If it is a group, have everyone in the group draw a card.

If there is no specific question, ask, "What does the querent need to know for their highest and best good?" If there is a specific question, ask the question in your mind's eye or repeat it out loud.

Set any intention ahead of time. You decided how to set intentions for your readings in part 1 of your handbook.

Look at the postcard or greeting card and receive any information. Do not second-guess yourself. You can consider anything on the card in your reading. There are no rules when it comes to what you can consider on the postcard or greeting card. Perhaps the card is torn. You may or may not want to take that into consideration. It is totally up to you.

Write down or verbally deliver the message.

Exercise: Psychometry Readings

The purpose of this exercise is to practice your clairtangency or psychometry.

Although psychometry and clairtangency are not necessarily the same thing, psychometry exercises are beneficial for increasing your clairtangency. This exercise can be done by yourself or with a group, but you will need at least one item and someone to provide the history behind it. You will need a sheet of paper or index cards to write down the information you receive. This exercise can also be done involving a large object such as walls in a building. The idea behind psychometry is that it is the touching of the object that triggers the message. Many people think holding an object to feel its energy is just used for mediumship. While clairtangency may be used for mediumship, it is not limited to such a reading.

Equipment: Items with known backstories, a sheet of paper or index cards, pen

Instructions:

Have someone pick out an item they know the history of. The more history they know about the item, the better.

Take the item and hold it in your hand. You may choose to look at the item or not. If you look at the item, you might think that will make it easier to write things about the item; however, sometimes it inhibits you because you might think what you are writing down is too obvious. Set that inhibition aside and write down the obvious things, such as "It is a watch." Then, begin to go deeper. Do not hold back. Write down every thought, color, feeling, or picture that comes into your mind. Remember not to second-guess it. Give yourself no more than two to three minutes with the item to write down the thoughts or feelings that first come to you. I often count down from three to one. Then, I instruct people to stop writing to avoid them overthinking.

If you choose not to look at the item, note whether it is wrapped in something to disguise it from you. Consider that you may pick up on the energy from the packaging that it is wrapped up in.

Once you have noted all of your impressions, ask for the meaning associated with the item. This comes from the person who knows the history of the item. The associations can involve many different aspects, including who owned it, where it is from, all the people it has passed through, who manufactured it, and all the energies surrounding any aspect of the object.

Do not consider anything you wrote as wrong. Many people may think this is contriving a correct answer and is a scam. To the contrary, when you are learning, you must be willing to make what seem like mistakes and then see how these perceived mistakes are ultimately accurate. When you are learning, you must be willing to make mistakes (usually in the reading or relaying of the message). You may not always be accurate, but there might be times when it seems like you're incorrect and later find out you were spot on.

Exercise: Hot/Cold Readings

The purpose of this exercise is to learn to use your psychic knowingness to find a hidden object. This exercise is ideal to help you overcome the feeling that you are guessing, which many people feel when they are practicing their psychic knowingness. It is one of the biggest opponents in your handbook—feeling like you are making it up. This exercise helps you learn to trust your inner guide or inner pendulum.

Equipment: Something to hide, a room or area to hide it

Instructions:
Find an item to hide. It does not make any difference what it is. First, show the item to the seekers—the ones that will be looking for the item. Let the seekers hold the item if they so desire. Then, with the seekers in another room, hide the item.

Bring the seekers one by one into the room and tell them to begin seeking the item. Instruct them not to touch anything.

As the seeker gets close to an item, tell them they are getting warmer, or even hot if they are right by the item. Therefore, it is best to bring them in one by one because once you tell them they are warm or cold, everyone in a group will know. The alternative, if you have a large group, is to whisper to them.

Once the seeker is hot, have them make a guess. If they are in a group, find a way for them to do this discreetly or the exercise is somewhat ruined for everyone else. Another reason to allow one seeker at a time is because I have seen people become discouraged in large groups, which is the opposite of the purpose of the exercise.

A more advanced version of this exercise is to not let the seekers know what they are seeking. Let them know they are seeking something that you have hidden. Once they make their guess and are close enough, have them sit near the area of the hidden object and write down their intuitive impressions about the hidden object. Remind them to describe the object instead of stating what it is.

An alternative to the inner pendulum (using your body as a pendulum) is for the seekers to use an actual pendulum. I often do this exercise at the end of a pendulum class. Students use their pendulums to guide them to the hidden object. They can either ask yes-or-no questions, such as "Is the hidden object in this direction?" or ask the pendulum to point to the hidden object by swinging or pulling in the direction of the object.

Exercise: Crayon Readings

The purpose of this exercise is to use randomly drawn crayons to practice all different types of readings involving color. Chakras, auras, and candle colors immediately come to mind, but you could get even more creative.

Equipment: Box of crayons, paper or index cards, pen (I suggest starting with a smaller box of crayons and advancing later to the large boxes.)

Instructions:
Have the querent draw a crayon. Then, based on the crayon they draw, the reader will give a message regarding the associated chakra, the aura color, or even a candle color and why it might be of use. You could also have the querent choose a few colors and ask them to draw a picture. Give them a time limit because some will want to draw for hours. Then, give a reading based on what they drew.

Exercise: Scrabble Readings

The purpose of this exercise is to use your various means of intuition to give a reading based on the letters and numbers on Scrabble tiles.

Equipment: Scrabble tiles, Scrabble board

Instructions:
Have the reader or querent randomly draw four to five Scrabble tiles. Then, the reader gives a reading based on what they intuit from the letters and numbers on the tiles. The reader may decide to have the querent draw a couple more tiles, but the goal isn't necessarily to spell a word.

If you have a Scrabble board, the querent might be asked to place the tiles intentionally or randomly on the board, and then the reader could give a message. Another alternative is to have two to four people play a short game of Scrabble and then give readings for one another based on the game.

Exercise: Tangible Element Tool Readings

The purpose of this exercise is to integrate elements with tarot using various modalities. Each suit in the tarot relates to an element. This exercise will show you how to draw upon that element to help you or your querent course correct after a reading. Once the tarot has spoken, you have an opportunity to act based upon the message delivered. This exercise will introduce tangible elemental tools (candles, crystals, herbs, and essential oils) corresponding to the suits and individual cards to integrate in readings as a means for querents to become active in their intention setting, goal making, self-healing, life navigating, and course correcting. This is a scent-sual exercise. The goal of this exercise is not necessarily to name a different tool for every card, but to utilize the best tool for growth and healing.

Equipment: Tarot cards, herbs, crystals, essential oils, and candles

Instructions:
First, go over a brief recap of the suits and the elements associated with said suit. This is merely the foundation. The four suits in tarot are pentacles, swords, cups, and wands. Pentacles are associated with the element earth. Swords are associated with the element air. Cups are associated with the element water. Finally, wands are associated with the element fire. (Please note that some practitioners switch wands and air, but we will stick with the correspondences listed above.)

This is an advanced exercise where you will assign various herbs, crystals, essential oils, and candles to each of the cards. I suggest doing this as intuitively as possible and then layering in outside research regarding various herbs, crystals, essential oils, and candles. If you prefer to substitute another correspondence, such as land mammals for pentacles, birds for swords, water beings for cups, or amphibians or reptiles for wands, feel free to do so.

The pentacles are an earth element. We will use herbs to represent the element of earth. Each card has a corresponding herb and explanation of use for attracting health, wealth, and abundance. Use your intuition and research skills here. For instance, the Six of Pentacles is associated with thyme. The Seven of Pentacles is associated with dill.

The swords are an air element. We will use crystals to represent the element of air.

Each card has a crystal for clearing conflict and inviting clarity of thought.

The cups are a water element. We will use essential oils to represent the element of water.

Each card has an essential oil to help draw in loving support.

The wands are a fire element. We will use candles to represent the element of fire. Each card has a candle and ritual to ignite necessary passion put to action.

Additionally, the twenty-two major arcana cards may express one or all four elements, which will help connect to the archetype(s) that arise in a reading.

Once you have assigned correspondences to each card, then you can begin this exercise. Ask, What will you do with this information? What do the elements have to tell you, and how do they tie into something tangible you can use in your life to stay the course or course correct?

Next, you can use what you have created in a spread. Divide your cards into four suits and the major arcana. You should have five piles of cards. Shuffle each pile and draw one card from each of the minor arcana and one from the major arcana. Place the chosen pentacle card at the top, the chosen sword card to the right, the chosen wand card on the bottom, and the chosen cups card on the left. Finally, place the major arcana card in the middle.

The pentacles represent physical matters, material matters, mundane matters, health, wealth, and what roots and grounds you. Look at which pentacle card was drawn and the corresponding herb. Take this all into account to see what may need course correction. The herb can be integrated into the message. Alternatively, the herb may be what you need to help stay the course or course correct.

The swords represent intellect, thoughts, well-being, communication, conflicts, and one's mental attitude about the situation. Look at which sword card was drawn and the corresponding crystal. Take this all into account to see what may need course correction. The crystal can be integrated into the message. Alternatively, the crystal may be what you need to help stay the course or course correct.

The wands represent willpower, determination, projects, creativity, and passion. Look at which wand card was drawn and the corresponding candle. Take this all into account to see what may need course correction. The candle can be integrated into the message. Alternatively, the candle may be what you need to help stay the course or course correct.

The cups represent feelings, relationships, and the possible emotional state of yourself and others. Look at which cup card was drawn and the corresponding essential oil. Take this all into account to see what may need course correction. The essential oil can be integrated into the message. Alternatively, the essential oil may be what you need to help stay the course or course correct.

Finally, look at the card in the middle. The major arcana card represents an archetype or major life matter. It will help you know the overriding issue that may need course correction in your life.

Exercise: Forecast Readings

Forecast means to predict, calculate, foreshadow, declare, foretell, or prophesy in advance. The purpose of forecast reading is to provide a querent with a snapshot of the next six or twelve months. Some people think these readings must be started at the new year, but they can be started anytime. These readings help the reader tune in to a brief snapshot of the most important thing the querent needs to know for each month. It also helps the reader to layer and find correlations in the overall reading. I have clients that return every year to receive these readings.

Equipment: Paper with squares like a calendar, whatever you are going to read with: tarot cards, oracle cards, crystals, animals, etc., and a timer

Instructions:
Set aside thirty minutes for a six-month reading and sixty minutes for a twelve-month reading.

The first month is the month when you are giving the reading. The only exception is if the month is over in a week or less. Label the month at the top of each square on your calendar. Decide what modalities you want to use. I suggest using tarot or oracle cards. Have the querent draw six or twelve cards, one to represent each month. Write the card drawn for each month at the top of each square on the calendar sheet. I give the reading month by month. Write a few bullet points in the square. Remind yourself and the querent that this type of reading does not allow time for a lot of questions, nor does it address everything that will happen in that month. It is a snapshot of what the reader receives. Then, layer with whatever you choose. I usually give one animal to work with for the time period by drawing an oracle card. I also have them randomly place two crystals on two different months if it is a six-month reading or four crystals if it is a twelve-month reading. I integrate those crystals into the reading and then gift them to the client.

Exercise: Tapestry or Quilt Readings

The purpose of this reading is to use several of your clairs to read a quilt or tapestry.

Equipment: Quilt, quilt swatches, quilt book, tapestry, or tapestry book[102]

Instructions:
Have the querent pick a pattern. Then, read the pattern based on shapes, images, texture, colors, and more. Deliver your message.

. . . .
102. Amy Zerner and Jessie Spicer Zerner, *The Dream Quilt* (Charles E. Tuttle, 1995); Monte Farber, *Enchanted Worlds: The Visionary Collages and Art Couture of Amy Zerner* (RedFeather Mind, Body Spirit, 2021).

PART 3
CONCLUSION

Now, you are on a roll. Whether you practiced all the exercises in part 3 or only a few, you now see how fun and accurate layering modalities is. You can have psychic circles and parties or even teach classes using the information you have just added to your handbook. Let's wrap it up with the Eight E's of Psychic Success.

PART 4
THE EIGHT E's OF PSYCHIC SUCCESS

Throughout *A Psychic's Handbook,* you have developed your own psychic style. I hope you feel some measure of satisfaction from the work you have put into developing your personal handbook. It is quite an accomplishment that will be of use in your life, whether you decide to use it in your daily life or as a professional psychic. Obviously not everyone wants to be a full-time psychic, but everyone can use the following Eight E's in their life. Thinking intuitively is becoming more and more accepted by the public and corporations. We all benefit by using our intuition at least as much as we use our logic.

With this new perception of intuitive or psychic abilities comes a responsibility to represent our psychic selves in the best manner possible. Doing so will lead to long-term success rather than short-term glory. I realize that not everyone in the profession agrees on all matters that will be discussed in this section, but I do know that at some point, there will need to be a governing body of some sort. If we do not impose one on ourselves, make no mistake, one will be imposed on us. It does not take a psychic to figure out that you simply must follow the money to see when and where the government intervenes. So, with that said, let's get on with it, shall we? The Eight E's of Psychic Success include education, experience, ego, energy, empathy, ethics, entertainment, and excellence. Keep the Eight E's in mind while developing your handbook.

1. Education

To be excellent in any endeavor, you need some form of education. I will be blunt: Buying a deck of tarot cards one day and calling yourself a professional reader the next day with no education or training does not pass muster. You need to decide if you want to be considered someone who uses your psychic knowingness for your own benefit in your daily life or want to be a professional. If you want to be a professional, let's look at what that word means. A *professional* is an expert in their field or belongs to one of the learned professions such as theology, law, or medicine. Some people add that if someone decides to do a job for gain, then it is their profession. I propose there is a difference between a profession for gain (a job) and acting in a professional capacity (a career). Besides expertise, the difference is one's mentality toward the work. Do they take pride in the work and the field they represent? Do they set high standards for themselves no matter how much they are paid? Recently, I asked someone what would make them happy in a career. This client has never claimed to be happy in their job. They said a paycheck. I quickly pointed out that is what they will get—just a paycheck. They will merely get what they asked for instead of the happiness they also seek.

I also submit to you that someone who calls themselves a professional psychic should be educated in the modalities they are using for profit or gain. Before you jump to conclusions, note there are many kinds of education. Education may come from your grandfather and his friends teaching you to play dominoes. You can also get a great education by self-teaching in a modality by watching and reading the experts in the field and from those who perhaps teach you how to avoid common pitfalls. You can read books, attend classes, and attend conferences. The key is to never stop learning.

I am not alleging you must spend a lot of money, especially on certifications. Some certifications are only worth the paper they are written on because they may be taught in one weekend with no assessment of skills or hours of practice required to receive the certification. In the absence of rigorous study, assessment, and follow-up hours, it is wiser to award a certification of completion. These are the certifications I feel comfortable awarding. It merely means the certificate holder has completed the class. The key to education is to know that you always have more to learn.

2. Experience

Start by asking yourself whether you get readings from professionals in the field. If you do not, think about why not. Is it because you can read for yourself? (Which I agree, you can.) I encourage you to get readings from other readers no matter how many years you have read or how psychic you believe yourself to be. Why? Because you can always learn something from those with experience, whether that experience is more or less than yours. With experience, you'll also know how to handle situations such as clients that come to you who need to be referred to another type of professional, such as a psychologist, a doctor, or an attorney. With experience, you also learn how to handle clients that ask you to do unethical things. In short, you have enough experience that you are prepared for almost anything. You see, being an experienced professional reader goes way beyond knowledge of your modality. It comes with seeing thousands of clients and having some life experience to know how to handle real-life situations of clients that sit with you for a message.

3. Ego

To be an excellent reader, you need to acknowledge that the reading is not about you. It is about the querent. You want to step out of your ego self and into the higher version of you called your higher self, which is connected to the universal consciousness. Your readings should not come from ego. Some examples of ways you know you are in ego include giving personal advice, going with the odds (they cheated three times, so they certainly will cheat again), or merely reading body language. These are not psychic readings. They are opinions or advice based on your experiential filters.

Some might add the word *empowerment* to the E's. Many claim their role as a psychic messenger is to empower their clients. While such a purpose sounds noble, I have thought long and hard about that statement. While I hope my messages empower my clients, I cannot say that it is my job as a psychic. My job is to deliver the message imparted to me. Hopefully, I relay it in the tone I am led to use with each querent, but unless I am given a message to empower, I cannot claim it is my role or purpose as a psychic. My purpose is actually quite simple: it is to deliver the message I am given. I have had experiences with clients where the message I relayed raised their spirits because the message gave them a plan to proceed in what began as a seemingly hopeless situation. On the other hand, I have had clients who were dishonest with themselves and with me. (Makes you wonder why they come to a legit psychic.) There was an occasion when the messages I relayed did not empower the querent, but instead let them know they needed to work on things to stop controlling others. Those messages were not empowering to that client, but I did my job. Some will argue that those messages will ultimately help empower the client.

Frankly, who knows? But my job is to request (ask), receive (get the information, like gathering the facts and evidence), read what I received (interpret), and ultimately relay (deliver) the message. Like the ancient oracles, soothsayers, sphinx, and shamans, it is not up to me to twist that delivery into anything more than what I was given.

4. Energy

It is important that you be at your best to maintain your excellence. One way to do this is to manage your own energy by doing a body scan before every reading. This allows you to know what energy belongs to you and what energy belongs to the querent. Not only does this help protect you from absorbing energy that might not be good for you, but it also keeps you from mistakenly reading your own energy and attributing it to the querent. An energetic body scan consists of scanning your body physically, mentally, emotionally, and spiritually (see part 1, chapter 3 on energetic body scans). At each phase, take note of what belongs to you. For instance, physically, you might have a slight headache, so you know that is yours not the querent's. You do not have to be perfect to read, but you should know what energy belongs to you and what energy is not yours. This will help protect you and any potential querent.

5. Empathy

To be an excellent reader, it is not your job to fix the querent's issues or absorb their energy. Don't fix it; just read it. I do not give advice unless said advice is shown to me by a modality or is clearly coming as a message to deliver to the querent. Remember that the querent is coming to you for psychic information, not for your opinion. However, free will and the reading can show the querent a way to course correct or pivot once they are shown a direction that perhaps they would like to change. This should be determined with your psychic abilities, not your opinions.

6. Ethics

Laws vary by county, state, precinct, providence, and country. So it is important for you to know the laws governing your divination practice. The remarks in this section are limited primarily to the US. However, it is interesting to note that Canada had a particularly strict prohibition against psychics dating back to the inception of their criminal code in 1892. The law was repealed in 2018. Before its repeal, people were charged under Section

365 of the Canadian Criminal Code for fraudulently pretending to exercise witchcraft, sorcery, fortune-telling, or conjuration.

The US psychic industry has grown at an incredible rate since the turn of the millennium. And guess what? Where there is money, government bodies often find a way to regulate, even if just by a license, registration, or certificate. I fully predict more states will want a piece of that pie. Some states have strict regulations, so it is up to you to check the laws in your state or province. For example, states such as New York, Pennsylvania, Maryland, and Oklahoma have laws on their books about fortune-tellers or related activity. But some states have struck down their fortune-telling laws as unconstitutional limits on free speech. Currently, removing curses seems to be the biggest area where fraud is alleged against psychics.

The internet makes much of our work fall under interstate and international commerce. This is a good way for the government to bump a charge to federal versus state jurisdiction. So even if your state doesn't require it, it is smart to put "For entertainment purposes" on your website and on any sign-in sheets.

An ethical code or a professional code of conduct must be followed in professions such as law and medicine. Lawyers and doctors have a professional code of ethics that if violated may result in fines, suspension, or loss of license. Many professions also require continuing education that includes ethics. With no governing body implementing a code of ethics for psychics, stores, or events, where you work may have their own written rules or a professional code of ethics. Always ask for a copy and make sure it aligns with your moral compass. For example, I offer continuing education for readers and energy workers. I am pleased with this program if you would ever like more information.

A *moral compass* is your personal set of values that guide you in your ethical behavior. Your morals are the basis for your ethics. Consider this: Ethics aren't always moral. The mafia has a code of silence. Just because they have this code of ethics does not mean it is moral. On the other hand, morals aren't always ethical. A lawyer telling a judge their client is guilty may be moral, but it goes against the legal code of ethics. The most important thing is that you decide what your moral compass is as a psychic. In the age of social media, this is perhaps more important than ever.

There is no reader-client confidentiality privileged communication under the law, but you can get a minister's license from the Universal Life Church. In other words, you may be an ethical reader and keep confidences, but there is nothing that legally binds you to do so unless you are a minister and acting in that capacity. There is also no protection under the law from you being subpoenaed for the information you know. There is no reader-client privilege. I do not keep notes, and I do not recall my readings. I keep confidences because I have clergy- and parishioner-privileged communication with my clients.

7. Entertainment

Note that this section is not necessarily referring to reading at parties or big events; however, the same applies no matter where you read, including social media.

While the entertainment factor is an important part of excellence in that psychics are providing an experience for their clients, it is perhaps more important now than ever to know two things: What type of style does your client expect, and how do you want to represent yourself as a reader? With everyone on social media clamoring for attention, it is imperative that you decide who you want to be and subsequently how you want to be perceived.

I have heard many theater teachers through the years ask their students, "Do you want to be an actor, or do you want to be famous?" This is not to imply there is a right a wrong answer, but it helps to know what you want to accomplish with your career.

Once you are honest with yourself about why you read, you will know what you want your readings to look like.

8. Excellence

The first seven E's, if carefully formulated and followed in your psychic journey, will lead to excellence. There are always bumps along the way. We are not perfect. But as long as you are striving for excellence (not perfection) you will always feel you have done the best you can. Excellence, in psychic development, is not competing to be better than others. In fact, if you fall into comparisons and competition, it defeats the whole purpose of this book. You have your personal, one-of-a-kind psychic journey. Focus on your psychic development and how you want that to show up in your life. In this case, focusing on yourself will lead to your standards for excellence.

Exercise: Excellence

The purpose of this exercise is to encourage contemplation regarding what kind of psychic you want to be so that you can maintain excellence in your use of your psychic knowingness.

- What does the word *professional* mean to you?
- How do you continue your psychic education?
- Is experience important to you? Can you think of scenarios where it might be important?
- Do you believe you should give personal opinions and advice in readings?
- How do you keep an eye on your energy?
- How do you not take on the energy of your querent?
- What is your moral compass regarding psychic readings? Make a list.
- Do you operate under some written code of ethics?
- Do you know the laws for psychics where you live?
- Do you have waivers and disclaimers?
- Do you believe psychics should have some sort of governing body?
- How do you view yourself as a psychic or reader? What kind of psychic or reader do you want to be? This is comparable to your zodiac Sun sign, which is how you present yourself to the world.
- How do you feel about yourself as a psychic or reader? This may include things you don't share with others. This is comparable to your zodiac Moon sign, which is often what you do not show others.
- How are you perceived as a psychic or reader? This is comparable to your zodiac rising or ascending sign, which indicates how you are perceived by others.
- How do you rise above the noise, or do you shut it out?
- What is your goal as a psychic or reader? Look back at part 1, chapter 2.

Exercise: The Reader in Me

This exercise aims to integrate a divination modality into your contemplation of who you are or want to be as a psychic. The modality used here is tarot, but try other modalities as you prefer.

Randomly draw three tarot cards. Place each card left to right as you draw so that there is a left, middle, and right card. Look at the meanings of each card in relation to where the card is positioned. Read and relay the message to yourself or the other querent.

Card 1: What kind of reader do I want to be?

Card 2: What kind of reader am I?

Card 3: What kind of reader am I perceived to be?

Journal Prompts: The Reader in Me

1. Do I get readings? Why or why not?
2. What is important to me when I get readings?
3. What kind of reader do I want to be? Why do I read? (Sun sign)
4. What kind of reader am I? (Moon sign)
5. What kind of reader am I perceived to be? (rising sign)

Exercise: The Eight E's of Psychic Success

This exercise aims to help you ascertain where you are with your Eight E's. The exercise integrates a divination modality. Tarot is the modality used here, but try other modalities also as you become more familiar with varying types.

Card 1: Education

Card 2: Experience

Card 3: Ego

Card 4: Energy

Card 5: Empathy

Card 6: Ethics

Card 7: Entertainment

Card 8: Excellence

Randomly draw eight cards and place them in the shape of an E.

Each card represents a different *E* word that makes up the Eight E's of Psychic Success. Assess where you are. There are also cards that may represent one of the Eight E's of success. If you draw one of those cards and it is in the spread position directly related to that *E*, then you can be certain it is an important area for you to consider working on or paying attention to at this time. Some examples for the indicator cards are listed below, but please know that you can change or add to these initial suggestions.

Education: The Hierophant, Experience: The Hermit, Ego: The Fool and The High Priestess (represents the higher self instead of ego), Energy: Temperance, Empathy: The Empress, Ethics: Justice, Entertainment: The Magician, Excellence: The Sun.

Journal Prompts: The Eight E's of Psychic Success

1. What card did you draw for education? How do you interpret the card?

2. What card did you draw for experience? How do you interpret the card?

3. What card did you draw for ego? How do you interpret the card?

4. What card did you draw for energy? How do you interpret the card?

5. What card did you draw for empathy? How do you interpret the card?

6. What card did you draw for ethics? How do you interpret the card?

7. What card did you draw for entertainment? How do you interpret the card?

8. What card did you draw for excellence? How do you interpret the card?

9. Did you draw any cards that seemed to directly represent one of the Eight E's? How does that layer into your reading?

Exercise: Putting It All Together

The purpose of this exercise is to use your psychic style in a divination. Pick a modality and do a reading for your progress in *A Psychic's Handbook*. At each point, ask how the Eight E's, Four R's, and Three C's tie into your readings.

First, pick a modality or tool. Consider the Eight E's. Note those that help you with the modality you chose. For example, maybe you like charm readings because you have *education* and *experience* with charms. You might also find they are a good way to *entertain* the querent or keep them engaged.

Then, consider the Four R's. You will actively use each of them in this exercise. Consider the Three C's as well. Let them help activate your flow of information.

Put up any protection you have found is best for you and do any introductory rituals that you desire.

Request: What are my next steps in using my psychic knowingness? What do I need to know about the words I use for psychic knowingness? What do I need to know about my overall spiritual pursuit? Am I utilizing the proper psychic defenses? How am I at letting go of my need to be right or spot on? Am I working with guides? Do I go straight to my higher self or Source? Which clair do I utilize the most? Which chakra gives me information about my psychism? How am I doing with requesting, receiving, reading, and relaying information? (You can use four tools to answer this one. If you are casting charms, you can pull a charm to represent each of the Four R's.) What do I need to know about working with auras? What is my aura right now? How does this influence my psychic knowingness? What meditation or ritual is best for me to use at this time? How am I doing with learning my tells? Is there one I can glean from this exercise? Is there someone I need to get in touch with who has passed and has a message for me regarding stepping into my psychic knowingness?

Receive: Once you have requested the information, you now need to closely observe what you receive as your answer. Simply note the information at this point.

Read: Once you feel you have received your information, now put it all together. Interpret the information. Remember this is where most mistakes are made. Put aside all preconceived ideas by using windshield wipers on your third eye. Now, you can read clean and without bias.

Relay: Relaying the information is the point of divination. How will you relay the message? Is there anything you need to know about pairing your psychic style with that of a querent?

PART 4
CONCLUSION

The Eight E's of Psychic Success are always in play. They should always be at the forefront of everything you do as you lean more and more into your psychic knowingness. The best thing is that you can make the E's unique to you. Even with the various E's, no two handbooks should be alike. Your approach is uniquely and perfectly suited for you. Stay out of ego and relay the messages you are given. If you have followed the exercises in this book, you will never have to doubt yourself. It is only when you step in as fixer, which is not your job, that you may venture into precarious situations. Always remember, you are the messenger. You are not life coach, counselor, or fixer. You are the psychic, and you are a darn good one.

CONCLUSION

There are so many different things I would like to emphasize in this conclusory note to you, but the most important thing is to encourage you to have fun with your psychic knowingness. I realize it can sometimes be an incredibly overwhelming feeling to know things others don't. A judge that I'm close to recently said to me, "I don't know how you know what you know, but I know you know it." When you realize the world is not flat or linear, but a big, swirling, interconnected ball of energy, it helps you see things from a much different perspective. It may seem tough at times, but the key is to stay in gratitude and have fun. It is all right to laugh and have joy in the midst of your journey here on earth. As a lifetime psychic, I have learned that I am different than others. As I wrote this book, I went through some of the most difficult times of my life. But I know there is more to our souls than this life on earth. Writing this book and not shying away from my abilities helped me to know that although I am different and it is difficult, I have helped many people. That is what is most important to me, and I hope will be most important to you.

Remember to check out all the bonus materials I provide on michellewelch.com because you will continually grow and expand your handbook. Make sure to share it on *A Psychic Handbook*'s social media platforms so that others can see your psychic style.

I can't wait for everyone to feel the freedom that comes with writing your psychic script instead of following a cookie-cutter one that perhaps doesn't fit you. Remember that you are connected to everyone and everything, but you are also unique in your psychic style. You know that practice makes psychic, and you are ready for psychic success!

RECOMMENDED RESOURCES

Included in this list are books and websites of other practitioners.

Books

Ambrose, Kala. *The Awakened Psychic: What You Need to Know to Develop Your Psychic Abilities*. Llewellyn Publications, 2016.

Auryn, Mat. *Psychic Witch: A Metaphysical Guide to Meditation, Magick & Manifestation*. Llewellyn Publications, 2020.

Chestney, Kim. *Radical Intuition: A Revolutionary Guide to Using Your Inner Power*. New World Library, 2020.

Fox, Karen. *The Psychic Workbook: Tools and Techniques to Develop Reliable Insight*. Schiffer Publishing, 2015.

Greer, Mary K. *Archetypal Tarot: What Your Birth Card Reveals About Your Personality, Path, and Potential*. Weiser Books, 2021.

Hoffman, Enid. *Develop Your Psychic Skills*. Schiffer Publishing, 1981.

Katz, Debra Lynne. *You Are Psychic: The Art of Clairvoyant Reading & Healing*. Llewellyn Publications, 2004.

Kenner, T. A. *Symbols and Their Hidden Meanings*. Thunder's Mouth Press, 2006.

Pamita, Madame. *The Book of Candle Magic: Candle Spell Secrets to Change Your Life*. Llewellyn Publications, 2020.

Phillips, Lesley. *Intuition and Chakras: How to Increase Your Psychic Development Through Energy*. Llewellyn Publications, 2020.

Reed, Theresa. *Astrology for Real Life: A Workbook for Beginners*. Weiser Books, 2019.

Roberts, Billy. *So You Want to Be Psychic? Develop Your Hidden Powers*. Watkins Publishing, 2010.

Schulz, Mona Lisa. *Awakening Intuition: Using Your Mind-Body Network for Insight and Healing*. Harmony Books, 1998.

Sturgess, Stephen. *The Book of Chakras & Subtle Bodies*. Watkins Publishing, 2014.

Websites

Carrie Paris: https://carrieparis.com/

Devin Hunter: https://modernwitch.com/devin/

Divine Hand Jim: https://www.thedivinehand.com/index.html

Enchanted World, Monte Farber & Amy Zerner: https://www.enchantedworld.com/

Ethony Dawn: https://ethony.com/

Higgypop: https://www.higgypop.com/

Intuitive Specialists: https://intuitivespecialists.com

Michelle Welch: https://michellewelch.com/

World Divination Association: https://www.worlddivinationassociation.com/

Client Help Resources

The categories below are resources for you to share with clients if needed.

Suicide

1-800-SUICIDE or 1-800-784-2433

1-800-273-TALK or 1-800-273-8255

TTY 1-800-799-4889

Text HOME to 741-741 for free twenty-four-hour support from the Crisis Text Line

Outside of the US, please visit the International Association for Suicide Prevention for a database of resources.

Domestic Violence

1-800-799-SAFE (7233)

TTY 1-800-787-3224

Text "START" to 88788

National Sexual Assault Hotline

1-800-656-4673 (HOPE)

Trans Life

1-877-565-8860

BIBLIOGRAPHY

Akhtar, Shazia, Lucy V. Justice, Catriona M. Morrison, Martin A. Conway. "Fictional First Memories," *Psychological Science* vol. 29, no. 10 (2018), https://doi.org /10.1177/0956797618778831.

Augé, C. Riley. *Field Manual for the Archaeology of Ritual, Religion, and Magic.* Berghahn Books, 2022.

Bolton, Henry Carrington. *The Counting-Out Rhymes of Children: Their Antiquity, Origin, and Wide Distribution: A Study in Folk-lore.* D. Appleton & Co., 1888.

Buckland, Raymond. *The Buckland Gypsies' Domino Divination Deck.* Llewellyn Publications, 1999.

Buckland, Raymond. *The Fortune-Telling Book: The Encyclopedia of Divination and Soothsaying.* Visible Ink Press, 2004.

Cheung, Theresa. *The Element Encyclopedia of the Psychic World.* HarperElement, 2006.

Farber, Monte. *Enchanted Worlds: The Visionary Collages and Art Couture of Amy Zerner.* RedFeather Mind, Body Spirit, 2021.

Freud, Sigmund. *The Interpretation of Dreams.* Edited and translated by James Strachey. Avon Books, 1965.

Grasse, Ray. "Synchronicity and the Mind of God." *Quest* 94, no. 3 (2006): 91–94. https://www.theosophical.org/publications/quest-magazine/synchronicity-and -the-mind-of-god.

Guiley, Rosemary Ellen. *The Encyclopedia of Magic and Alchemy.* Facts on File, 2006.

Hall, Fitzedward. *Modern English*. Scribner, Armstrong & Co., 1873.

Horwitz, Elinor Lander. *The Soothsayer's Handbook: A Guide to Bad Signs & Good Vibrations*. J. B. Lippincott and Company, 1972.

Jung, Carl. *The Structure and Dynamics of the Psyche*. 2nd ed. Vol. 8 of *The Collected Works of C. G. Jung*, Bollingen Series 10. Edited by Herbert Read, Michael Fordham, Gerhard Adler, and William McGuire. Translated by R. F. C. Hull. Princeton University Press, 1972.

Kieckhefer, Richard. *Forbidden Rites: A Necromancer's Manual of the Fifteenth Century*. Pennsylvania State University Press, 1998.

Musruck, Alexandre. *The Art of Lenormand Reading: Decoding Powerful Messages*. Schiffer Publishing, 2018.

Naifeh, Steven W., and Gregory White Smith. *Jackson Pollack: An American Saga*. Clarkson N. Potter, 1989.

Pickover, Clifford A. *Dreaming the Future: The Fantastic Story of Prediction*. Prometheus Books, 2001.

Puhle, Toni. *The Card Geek's Guide to Kipper Cards*. Published by the author, 2017.

"Spirituality Among Americans." Pew Research Center. December 7, 2023. https://www.pewresearch.org/religion/2023/12/07/spirituality-among-americans/.

Styler, Laura. *The Little Book of Aura Healing: Simple Practices for Cleansing and Reading the Colors of the Aura*. Rockridge Press, 2020.

Welch, Michelle. *The Magic of Connection: Stop Cutting Cords & Learn to Transform Negative Energy to Live an Empowered Life*. Llewellyn Publications, 2021.

Welch, Michelle, and Roger Welch. *Pendulum Palooza*. Published by the authors, 2018.

Welch, Michelle. *Spirits Unveiled: A Fresh Perspective on Angels, Guides, Ghosts & More*. Llewellyn Publications, 2022.

Wen, Benebell. *I Ching, The Oracle: A Practical Guide to The Book of Changes*. North Atlantic Books, 2023.

Zerner, Amy, and Jessie Spicer Zerner. *The Dream Quilt*. Charles E. Tuttle, 1995.